TRADE
WARS

TRADE WARS

The High-Technology Scandal of the 1980s

Kevin Cahill

W.H. ALLEN · LONDON
1986

Copyright © 1986 Kevin Cahill

Photoset in Imprint by
Phoenix Photosetting, Chatham
Printed and bound in Great Britain by
Mackays of Chatham Ltd, Kent
for the Publishers W.H. Allen & Co. Plc
44 Hill Street, London W1X 8LB

ISBN 0 491 03095 9

CONTENTS

AUTHOR'S NOTE

The opinions expressed in this book are my own and not those of Paddy Ashdown MP or anyone else except where they are quoted from their own speeches or writings.

To thank everyone who helped me to write this book would run to many pages, but a special thanks is due to the following who directly encouraged or helped me to keep going with the story: my editors, Ron Condon, Simon Timm and David Craver; all my colleagues on *Computer Weekly* and *Computer News*, and John Murphy on *Computing*; Jack Saltmann and Mike Chrissman on *TV Eye*; Philip Beresford on the *Sunday Times* and Della Bradshaw on *Electronics Weekly*; Nick Anning, Celina Bledowsky and Linda Malvern for help with the research; and Joe O'Reilly at W.H. Allen.

To Kevan Pearson, a special thanks, and finally a very special thanks to Paddy Ashdown MP, Michael Meadowcroft MP and Spencer Batiste MP, each of whom has taken a special interest in this issue and who have introduced me to the House of Commons and its workings.

INTRODUCTION

THE UNITED STATES OF AMERICA is embarked on an attempt to gain control of all high technology in the free world. To this end, to cite but two examples, the Austrian government, under intense US pressure, recently passed a law making it an offence in Austria to break American law in relation to the use and movement of high technology products. In an attempt to drive socialist Spain into the same corner, the US has placed Spain's largest electronic company on a published United States blacklist, denied the company supplies from the US, and mounted a strenuous campaign, from the US embassy in Madrid, to persuade the Spaniards to toe the US line. The American campaign to get control of Western technology began with the foundation of NATO in 1949, but since 1979 the campaign has taken on both new dimensions and a global goal.

The campaign, ruthlessly pursued by senior figures in the American military establishment, has as its ostensible aim the denying of all significant technology to Eastern Europe and various other regions the US disapproves of. The ostensible purpose of the US campaign, and its real intent are, however, two radically different things, linked only by the fact that the US supplies Europe with over 80 per cent of all its high technology needs. Around the rest of the world, excluding the USSR and its allies, but including China, the US is the majority supplier of high technology. Based on this massive dependence, and other inter-linked trade and economic factors, the US is in a unique position to make its will prevail, and it does.

The practical consequences are, however, very different from those with which the world has become familiar through a somewhat similar dependence on oil. In the case of the US, a high price for its product is but one of the consequences of its policy and, as this book will reveal, a minor one at that. The heart and soul of US policy in relation to high technology, to computers and to electronics, is ideological. The people who make, sell, buy and use these engines of the new age, are all instruments to be subordinated, to the defeat of communism under the direct leadership of the US military authorities, particularly in its Soviet manifestation. The current ideological impulse in US politics is new, not in its occurrence, for US politics has always had a substantial ideological potential, modified only by the great diversity of viewpoint incorporated into the political map via its pluralist constitution, but in its articulation, and in its implementation, particularly in American foreign policy. The foreign policy of the United States is no longer simply an amalgam of commercial opportunism, military jingoism and a smattering of anti-communism to keep the folks back home sweet. It is a fully dedicated, carefully honed weapon whose sole aim is the defeat of communism everywhere by every possible means, legal and illegal. It is, to put not too fine a point on it, on a war footing, and as we all know, wars are emergencies during which the finer points of civilisation like individual freedom, freedom of speech and movement, and many other laudable goals, are lost. Such is now the case, certainly within the computer community, and such is the message of this book. The soldiers in this war, the technology workers in the Western world, have been press ganged into this campaign, however, without their consent; often without their knowledge.

The US has embarked on what is effectively a military crusade with a destructive, not constructive, aim in view. High technology is a critical part of that crusade, for a variety of reasons, some real, some illusory, and the most real of all is the fact that worldwide dependence on US technology is now at its apogee. Among the 'window of opportunity' strategists, a very popular school of thought in the US, the vision is of an open window, which will soon narrow significantly, particularly as Japanese strength in high technology grows. To this correct perception is added, particularly by the US military, a converse premise that is at first difficult to refute. This is the claim that Soviet technology, particularly in computers and electronics, is five to ten years behind that of the US, and totally dependent on it for its blueprints, plans and data, all of which are stolen from the US. Not only is the claim unfounded and compounded with genuine lies and deceit; it is profoundly dangerous. It is dangerous because in a world that is two minutes to midnight on the clock of nuclear Armageddon, we in the West may find ourselves at war with the Soviet Union. Fifteen minutes into World War III is not the moment to find out that what the Pentagon fed the world, often through the US State Department, was trash, back and front.

The Soviet Union, and most particularly its military, are not dependent on the US for anything, except the occasional opportunity not to reinvent the wheel. The Soviet military ordnance industry is able to supply, not only the Soviet military, but also some Soviet civilian sections, with all their electronic and computer needs. What is not supplied within Soviet Russia itself is, for the military at any rate, readily available from the Soviet Union's trading partners in Comecon, the East European version of the EEC.

Sadly, not only is the Pentagon's estimate of Soviet military high technology seriously at fault, so is its estimate of the effectiveness of high technology in its own weapons. To take but one claim: that of accuracy in its minuteman missile fleet. The Pentagon puts around to the press the idea that minuteman, on average, is accurate to within 100 feet of any target. What it fails to add is that this figure is good only for the one out of every six minuteman missiles that is ever expected to get within even nuclear blast range of any target. For ten years the Pentagon and NATO relied on an early warning system which produced major computer breakdowns every thirty minutes, and attack alerts every other day – though big attack alerts only every ten days or so. High technology remains a very uncertain component in weapon systems, as facts show, but to the true believers in the Pentagon it is the path to glory and a crucial tool in the bid to contain and strangle the Soviet Union. This is where the Pentagon, and much of the current US administration, have gone beyond the remit of, first, the US Constitution and certain laws derived directly from it, and secondly, have sought, in some cases very successfully, to militarise the Western world's high tech industry, and to impose US law throughout the Western world, even within countries such as the UK. Indeed it is within the UK that the US has been most successful in perverting and usurping the local constitution, and is actually implementing its writ throughout the country.

If the Austrians passed a dubious law under doubtful circumstances and as a result of intense US pressure, the current UK government has neither stepped in to defend its citizens, nor acted to restore its own eroded legitimacy. In an abandonment unique in English history of its most central function, the protection of sovereignty on the UK mainland itself, the British government has gone further in compliance with US policy than any other country in the world. It has abandoned jurisdiction over thousands of large computer sites around the UK, and over the UK citizens who work there. It has abandoned almost half a million citizens, in mainland Great Britain, to US law in relation to their work, to the goods they produce and traffic in, and to their ability to export from the UK.

[3]

CHAPTER 1

The Story Breaks

THOUGH LONG IN OPERATION, and just as long ignored, the situation finally came home to roost on the first working day of 1984.

That morning thirty-two UK managing directors, all engaged in the business of buying and selling computers, found a slim, two page letter from International Business Machines (IBM) sitting atop their mail piles. Letters from IBM, the largest computer supplier in the world, were hardly a novelty – most of the recipients dealt in new or second-hand IBM machines and had frequent contact with the company, but the letter IBM had sent out on Christmas Eve 1983 was unique.

The second sentence in the letter said: 'As you are aware, transactions *within* the United Kingdom involving "Advanced Systems" are also subject to the obtaining of US export licence approval. Such transactions include not only the initial installation of a new machine with a user, but also any subsequent dealing or transfers in such machines.'

The more sophisticated amongst the recipients admitted shock at the singular bluntness of the letter, though not surprise. According to John Fulston, managing director of Atlantic Leasing, a large trader in IBM equipment and a company publicly listed on the Stock Exchange, the whole thing was a storm in a tea cup. 'We've had an office in New York with two people getting our licences for some time,' he said.

Norman Tebbit, the Trade and Industry minister, speaking on a radio programme some weeks later, gave comfort to Fulston's view. He noted that the situation had been going on for some time, without causing any problems. He advised companies to look after their commercial interests. But not everyone was as nervous as Fulston, or as indifferent to constitutional impropriety as Norman Tebbit.

The morning the letter arrived, Nigel Green[1], the managing director of one small company, also involved in handling IBM equipment, was at first appalled, then outraged, at what he read. He pondered what to do for five minutes, then got on the phone to a computer industry trade paper in London. His choice of journal, and the editor he reached, were crucial.

There are three major trade weeklies in the UK computer industry: *Computer Weekly*, *Computing* and *Computer News*. Each is mailed weekly to 100,000 or so of the industry's key workers, managers and directors. The oldest of the three, *Computer Weekly*, based in the Surrey town of Sutton, is staid, comprehensive and very reliable. It seeks, and generally succeeds in covering, somewhere in its twenty-odd newspages, most of what's going on in the industry, even the boring bits. The paper is not noted for its journalistic aggression or a campaigning style, though it occasionally has bouts of both. *Computing*, on the other hand, is a paper with an approach that's hard to categorise. Linked to the British Computer Society, the magazine seems to aim at sensation as much as comprehension. In some ways it is the magazine the industry loves to hate, due to its frequent attempts on the jugulars of the many colourful personalities who make up the industry. Like *Computer Weekly*, the paper has no history of campaigning, and an evaluation of its pages would not easily reveal what the key issues of contention in the UK computer industry are.

Computer News, however, stuck out like a sore thumb. Launched in 1983 on a near-shoestring budget, the paper lit up its first edition with a campaign headline that has defined the core of the paper's 'voice' throughout most of its life to date. 'US military threatens Europe's hi-tech trade.'

The paper had gone to press on the 6 October 1983, to tell its readers that the US military were trying to take control of the European computer industry. The story, which in fact was something of a Hobson's choice for the small team of six journalists faced with finding something 'hot' for the lead in their first issue, proved a godsend in the case of the IBM letter.

Nigel Green rang *Computer News* at ten past nine that morning. His information faced me with an acute quandary. I was certain it was a sensation, or rather, a sensational development in a case that was already underway. The problem for me, and for my editor, Ron Condon, was that we had already run the story. On 11 November we had printed a lead story, forecasting a direct collision between IBM UK and the government over this very issue. The preamble to the 11 November article was a series of conversations between the IBM press office and myself, each conversation culminating in an insistence by

[5]

IBM that they had no difficulty in implementing both US and UK law, in the UK. This assertion is nonsense, and, having given IBM's press office time to talk to their lawyers and confirm that the imposition of two sets of laws in one country was indeed IBM policy, we had run the story.

The point of the 11 November story was evidently ignored by IBM, who, instead of spotting the legal, and ultimately the political implications, had simply gone ahead with what was intended as a clarification, in their 22 December missive. The clarification was all that was needed to turn an obscure legal row in a trade paper into an issue that was to reach 10 Downing Street, and the White House itself, within a few months.

The immediate problem for Ron Condon and myself in our offices in Gray's Inn Road, opposite the imposing mass of *The Times* and *Sunday Times* buildings, was what to do with the story. We couldn't get a good copy of the letter from Nigel Green in time to splash it across the front, and thereby fill the blank that would be created if we pulled out the existing lead story. In the end, Ron decided to squeeze onto the already complete front page, a short version of the letter leading up to an announcement, with picture, that Edwin Nixon, IBM UK's chief executive, had been knighted in the New Year's honours list. He decided that we would print the letter the following week, in a news analysis piece on the issue. In the face of our own earlier lead in November, and the sheer mechanics of getting the paper printed, there was little else we could do, even though I felt that we were allowing the mechanics of production to dictate a down-playing of what I believed was a sensational document.

In the overheated moments that always follow the going to press of a newspaper, Ron and I sat at his desk looking straight across the road into the foyer of *The Times*. After a few minutes of wind-down chatter, I told Ron that I thought *The Sunday Times* might be interested, and perhaps BBC Radio 4 as well.

For the first time I tried to assemble for myself a picture of the story, and perhaps more importantly, just where I thought it was going. The apparent core of the story was the huge and real infringement of UK sovereignty by the US, now fully evidenced in the IBM letter. The letter itself covered about 1,400 large IBM sites throughout the country, many of them in government departments, including the Ministry of Defence. The total number of people affected by the regulation, excluding IBM's own staff, would number up to 30,000. And the reason for sending the letter at that juncture? Well, that was

[6]

clear enough. Since the early summer of 1983, companies dealing in computers, particularly those who leased rather than sold the machines to customers, had either been transhipping the machines through Sweden, or round-robinning the machines out of the UK to Sweden and back again.

The reason was simple. In order to encourage capital investment, the Swedish government had created a thirty per cent capital allowance for major items like computers, bought by Swedish companies. The allowance was open ended in that the Swedish purchaser, once delivery of the machine was made, did not have to make any further accounting for the device. A number of nimble Swedish financial institutions, with fat profits awaiting the taxman's severe bite, saw a way of reducing the handout to the state. They would buy in mobile capital equipment, such as a computer, take it on the books at full value, prepare the thirty per cent claim, depreciate the machine by thirty per cent and return it to the supplier at the depreciated price, plus a fee, and everyone was twenty to thirty per cent better off. The UK companies in particular, could use the Swedish loophole to create a significant advantage over IBM, the original supplier.

IBM not only got to hear about this, but also, it was rumoured, got in on the act itself, something the company strenuously denied. Whatever the truth might be, IBM did have another way of stopping the trade through Sweden. The company invoked the US law it had cited in its letter, thereby forcing the leasing companies to disclose Sweden as one of the destinations. The supply of US export licences for such shipments, ostensibly originating from the US commerce department in Washington, dried up. But the Swedish transhipments did not halt altogether. One or two of the leasing companies continued to buy IBM machines through Sweden on UK export licences, which are issued, at least theoretically, on a completely independent basis by the UK Department of Trade and Industry. The leasing companies argued that, as the ultimate end user and destination was the UK, there was no need to go back to Washington for a new export licence. IBM didn't agree, and the use of the word *within* connected with the word *transaction* in the letter was meant to make crystal clear the fact that the US government retained total control over all transactions affecting the machines listed in the letter.

At that stage very few people were aware that the US government and the Kingdom of Sweden were, right up to the level of King Olaf himself, involved in one of the most bitter rows for years. In 1980 a Swedish company called Datasaab Computers had accepted a contract to build an air traffic control system for a commercial airfield near Leningrad. About nine per cent of the components to be supplied were of US origin, and Datasaab failed to get a US export licence for those components. In fact, as the installation neared completion Datasaab executives were weekly taking components out to Russia in their brief-cases; again, some were of American origin. The contract did have an export licence from Sweden, and to all intents and purposes was fully supported by the Swedish government. By 1983 Datasaab had become a subsidiary of L.M. Ericsson, a massive Swedish electronics con-glomerate with substantial commercial interests and prospects in the US. Ericsson was the pressure point crudely chosen by the US, alongside an equally crude threat to cut off vital electronic components for use in Sweden's military aircraft industry, to make the Swedes behave and accept the imposition of a massive fine on Datasaab.

In addition to the problem over Ericsson, US customs authorities had also claimed that a Swedish company, Sunitron, was a major diversion point in a sophisticated international smuggling ring, which was shipping allegedly vital US computers to the Soviet Union. That autumn, the Kingdom of Sweden was under the gravest suspicion in the US, which was issuing high technology export licences to Sweden at what can only be called embargo pace. Aware of this background, IBM was very anxious to ensure that none of the UK machines merry-go-rounding through Sweden got lost and wound up in Russia. In fact, IBM's fears went further than that. With Sweden virtually in quaran-tine from a US point of view, IBM UK did not want to appear, however indiscreetly, as an embargo breaker.

Like the Austrian and UK governments, the Swedish government either failed, or refused, to face the legal issues involved, and attempted to reach a political agreement with representatives of the US, a move that was to cost L.M. Ericsson dear, and very nearly cost the Swedish Economics Minister, Matt Helstrom, his job, when the US welched on the deal. But that comes later in the story. What I had established for myself by the time I went up the road to the Blue Lion pub on the evening of 3 January 1984, was that someone, somewhere in IBM, was so worried about getting caught in the Swedish situation that they had broken cover on the implications of the US laws to which the letter referred. This is the US Export Administration Act of 1979. It is a long and complex Act but it makes two claims that are unique in the laws of any country outside the Soviet bloc.

The Act claims that US law applies, in full, wherever the goods specified in the Act are to be found, and no matter how many transactions the goods have gone through. The EAA claim on behalf of the US deems itself to precede any claims to ownership anyone may acquire by right of purchase. The natural comment here is 'absurd', but only if one had never seen the IBM letter or knew how effective was the threat inherent in it. The second highly unusual claim in the Act is to the ownership of all data of US origin, however diluted or comingled, including the data in people's heads. Over that data the US claims the right of legal jurisdiction all over the world.

When Nigel Green told me the contents of the IBM letter, I phoned the American Embassy, who, like the Department of Trade and Industry, refused to comment until they saw the letter. We solved that problem by sending both the Embassy and the DTI a copy of the document, without Nigel Green's name and address. The Embassy's reaction was that IBM were interpreting the US law in far too narrow a fashion. My intuitive feeling, based on a superb analysis of the Act leaked to me by ICL years before, was that IBM was right, and that the Embassy was deeply uncomfortable, but wrong.

From the Blue Lion, I phoned across to *The Sunday Times* and asked to speak to Philip Beresford, the acting computer correspondent. I had made Philip's acquaintance on a long trip to Wales in 1983 and he had moved to *The Sunday Times* about the same time *Computer News* had opened its doors on the other side of the road.

I showed Phil the letter and he instantly recognised the implications. The advantage of having kept it small in our paper now became clear. It gave Phil a clear shot at a story of substance which he would have no difficulty rendering exclusive with his own material. *The Sunday Times Business News* editor, Roger Eglin, took the same view as Phil. The item led the *Business News* that Sunday, and with that our story began to take shape as an issue. The implied campaign we had been running for three months was now explicit, the more so when Radio 4's *Today* programme, for the third time, took up the story too. They persuaded the Trade and Industry minister Norman Tebbit and the American Embassy into a confrontation over the early morning airwaves, with something like 2½ million listeners.

Tebbit barked his opposition to US law in the UK and threatened IBM, but ran for his burrow when asked what UK companies should do. 'I would advise them to look after their own commercial interests,' he said.

Most listeners heard the bark of opposition to US imperialism and the threat to IBM. Only the small band of those affected by the letter, and those of us involved in writing the story, heard the cowardice in the key piece of advice.

[9]

Tebbit, a very adept politician, either was not briefed as to any practical course of action, or there was something else. Something so serious that he was not prepared to act to restore UK sovereignty in the face of US opposition. From his concluding remark on the Radio 4 programme, it was obvious that he intended to use IBM in his feeble attempt to oppose the US. He warned IBM that if the situation did not change, it would be bad for IBM's business – a claim he was later to make good on[2]. The Embassy spokesman was a US military man who assiduously confused the listeners by refusing to address the issue or the letter, but whose rank and origin should have warned us all, even then, that we were dealing, not as we had imagined, with the US Department of Commerce, but with the Pentagon. Norman Tebbit, a civilian of ministerial rank, rated at least an Embassy First Secretary, if not the Ambassador, but the Pentagon, in defence of what were all too clearly its policies, sent along a low ranking, semi-incoherent soldier. So much for the US view of the number three in the British Cabinet.

An intriguing coincidence that overshadowed all these events was Tebbit's planned visit to the US and his meeting with the President of IBM, John Opel, which was part of the schedule for his visit.

But behind the scenes in the UK, purgatory, if not hell, was breaking out. IBM, while accepting that the letter had the full backing of the entire UK management of the company, categorically denied our assertion that the letter had been sent out on the orders of IBM World Trade in the United States. Our claim had been based on a good source, which had been corroborated, but which suffered from the same defect as does all reporting about IBM. The company, the seventh largest in the world, is more secretive than many military establishments. The official press offices of IBM will never engage in background briefings, off the record discussions, or anything other than the issue of press releases to support events such as new product releases or annual results.

For stories about IBM the press rely on a small army of IBM watchers, mostly American, usually financial analysts, and much of the reporting is on the basis of rumours, sources close to the company, etc. This gives the task of following IBM's doings something of the quality of *Alice in Wonderland*. 'Maybe she will, and maybe she won't. Maybe she did, and maybe she didn't.' It gives a reporter a lot of scope for elaboration, for inaccuracy, and very little chance of being proved right or wrong, since IBM tend not to react one way or the other. Why should they? Very little that's written has any bearing on the company or its status or, perhaps most importantly, on its shares, where a $1 shift moves the value of the company up or down by over half a billion dollars. But the publicity afforded the letter stung IBM as few things have ever done. Alongside the story that the letter had been sent out on the orders of World Trade, we had also heard that IBM were blaming us for the destruction of a very expensive PR campaign the company were running to persuade the UK and Europe that they were indeed a truly European company, as much a part of the UK as Marks & Spencer and IK Brunel. The campaign was based on full page ads in all the leading papers. To say that publication of the letter blew the campaign is to put it mildly.

First off the mark behind the scenes was the Department of Trade and Industry. In the footsteps of its boss, the department blandly announced that, 'no, they had not asked IBM to withdraw the letter and yes they were keeping the situation under review'. Whatever measures had been used to steer Norman Tebbit away from the substance of the letter, the breach of UK sovereignty had also been successfully deployed within his department. 'No, the relevant body of UK civil servants were not going to do anything about "an unwarranted encroachment on UK jurisdiction", as Sir Michael Havers, the Attorney General, was later to call it and no, they were not going to do anything about the restraints this imposed on UK exports.' It was an attitude and a response that I was to get more and more used to as the year wore on and even more serious issues emerged.

Computing, our real rival as we did not have the manpower or the newsprint to compete directly with *Computer Weekly*, were forced to waste a quarter of their front page on a grovelling apology forced on them by IBM. (They had reported the DTI demanding the withdrawal of the letter.) It gave me no pleasure not to have been approached by IBM, even though we had printed a very short, but identical story, based on an identical statement from the DTI. IBM readily admitted to me that the DTI statement could have been misleading. It was, and it was now obvious that one of IBM's defences, and a tactic that both the US Embassy and the DTI would try and deploy later, was to confuse any journalist not intimately involved in the story, on the basis that journalistic ignorance and uncertain information, would achieve what silence and a denial never would. They were all too right, as time and again national newspapers were steered away from developing elements of the story by a confused statement from the US Embassy, followed by a semantically contrived denial, which upon analysis seldom proved to be a real denial at all. But that analysis depended on an appreciation of the issues. The nose to nose exposure we got gave us that understanding, but denied it to our colleagues who had many other things to cover

[11]

besides a virtually metaphysical contretemps, affecting only the computer industry, which was far too complex for most of them anyhow.

Then the Embassy decided that it was time it too had a go at IBM. This incident went unnoticed at the time, as does much of the often extraordinary involvement in UK affairs that goes on at the US Embassy. The letter, more than almost any recent incident, upset at least three different groups inside that tank proof block on Grosvenor Square. The CIA, in the middle of a series of highly illegal operations investigating UK computer companies, felt that the row caused by the letter might lead to the exposure of their activities. The State Department, the nominal occupants and bosses of the building, were upset because IBM had neither consulted the Embassy before the letter went out nor contacted them afterwards. Finally, a group of US Customs officials, lodged in the Embassy, and also engaged in a series of operations against UK computer companies, were worried that any political fallout from the letter could lead to a diminishing of the slavish cooperation they had so far elicited from UK Customs.

Sir Edwin Nixon chose not to visit the Embassy himself. Instead he sent his number two, a tough, hardened manager called Tony Cleaver. Cleaver had a reputation inside IBM as an efficient trouble-shooter with something of a name for ruthlessness, but not for diplomatic expertise. With Cleaver went two lawyers and the party arrived in Grosvenor Square at a little before 11 am on a cold January morning, with the echoes of the Radio 4 programme still ringing around the Embassy. The omens were not auspicious when Tim Deal, the Economic Counsellor at the Embassy, asked Cleaver if he could have a copy of the letter. The request was a formality. Deal already had the copy we sent him. But Cleaver, retreating to the lawyers, said no, that he hadn't anticipated Deal's request and he would have to discuss the issues both with the lawyers and his own management. It was obviously a stall, and there was no rancour when Cleaver left to do his 'discussing'.

What the Embassy did not know was that Cleaver and IBM management were bent on taking their discussion outside the UK – to Washington. Early that afternoon Deal got a call from Washington. He was stunned, so stunned that he told the story around the Embassy, which is how we heard about it. Deal it seemed had been told to lay off the company. The matter was being dealt with in Washington. That was it. IBM were now free to handle the issue as they saw fit, which was by silence, with Washington giving cover, although which particular government department in Washington, no one ever found out. The

Embassy meanwhile was left to catch the growing flak, which had now moved to Parliament. But in our office a new issue had emerged.

In 1981 and 1982 a fashion for computer associated espionage had arrived from the United States. The Pentagon, which began its bid to militarise the entire high tech industry sometime in the late seventies, but only really got wheels under the campaign with the arrival of the Reagan administration in 1980, had solved the problem of its legal exclusion from commercial affairs by funding a section of US Customs to the tune of $30 million. This happened in 1981, following a very carefully orchestrated campaign, driven by Richard Perle and Larry Brady, against alleged slackness in the licensing division of the US commerce department. Perle, a rising political bureaucrat on the Washington scene, had based his career on vitriolic anti-communism, compounded with a hardline attitude towards the Soviet Union and all forms of arms control. A so-called Democrat, he had managed, almost single-handed, to get Senator Scoop Jackson to insert the human rights clause which allegedly caused the Soviet Union to walk out of the 1984 arms talks. By careful manoeuvring Perle seems to have suffered no significant flak from the fact that, along with ending participation in the arms talks, the Soviet Union also virtually cut off all Jewish emigration from the USSR, which was the alleged object of Perle's human rights clauses. His enemies, and Perle has plenty, now claim that the Scoop Jackson amendment to the 1974 Trade Act which Perle helped to formulate and table persuaded an angry Soviet Union to virtually end Jewish emigration. This was the exact opposite to what he intended.

Perle, who is the son of Russian-Jewish emigrants, has two other major failings, which are all too visible to those who have had to deal with him in Europe. He is extremely arrogant, and often fails to conceal from his audience the evident contempt in which he holds many of the NATO allies and their institutions. Not something likely to hurt him in an administration notable for its gross insensitivity in foreign affairs. The second quality is harder to specify; suffice it to say it seems to stem from a philosophy of ends justifying means and manifests itself as a penchant for saying one thing in Washington and something close to the opposite when faced with any opposition elsewhere. He is also noted for a close to 180 degree divergence between his private and public comments, especially when in close proximity to those his comments were about.

Perle got behind a programme in 1981, aimed at exploiting a very narrow difference of functions between agencies of the US government. The Commerce Department are charged with handling

[13]

all the commercial affairs of the United States. Customs, on the other hand, have the task of overseeing all imports and exports. The Pentagon, under Perle's direction, decided to improve the US Customs' bite when it came to overseeing high tech exports, by voting $30 million to a special Customs operation called Operation Exodus.

The justification for Operation Exodus was threefold. In the first place, the Pentagon alleged, the USSR was engaged in a monumental raid on US technology. Proof of this was adduced from a number of marginal espionage cases, all involving high technology such as computers or lasers. The cases were few in number and the link to a Soviet effort involving 20,000 spies was tenuous to say the least. Nonetheless, a very limited number of cases of smuggling remain the key element of proof in the Pentagon's case. The second arrow in the Pentagon's quiver was a claim by the CIA, never substantiated, and rejected privately by most Western governments, that the Soviet Union has no less than 20,000 operatives in the field, committed solely to stealing US technology. From those two very shaky premises comes an astonishing and deeply flawed conclusion: because the USSR is spending such mighty effort on stealing US technology, it therefore follows that the USSR is totally dependent on the US for its technology, which is based entirely on stolen US plans and blueprints. As the USSR copies everything it makes from the US, the theory runs, it is five to ten years behind the US in its high technology.

From those premises, buttressed by an astonishing CIA document which was declassified to Congress in 1982, Perle moved to his most ambitious target of all – the binding of all the nations of the NATO alliance, including Japan, to the US and its perception of the role of high technology in the coming world of total mobilisation against the Soviet Union. When the Pentagon couldn't prove a direct connection between high technology and munitions, the scientists in the Pentagon came up with the concept of dual use. Under this concept, the claim that high technology might have a military use, was sufficient to make it de facto, military high technology. In this way did Perle further extend the reach, not of the US, but of its military regime.

As the initial propaganda for Exodus and for Perle's campaign wafted across the Atlantic, I refused to take an interest. I was an associate editor at *Computer Weekly* at the time, and most of the spy cases that came our way were either second-hand, ancient history, or blown out of all proportion to their real importance. All except one.

On 20 November 1982 the issue of UK membership of the International Institute for Applied Systems Analysis in Vienna came

[14]

up for review. Notice that the UK was reviewing its membership of the only International Computer Institute of standing in the world arrived in a most curious way. I saw it in the *Daily Telegraph* and was stunned. The piece opened with an American claim that Soviet staff at IIASA were using the Institute's computer facilities to creep across the international phone lines, break into the UK Ministry of Defence super-computer at Reading and model Soviet nuclear weapons there. The claim was utterly preposterous. There is no MoD super-computer at Reading. The super-computer owned by the Atomic Weapons Research Establishment at Aldermaston is not connected to the outside world, nor are international phone circuits suitable or properly capable of transmitting scientific data relating to nuclear weapons. Finally, the super-computer at Aldermaston, like all such machines, stores all its work on a spare memory system every two and a quarter hours. So, if the Soviets were modelling nuclear weapons in the UK, they were, of necessity, leaving all the details behind.

The story was picked up by the UK media from an American magazine called *Parade*, a Sunday colour supplement, and the author of the piece, Tad Szulc, claimed a CIA source for it. Having established that the story was technical garbage, it didn't take all that long to source it because, within days of its appearance, another story surfaced, saying that the US was getting out of IIASA on the orders of the White House, which was where the *Parade* story started. In its report to the US member of IIASA, the National Academy of Science, the Office of Science and Technology at the White House had included an appendix containing an assertion similar to the one published in *Parade*. That version of the OST report was rejected by the NAS, but that body was forced out of IIASA when the White House ordered a withdrawal of the funds used to maintain the IIASA membership.

The UK, with no explanation to Parliament or public, followed the US out of IIASA. Only the UK left alone. No sooner had the National Academy of Science cut loose, than the American Academy of Science and Letters stepped in, renewed membership, and the US subsequently took over the directorship of IIASA in 1984.

In the wake of the IIASA scandal, it became essential to consider, with some care, just what US intentions towards the UK were, at the administrative rather than the directly political level. With Norman Tebbit's visit to the United States only weeks away, and the IBM letter headed for Parliament, an undercurrent of rumour began to grow. Prominent among the rumours were a spate of stories about un-identified US officials visiting UK computer companies up and down

[15]

the country. Allied to the rumours were a series of statements made to the paper by an incautious Pentagon official a few weeks after we published the IBM letter. IBM had consistently refused to say what would happen to a company that ignored the advice in the letter. The frustrating element of this was that I knew the answer but, abiding by journalistic conventions, I only had a story when IBM would tell me the answer. In desperation I turned to Washington, and got a few frills added to the information I already had.

Yes, I was told, any company that moved equipment in the UK without US permission would get put on the US Export denials list. No US company, and no subsidiary of a US company, would thenceforth trade with that company. But what of the British Ministry of Defence? 'What of it?' was the reply. 'If they move US technology without US permission, they would be in big trouble. They would be investigated.' I certainly had my story, but I also had something else, both more worrying and more puzzling. The US, I was told by a source I definitely could not reveal, had a complete list of every computer in the UK, and the US was in a position to carry out its threats.

This latter piece of information, taken with all the other material coming in to the paper, pointed unnervingly to an intelligence operation of some sort. For a start there is no basis for a list in the UK. There is no obligation on the purchaser of a computer to tell anybody, government or private body that he has a machine. The *Computer Users' Year Book* is hopelessly out of date and up to fifty per cent inaccurate.

My source again made plain that, not only was the Pentagon accurate, but it covered British built ICL machines, as well as American supplied machines. That apparently excluded the possibility that the Pentagon was simply using the Commerce Department export licence file to find out where computers were in the UK. The Pentagon had either persuaded or forced the US companies to part with their customer lists, or else something more sinister was afoot. As events were to show, all three conclusions were correct. The Pentagon did get access to the export licensing file and later got access to the company customer files, and the CIA had been put in too.

The Sunday Times, informally keeping an eye on us and our story, began to see the shadows down the road, and more than once, senior journalists there suggested that protection of some sort was in order. At that stage we were sharing with our colleagues across the road a lot more than we were printing. My own view, despite annoying evidence that both my telephones were periodically tapped, was that we hadn't got to

[16]

Watergate, yet. But we weren't far off. I wagered with Ron in the pub one night that we would get what I called 'brown envelopes'.

It was impossible to believe that the outrage Nigel Green had felt over the IBM letter would not also be shared by some of those who were being subjected to American snooping and interference. What I thought might be much more difficult to nail, and what I was proved wrong about, was the CIA connection. At the time of the IIASA scandal in 1982 I had reasoned that such a blatant smear against the UK security services, following so closely on the Prime scandal, would create for the CIA a couple of enemies in the UK security services, enemies who would be more than glad to shop any American 'cousin' found wandering around the UK, which would be a breach of inter-intelligence rules anyway. The shopping was indeed done, eventually, though very indirectly, and with most of the spadework left to *Computer News*. For small mercies however, much gratitude is owed.

The oddest thing was that conclusive proof of CIA activity in the UK was provided by the Director of the CIA, William Casey, confirmed by Richard Perle, and indirectly corroborated by the Prime Minister, Margaret Thatcher. In the end the task of nailing the spooks was easier than we had persuaded ourselves it would be, thanks mostly to those three people.

But more of that later. In February 1984 Norman Tebbit prepared to leave for the United States and before doing so he made himself an uncharacteristic hostage to fortune. He told reporters before he went, in ringing tones, that he would be raising the IBM letter with the company chairman and the issue of extra-territoriality with US officials. He implied clearly that he would do so in the strongest possible terms. He laid his political credibility with the computer industry on the line, by telling the people who worked in it that he would face up to IBM.

He laid his credibility on the line and he lost. He took a nose-dive of unusual political depth by admitting, within ten days of his brave assertions, to the same bunch of reporters he had spoken to on his outbound trip, that he had not raised the issue of the letter with John Opel. His lame explanation was that it was not appropriate to do so. End of scene.

At that stage of the game the computer industry was generally unaware that Norman Tebbit's personal political advisor was Michael Dobbs, a specialist in arms control, and a personal friend of Richard Perle. Had we known, perhaps we would have probed more deeply into the sudden simultaneous disappearance of Tebbit's fighting spirit, and his political nous. It was just that his retreat, coming so soon after his advance, and announced so abjectly, took us all by surprise. Prior to his trip I had, out of sheer frustration over IBM UK's refusal to tell me the consequences of disobeying the letter, sent a telex to Opel in New York. I told him of the reaction to the letter and said that having given such advice, the company was duty bound to state the consequences. IBM UK were refusing to do this, would he oblige? I also injudiciously asked for reaction to Tebbit's Radio 4 outburst, and quoted it.

I got no reply other than a call from IBM's UK press office telling me I was unwelcome at any IBM site worldwide. I had done myself a whole lot of no good with that telex I was told. Well, it seemed to me I was doing no worse than Norman Tebbit, only he'd got his come-uppance in public and I hadn't. Besides, I hadn't been to an IBM company premises for almost ten years. A few more years in the cold would hardly do me any harm. Not that things stayed that way. By spring a sense of sardonic humour had returned to IBM's press office and they were referring to the letter as 'Kevin Cahill's Christmas present'.

But no adequate post-mortem was ever done on Tebbit's retreat, which was widely picked up in the national as well as the Trade press. He had made himself a hostage, not only to the computer industry, but to a good many others as well. Few noticed a certain consistency in his behaviour rather than just his words. Faced with the choice of telling the Americans to remove their challenge to UK sovereignty, as his oath of loyalty as a Privy Councillor obliged him to, and of defending the UK computer industry from predatory US interference, Tebbit had opted out of his duty and left the industry to fend for itself. Faced with one of the most powerful executives in the US, Tebbit had once more bolted for cover. Why? Neither action was characteristic of the man. Did the Prime Minister order him to cool it after reading his pre-departure remarks in the *Financial Times* where they were quoted? Or did other counsels prevail? Was he told by his advisors that Opel did not want to discuss the letter and would be angry if Tebbit raised it? Either of the two is a real possibility.

Thatcher's love affair with Reaganite America has carried her into ill-advised flattery of the ageing US president, out of line with sentiment in the UK and to no practical effect. Does it also extend to her advice to her ministers? Does sentiment so cloud her judgment that she has let a year pass without removing an open challenge to UK sovereignty, on the UK mainland? The questions have to be raised, not only because she has failed to resolve the American challenge to the constitutional foundations of her government, but because she seems determined to

[18]

prevent her ministers from raising it anywhere in the US, where there might be a specific reaction, or incident, as with Opel. To whine away in public, in a general way so that no one hears or cares, as her ministers sometimes do – that is permitted. And that cuts no ice in the US. Whatever may be Margaret Thatcher's notion of the qualities of North Americans, she seems to know nothing at all of the merciless measure of seriousness they adopt in negotiations. And her illusions have either been imposed on, or are shared by, the UK team at Cocom, as described by one of their American adversaries on completion of the negotiations:

'I can't believe it,' the colonel said, 'they just rolled over on their backs, put their feet in the air and bought the whole deal. They bought the whole deal,' he almost shouted. The deal is a sentence of US control over most remaining technology in the Western world, and in the United Kingdom in particular. It is a death sentence on UK high technology exports, especially for small companies.

---

[1] Nigel Green's real name cannot be given because of fear of retaliation by IBM and the US Government.
[2] He refused IBM to form a special link with British Telecom in 1985.

CHAPTER 2

A History of Secrecy

A CENTRAL THEME OF THIS narrative is that the United States, whether by design or good fortune, has obtained a monopoly stranglehold on the world's most important market, that of high technology goods. This is not a benevolent stranglehold. It is a further theme of the narrative that the main victim of this situation is the continent of Europe, which no longer supports a single big (main frame) computer maker, unlike the United States which has at least nine, and Japan which has five. It is equally a theme of the narrative, and a piece of logical common sense, that this situation could never have occurred without the compliance of the victim states. This does not mean willing compliance. Neither does it mean informed comment on the part of any democratic institution within Europe. Coercion, as the evidence to be presented shows, has been the most common means by which the US has secured this unique situation. Secrecy on the part of the bureaucracies of the victim states has been the manner in which this extraordinary extension of one nation's control, and later of its laws, to virtually every country in Europe, has been achieved. But first there had to be a central mechanism separate from any form of democratic scrutiny or control, through which the US could transmit its orders to its secret servants within the European states. This institution is known as the Coordinating Committee – simply that. There is no identified object for its operations. It is known as Cocom for short and as early as 1954, four years after it was set up, a minor attempt to reform it by the UK initiated a major crisis between the United States and the Churchill government in England. The crisis was precipitated when Peter, later Lord, Thorneycroft moved unilaterally to shorten two of the many controlled lists imposed on Cocom by the United States. In response to Thorneycroft's move, encouraged by Churchill, President Eisenhower sent the following letter to the British Prime Minister in London on 19 March 1954. The

[20]

letter is marked SECRET and was delivered by hand in London by Governor Stassen, the then US Foreign Operations Administrator.

Dear Winston

I have studied carefully the proposals for relaxation of East West trade controls which officials of your Government gave to our Embassy in London on March 1st. I understand that those proposals have been personally approved by you.

As you no doubt realise, the United States Government has for some time been conducting a searching review of all aspects of East West Trade Controls. I can assure you that the United States is prepared to go a significant distance towards the contraction and simplification of those controls . . . objectives which we both share.

However, we do not believe we should go so great a distance and so suddenly as the United Kingdom proposals suggest. To do so would be, I think, to go beyond what is immediately safe or in the common interest of the Free World.

I appreciate the weight that must be given to the strong views in favour of decontrol that are held by the British public and by the British business community. I assume, however, that you equally realise the weight of public and Congressional opinion in the United States and the problems arising out of the Battle Act. It would be most unfortunate if pressures in either of our countries produced reactions adversely affecting Anglo-American relations – political, economic, and military – as well as the strength of the NATO coalition.

Ordinarily I would not insert into our correspondence any matter of detail that properly belongs to our respective diplomatic services. But because your recent speech indicates that you have personally considered some of the included questions of the broad general subject, I feel a slight deviation from our normal practice is justified.

I feel strongly that the control system must continue to include equipment and raw materials of high war-potential significance, whether or not they have wide civilian use, where the Soviet bloc has a serious deficiency which it cannot overcome in a short time. However, there is room for discussion as to the scope and severity of the controls which should be applied under this principle.

Whereas the United Kingdom proposals would appear to

[21]

eliminate international lists II and III, I am convinced that there is an area in which quantitative restrictions are the most appropriate control mechanism. Of course, I recognise that it may be desirable to narrow substantially the area to which such controls need be applied, but I do not think we can scrap them altogether.

These seem to me to be the main differences between us. Although the gap appears wide, we have resolved greater differences before this to our mutual advantage and will do so again. I suggest, then, that we ask our responsible officials to meet together very soon, presumably with their French counterparts, and try to find the common ground on which we can continue jointly to provide constructive leadership to this consultative group.

Finally, I have two other suggestions to make. For one thing, I think it would be very useful if our representatives and subsequently the members of the Consultative group, were jointly to examine and assess the meaning and direction of the Russians' new trade policy, including the much-publicised Russian profession of interest in consumer goods.

Secondly, I think it would be advantageous for our representatives to explore ways and means by which the Free World might exploit, in its relations with the Soviet bloc, any decision to relax existing controls.

As ever, D.E.
Sincerely yours,
Winthrop W. Aldrich

The Right Honourable
Sir Winston Churchill, KG, OM, CH, MP
The Prime Minister
10 Downing Street
London SW1

Remembering, as common men and women must, that Eisenhower's letter was initiated by advisors, drafted by Cabinet rank ministers and screened by lawyers, and sent from the most powerful man in the world to the second most powerful leader in the Western alliance, careful analysis is called for.

The tone, which purports to convey a measured and friendly response to the UK move, is in fact both urgent and, in terms of over-reaction, panic-stricken. Presumably, this was because the UK move at Cocom was less than a month away. But to suggest that the security of the free world, and the cohesion of NATO, were seriously threatened by the desire of the UK government to decontrol items such as scrap metal, argues for one of two things. Either the US was genuine in its concern, in which case the reaction can rightly be seen as unbalanced, or the US President, at the behest of his advisors, was attempting to protect US business interests. The latter is by far the most likely explanation, given the US interest in copper and nickel and its marginal degree of control of these minerals compared with the level of control over copper and nickel still in the hands of the UK. In the classic manner of the US bureaucracy in a hostile negotiating posture, there is mixed into the context a red herring in the form of scrap metal. The British Embassy in Moscow and other business sources had told the Board of Trade in London that there was no evidence of serious shortages of scrap metal in the Soviet Union. This information was readily available to the US Embassy in Moscow, but Eisenhower, or rather his advisors, chose to ignore it. Another common negotiating trick still regularly in use at Cocom is for the US team to reach for the President whenever the going gets rough. This allows for the red herring, or whole shoals of red herrings, to be deployed to dilute the effect of hard information, such as that at the disposal of Peter Thorneycroft and the Board of Trade.

Eisenhower himself admits what he calls a minor procedural shift in the letter, in that he reaches down to a level of detail that 'might normally be left to their respective officials'. This is not a minor shift, but it is one which earns a passive snub from Churchill, in that the reply sticks to the conventions, and politely reminds Eisenhower that the officials should be informed of the differences and then allowed to get on with it. But before moving to Churchill's very proper reply it is worth identifying the various 'thrusts' in Eisenhower's letter.

He argues, or rather, he mouths his administration's argument for 'Festina Lente'. Commonsensical though this advice may seem, it had become such a worn out tactic from the American side that Churchill fully supported Thorneycroft's exasperation and maintained his demand for urgency, based on a Board of Trade memo of 29 March 1954. In fact it is noticeable that most memoranda reaching Churchill on this matter within the UK are shorter than Eisenhower's letter to the Prime Minister. And in his letter Eisenhower, in what must have

[23]

seemed, even to Churchill's eyes, a specious argument, suggests that he would not wish to encourage hostility in Anglo-American relations by doing things which were deeply felt by the British public to be inimical, ie, opposing a drive for relaxation in export controls to the Soviet Union. There is no evidence that the British public knew or much cared about the issue, then as now. The prevailing tone in the Western media was thoroughly anti-Soviet at the time. In the United States the McCarthy era was at its apogee. Concern about trade with the Soviet Union was confined to those relatively few companies in a position to do trade with the Soviet bloc and a slightly larger number who might do business if the controls were relaxed. On the whole, the public had no real attitude to the matter, at most, they would have had to resolve the ambiguity of trading with a country held by the government to be deeply inimical to the United Kingdom and its interests.

The appeal in Eisenhower's letter to potential problems with his own Congress is far more real. Few Congressmen or Senators represented constituencies or companies which would so gain in jobs as a result of trade with the Soviet Union, that the political price of general opposition to US policy was worth paying. However, what Eisenhower was projecting, disguised as concern for Western security, was the ongoing dream of the US bureaucracy of obtaining dominant control of all the major resources in the Western world. If this sounds like imperialism in disguise, remember that the republics of Greece and Rome eventually gave way to Imperialism. Indeed, in the more recent past, it was the French Republic which created the French Empire, just as it was the parliamentary democracy of Great Britain which eventually created the largest empire of them all.

Imperial notions arise from internal perceptions of strength, of weakness in others, and from the possession of enough force of arms to project the former and to exploit the latter. Imperial pretensions are not curbed by Constitutions, parliaments or people. They can however be constrained by informed friends and a balance of strength with potential adversaries. In this latter respect Eisenhower was projecting one of the clearest perceptions ever to hold the changing mind of any bureaucracy over an extended period. From the twenties to the present day the American bureaucracy and establishment have united in seeing in the Soviet Union an uncompromising military threat, and perhaps more deeply, an ideological threat. In some ways the wartime necessity to unite with one form of totalitarianism in order to defeat another, left the central US establishment more determined than ever to try to end the political system that gives the Soviet Union its colossal strength.

[24]

The American establishment and its attendant bureaucracy, can tolerate anything except ambiguity. To have discovered that communism was not the major source of evil in the world, as the US had to do in World War II, left a deep trauma in the psyche of America's ruling élite, one which remains unhealed and unregenerate to the present day.

However, like all things American, this one proved to have some quite significant commercial advantages. It produced on the part of the elected representatives of the American people a permanent willingness to sanction peace time military budgets that have produced a wealth of jobs and profits for the armaments manufacturers and their attendant industries. In a generation that has seen the superpowers test their aggression only through surrogate nations such as Israel, Korea and South Vietnam, on battlefields far removed from the native soil of the sponsor powers, it has also given the United States the key corporations in most leading edge technologies. What Eisenhower was doing in his virtually unprecedented letter, was helping to secure the internal controls, in the hands of the US, that would ensure permanent domination of the West's key strategic economic activities. Periods during which one power is in the process of consolidating its control over others, especially when the operation is essentially clandestine, produce extraordinary sensitivity on the part of those conducting the exercise.

It is not hard to see why the US bureaucracy over-reacted and forced the President into over-reaction. They saw their precious game plan threatened by a bluff, robust, English politician who had the ear of his own Prime Minister, who in turn was not going to give way to any emanations of the anti-Communist hysteria then sweeping the US. Not only was the game plan threatened by the UK, so was the whole careful structure of duplicity, involving principally the United Kingdom and France but driven by the United States upon which the Cocom structure rested.

It is clear from the various Cabinet minutes now available that Cocom was merely the forum through which procedures and regulations originating in the US, bilaterally agreed with Britain and at a later stage with France, were imposed on the other members of the committee. There were two critical bodies through which the various US initiatives were moved on their way to Cocom. The first was the Paris group, the second the Consultative group. By securing British and French approval for Cocom proposals in advance, in these two bodies, there was nothing at all that the minor powers could hope to achieve in

[25]

Cocom. It is not clear to what extent either the NATO council or the governments of the other Cocom members knew they were being set up, or that Cocom was no more than a rubber stamp for US policy. Probably they knew quite well. Probably too, the minor-power bureaucracies possessed the same inherent willingness to perform the essential betrayal of their countries' interests by agreeing, via obscure detail, to compromises of principle that no civilised human being should accept.

At any rate, the sight of the UK delegation arriving in full flown and total opposition to the United States, at the Cocom meeting, would have many messages for the other members. The black flag of rebellion, flown with the authority of the one man whose lone stand against fascism had led to the liberation of Europe, would not be lost on those who'd suffered under fascism. Certainly the coherence of the Anglo-American position would be called into question. It would be assumed that negotiations in the Paris group, in the consultative committee and between the Prime Minister and the President, had failed. It might even be assumed that this minor laying down of the American yoke in so public a way before the whole Cocom group, signalled changes in the UK position more strategic than tactical. In particular, since trade, and not war, was the issue, it might even be assumed that Sir Winston was airing his well known personal hankering for what has now become the EEC. In fact, no such switch of stance initiated the UK position. Peter Thorneycroft's departmental supplicants had a raft of good solid orders from the Soviet Union to fulfil. The Embassy in Moscow had checked out the position inside the Soviet Union as to the Soviet deficiencies in these materials, and confirmed the general safety of the deals.

The US side chose to deal, instead, in the interior fantasies of power in its expansionary phase. They chose to believe that the UK position would be misunderstood, and that rebellion would follow. If that happened, the US bid to replace the old political empires with a new economic and industrial imperialism of its own would be frustrated. The war had given the United States the opportunity, and imposed the necessary expansion on its economy, so that it emerged both militarily victorious and economically on a par with the old but dying empires. By switching wartime controls, originally intended to deprive the axis powers of strategic materials, through 180°, and imposing them on trade with the wartime ally, Russia, the US entered the post-war period with a unique capability to organise the economic destiny of the Western world, provided the rest of the West agreed.

The first five years after the war when dependence on the US for dollars to get Europe out of its difficulties was genuine, also saw the gradual merging of those American and British wartime controls into the basic Cocom structure. In this exercise in national commercial suicide the UK bureaucracy played a full and willing part. Wartime import controls were not abolished, just applied to new and different destinations. Parliament was never consulted. The Labour Cabinet in the immediate post-war period seemed only dimly aware of what was happening, and seems to have been totally unaware of where US policy was taking the United Kingdom, in commercial terms.

By 1949 the US needed something more than secret agreements with the servant bureaucracies in Europe in order to consolidate its hold on the restructuring economies. NATO was formed, and a captive market for US armaments, disguised as a military/political alliance, was created. The USSR shortly responded with the Warsaw Pact, creating for the people of Eastern Europe and Russia, to mirror-image the West, a new tax burden to pay for the escalation of the arms race.

But in one key respect NATO failed the United States. The strategic materials control system did not make it as a proper legal part of the NATO structure. There were a variety of reasons for this and in one sense the US itself was the primary reason the control remained extra legal. The US bureaucrat has a natural inclination, even more natural than their inclination to pursue US policy, to keep secret that which is already secret. Briefly, it can be put like this:

The US was out to shaft everyone, friend and foe alike. The UK cut a slightly better deal, or so it seemed, at the time, by getting first in line for operation, 'screw you all'. It gave the UK an apparent advantage over its European neighbours, starting with the French. This pleased the UK civil service, which in total contradiction to the view held by the elected leader, Churchill, could not stand Europeans, least of all the French. Unfortunately, the minor pleasure of 'buggering the French' was hardly compensated for by the total rape of the UK industrial base, which can now be seen in all its naked squalor, but which commenced in those far off days of thirty years ago. So the UK stayed with the routine of bilateral, trilateral and finally Cocom controls. And the US settled for that procedure, first to protect the essentially dubious international legality of the exercise, secondly, in order to keep NATO free of the inevitable jurisdictional rows as GATT, EFTA and later the EEC, came into being.

But, going back to the third week of March, 1954, Eisenhower gets his reply.

[27]

Please pass the following personal and private message to
President from Prime Minister.
Begins
My Dear Friend
Thank you for your message of March 19 about the relaxation of
East/West trade controls. We shall be very glad to talk over with
your representatives the points set out in your message and I
would urge that the talks should take place as soon as possible. I
agree that French representatives should also take part. I
suggest that if possible our officials should be informed before
the discussions begin what variation in terms of items your
Government would wish to make to the revised list we have
proposed.
Winston
Encs.

As soon as the document hit Washington, with the implications of an
unchanged UK position, it was 'all hands on deck and man the pumps'.
A major diplomatic offensive was mounted with focus on London and
Paris. The fruitful outcome of this, from the US point of view, will be
seen later. In the meantime the inner US establishment reached for the
mailed fist and sent it direct to its counterparts in the UK.

TOP SECRET
From Department of the Army, Washington
To Ministry of Defence, London
OPERATION IMMEDIATE
Info American Embassy
29 March 1954
For US Joint Chiefs of Staff to British Chiefs of Staff Info.
Governor Stassen
Signed Radford
As you probably know our two Governments appear to be a
little far apart as to the extent of relaxation of east-west trade
controls which should be adopted now. At the Prime Minister's
invitation to the President, Governor Stassen, the United States
Foreign Operations Administrator, left for London Friday to
discuss with the tops of your own Government, on behalf of the
President, a reconciliation of these diverging viewpoints.
It has been made clear to the President, that from the military
viewpoint, and despite political and economic factors which

[28]

must of course be taken into account, relaxation of controls to the extent proposed by your Government would in our opinion constitute a grave security threat not only to the United States but to the Western world on the whole. Particularly we fear its effect both at home and abroad upon the support now afforded by its members to the NATO structure.

We do not presume to make any suggestion regarding the forthcoming negotiations, nor particularly with respect to means by which a common meeting ground between the two Governments may be reached. However, your attention is invited particularly to the following points which appear to bear on the matter in the military sphere.

(a) The United States Government fears that the drastic cutback currently proposed by the United Kingdom in east-west controls of trade would incur, if adopted, such strong Congressional reaction that our Foreign Aid Appropriations, soon to come up for action in the Congress, might be seriously curtailed below the projected program of the administration.

(b) With respect to our offshore procurement (OSP) program for European Defense, a number of both raw materials and goods which would be decontrolled under the United Kingdom proposal fall either in the same category or are identical with materials which have been allocated to NATO countries under either our end-item aid (MDAP) or OSP programs. Public reaction here to such a situation would, in our opinion, contribute nothing to continuing American support of those programs.

(c) We feel sure that your Ministry of Supply will recall that during World War II, lack or shortage of specific materials and production equipment from time to time created military production bottlenecks of sometimes drastic import. This situation today exists in the Soviet Bloc to a large extent, many of the items concerned, such as copper, mica, abrasives, bearings, nickel, machine tools and locomotives are among those proposed by the United Kingdom to be decontrolled.

(d) The United States considers that the present level of the security advantage of the West with respect to the Soviet Bloc is minimal, if not less. Further relaxation of control, we feel, consequently would require either additional production or expenditures which we can ill-afford, or else the acceptance of a further reduction in the security advantage of the free world.[1]

Here indeed is the parent bureaucracy playing the nanny to the wayward British government. The US Chiefs of Staff knew, obviously in advance, that a major crisis between the two countries was not only in the making but actually in progress. From material available from MoD (Ministry of Defence) files in the Public Record Office it is not clear whether the UK Chiefs of Staff knew of the crisis. Certainly there is no evidence at all, until the arrival of this telegram, that they appreciated that the situation was in crisis. And it is equally unclear to what extent the MoD took the missive seriously. Certainly Churchill and Thorneycroft found the pressures inside the system mounting irresistibly.

But what were the arguments from the Pentagon? Are they as they should properly be, military arguments? The answer is no. The line in some ways is very similar to that taken in Eisenhower's letter, which is hardly a surprise since the initiative for Eisenhower's letter came from a level in the American bureaucracy in which the US Chiefs of Staff have participation. However, it comes much closer to recognising that if the UK maintained its posture, then there could be repercussions within the NATO structure. Despite the fact that Cocom is not a part of any NATO structure, a revolt in that forum by the UK would lead very quickly to a questioning of the relationships which constitute the key elements of NATO. If the US estimate of what constituted a strategic threat were rejected by the UK, the other members of NATO could hardly continue to repose such confidence in US views, particularly on the issue of strategic goods.

In arguing that the UK view posed a threat to the US the Joint Chiefs of Staff were at least being truthful. The linchpin of US grand strategy in the economic field lay in the control of key commercial goods, under the guise of security controls. The particular point at which the UK chose to make its challenge was utterly critical. It was already becoming clear in 1954 that economic activity in Germany, Japan and the UK was reaching a point at which any of the three economies might achieve independent take off, thus lessening dependence on the US and consequently diminishing US control. If that happened, any of the three economies might begin to generate significant commercial competition for the big US corporations, something the US has always been anxious to avoid. Indeed, as we shall see, US action in 1954 postponed the inevitable for almost thirty years, and did leave two of the target economies, those of the UK and West Germany, still very dependent on them and well within the ambit of exercisable control. Japan, on the other hand, has achieved virtual independence of the United States certainly in terms of its high technology development capacity, and in its

[30]

trading freedoms. But in 1954 the US Joint Chiefs of Staff were proposing essentially political and aid/commercial arguments in favour of the
UK military lining up against Thorneycroft and Churchill. As with the
Eisenhower letter, the US military argued potential congressional problems and cuts in the aid procurement budget. The latter argument in
particular seems utterly specious. NATO was into a purchasing
situation with the United States which can only be described as a nine
lane highway from the US, with the return traffic confined to the hard
shoulder.

Again, it is very difficult to know what the UK Chiefs of Staff
thought of the matter – their lobbying may have been confined to a few
remarks between ministers and soldiers in their club, the usual English
thing. At lower echelons of the civil service, but still at the highest levels
of power in the UK, the military threw in their lot against the elected
representatives of the people and sent around the word that Thorneycroft was rocking the boat. In due course the Foreign Office became
appraised of the lie of the land at the MoD and then faced a direct lobby
from the US Embassy. This combination of pressures gradually paved
the way for the dissolution, by civil service action, of the Thorneycroft/
Churchill initiative.

But the argument about national security was made, if in general
terms. The US Chiefs of Staff argued for control as a means of maintaining bottlenecks and critical shortages inside the Soviet Union.
Their argument was that such shortages had caused major problems to
the Allies during the war. The facts in this case being correct the flaw
has to be sought in the logic. The implication here is that the Soviet
Union is a war economy, forever in a state of attempted mobilisation
against the West. That is the kind of argument which has been used to
maintain the tempo of hostility between the two superpowers for the
past forty years, and which has caused the expenditure of untold
trillions of pounds, most of it to armament manufacturers, most of
them in the States. But it is an argument which should have been made
subject to critical analysis by the UK military which had, and still has,
considerable independent verification capacity in relation to the
situation in the Soviet Union.

Because the US argument in this case, though general in tone, was
addressing a specific situation, the MoD and the Intelligence Services
should have made the claim the subject of objective, factual analysis, as
well as medium-term strategic analysis. There is no evidence that this
happened or, if it did, that anyone took any notice of it at the higher
levels of the civil service. Most of the material shows the final decisions

being formulated and made as a result of cocktail circuit conversations (see page 33), very often with the predictable result of voiding Cabinet and Prime Ministerial decisions, as happened in this case.

The last argument (d) is a particularly curious one. In 1954 the West had, in reality, parity or better with the Soviet Union in terms of conventional forces. The forcible occupation of the Eastern bloc buffer states, by the Red Army, was foreseen in the Tehran, Rabat and Yalta summits and was the mirror image and proper military response to the existence in the West European buffer states of significant American forces. At conventional level the military balance, when administrative and reserve division are removed from the Soviet forces order of battle, was about symmetrical and equal. At the strategic level the situation was radically different. The US and by extension NATO, with its two independent nuclear powers, the UK and France, possessed overwhelming atomic superiority. There are still no independent nuclear powers within the Soviet empire and the Soviet Union in 1954 lacked a real capacity to defeat an atomic first strike from the West. The UK military knew that in 1954, just as they know the true nature of the superpower standoff now. In addition, it is clear from the material available to the UK Government, that what the Soviet Union really lacked and still lacks is organisation, particularly in the non-military, industrial sectors.

In 1954, the UK military essentially adopted a position in relation to both the government and UK trade, based on political arguments from the US side. There is no obligation on the UK military to support or agree with the government of the day. The only obligation in that respect is to speak up for what they believe to be the vital defence interests of the country and follow what orders they are given. In this particular case only the issue of opinion arises, since no military orders were issued on the matter. By supporting the US initiative however, the MoD showed a thoroughgoing inability to understand the issue at stake, or the UK interest in it. It would appear that the US telegram and its widespread dissemination within the UK bureaucracy, had the desired effect, with no evidence that either the Prime Minister or the President of the Board of Trade ever saw the original text. From the distribution list the Embassy was able to identify all the most sympathetic individuals in the UK structure, and apply pressure on them, which it did, both through normal channels and through the military attachés. This lobby within the system probably had a far more profound effect than direct American lobbying. Faced with many of their colleagues within far more influential ministries taking the American

[32]

line, support for the President of the Board of Trade within the Board, the Foreign Office and finally, within the Cabinet Office, faded.

How faded became clear two months later, when a series of clever manoeuvres by the US delegation on the eve of the Cocom meeting following on from the Paris group meeting on 13 April, led to the virtual dismissal of every element of the Thorneycroft proposals. It seems, from the final paragraph of the Coulson memo, that it was Reggie Maudling who wound up with the task of informing the hapless Thorneycroft that his brave effort to pave the way for normal trade with the Soviet Union to be dealt with as normal trade, was over.

First of all Coulson, perhaps without realising it, shows how the US disrupted the attempt to get machine tools off the list.

Decontrol
2   When the Delegation were on the point of putting a paper to COCOM proposing that COCOM should agree to the removal from control of the machine tool items whose deletion had been agreed, the American delegation made some difficulties and asked that the matter should be discussed with Mr Stassen before we put our paper in. This was in spite of the fact that we understood that this exact procedure agreed in London was satisfactory to the Americans. After some discussion and a slight revision of our paper, the Delegation sorted this out with the Americans.

But it didn't stay sorted out for long.

3   In addition however Mr Harpham arranged a lunch attended on the American side by Mr Gordon, Mr Loftus (the chief American East-West Trade delegate in Paris) and Mr George (Department of Commerce) at which Mr Dunnett and I were also present. The Americans confirmed that they were in agreement with our paper going in but expressed particular anxiety as to how we should handle the French.

Thus the UK delegation was adroitly pushed into lobbying a whole range of delegations who knew nothing of the deals struck between the UK and the US in London. The UK delegation were in serious trouble, but worse was to follow.

Procedure for Putting in our Lists.
9   At a reception given last night for Mr Stassen, he drew me aside and said he had just been informed of our decision to omit

the disputed items from the Lists which we were submitting to COCOM. He said that he regarded this decision as being a very serious matter and he must ask that it should be the subject of Ministerial consultation before we took action. He pointed out that copper, nickel and scrap iron were particularly delicate subjects for the Americans and he had indeed mentioned these three items particularly to the Prime Minister when he was in London. Scrap iron is apparently of particular political importance, although it is obviously an item which is essentially concerned with normal trade. I said that we would not put our paper into COCOM first thing the next morning, as had been our intention, and that we would consider his representations. He said the matter could be discussed in Geneva between Mr Eden and Mr Bedell Smith; between the Chancellor and himself in Paris; or any way we liked.

10 As Mr Maudling is a member of the relevant Ministerial Committee, I arranged for Mr Stassen to discuss the question with him. Mr Stassen spoke on the same lines and Mr Maudling, after pointing out that Russia could easily obtain her strategic requirements of copper from her own resources by squeezing the civilian uses, promised to give further consideration to what Mr Stassen had said. He proposes in fact to take the question up with the President of the Board of Trade.

J E Coulson
Paris 6.5.54

He did. The initiative died. Machine tools are still on the embargo list, though several Eastern Bloc countries now export machine tools to the West.

One document which shows with great clarity just how the US planned and executed its moves is an *aide memoire* from the American Embassy in London dated the same day as the US Chief of Staff's memo and obviously sent to the UK Cabinet Office, from whose papers it is extracted. There is no indication of author or recipient.

SECRET
The East-West Trade issue can be successfully handled without an adverse division between the United Kingdom and the United States with a bit of patience and a step by step review, as rapidly as possible and to be completed in the next three

[34]

months, of the present control list. We are in agreement that the present control list should be substantially shortened and that thus shortened can be and should be more effectively enforcable.

The United States considers it to be essential that the shortening take place step by step in the European Coordinating Committee (COCOM) with advance, step by step consultation between the United Kingdom and the United States.

The United States has not completed its internal, detailed, itemized review and is willing to revise first the categories which the United Kingdom wishes to place in priority.

An agreed instruction to the European Coordination Committee (COCOM) for a comprehensive review to result in a shortened list under new criteria, appropriate to the long haul and the current strategic appraisal, will be satisfactory and workable.

A precipitate tabling on 13 April of the very short United Kingdom list will cause unmanageable repercussions in the United States and will result in a procedure whereby the concerned Western European countries express opinions on a split issue between the United Kingdom and the United States.

The step by step technical review will result in a shortened list at an early date, with deletions to be made as progressively agreed, and will rapidly narrow the divergence between the United Kingdom and the United States. Remaining differences between us should then be resolved by high level bilateral consideration, not by multilateral decisions. On this basis the public understanding and essential Congressional support can be mobilised.

> *American Embassy London*
> 29 March 1954

While his proposal was slowly dissolving to death in the higher reaches of the British bureaucracy, Peter Thorneycroft was ploughing on with his plan. He gave way on the core of the American thrust and conceded the need to find a common meeting point. From an industrial point of view, and in perfect line with what the UK tried to achieve, he was still reaching for the keystone lists that the Americans needed to keep at all costs if they were to maintain their ultimate objective of US strategic control over key strategic materials.

Thorneycroft wrote to Churchill on 30 March 1954. 'If we accept the United States proposal (to proceed with an eight week review, and for the UK not to unilaterally introduce its list) there are two matters which I think we must make quite plain. First, we must say at the outset what we are going to do. It must be made plain that our objective is a substantial relaxation of the existing list. Secondly, we must throughout the operation reserve our freedom of action on our own short list.'

But Thorneycroft was making the very same mistake his predecessors had always made with the Americans, and that his successors continued to make, right up to the end of 1985. They were telling the Americans in advance just what they were going to do, thereby giving the thoroughly prepared and alert US negotiators plenty of time to plan ambushes that were as effective in 1984 as they were in 1954.

In Thorneycroft's 30 March memorandum to Churchill there were two sentences that express the essence of the UK mistake in Cocom, and the precise tactic the US has used to bloat lists that were large in 1954 into documents which are now several feet thick and which contain between 400,000 and 700,000 items.

> While we accept the genuineness of the United States proposal,
> past experience of these negotiations has shown that they
> generally lead to endless and fruitless debate. We have been
> debating some items for a year and have reached no conclusion yet.

There are items on the Cocom lists which have been there for thirty years and debated for thirty years and about which no conclusion has been reached, and which are still on the lists. But the real mistake in Thorneycroft's approach was to even begin to believe that the United States officials were being either genuine or by implication sincere. The US was genuine and sincere only in three things. Its remorseless defence of its existing and projected interests in the control of free world commerce, in exactly the same way the USSR controls the commerce of the Eastern Bloc countries; its hidden determination to wage all out continuous economic war against the Soviet Union, where it could not engage that country in direct surrogate military warfare; and finally, in wanting to strip the European powers of their former colonies, not for any good reason but in order on the one hand to deprive them of potential strategic materials and, on the other, to open up those strategic materials to exploitation by the big US corporations.

To a large extent, particularly in the overall global content, those plans have been remarkably successful. Where the US corporations have failed to get control, as the ideal objective would have dictated, no one else has. That is a very tolerable outcome. But the drive for this goal

[36]

would have been hopelessly frustrated if the Soviet economy had woken up and started to grow in anything like the way the US economy had. Taken together, the Soviet and Chinese economies, particularly in tandem, would have dwarfed the West in every sector. And the US had, and still has, every reason to believe that the two rival economies will one day explode into the kind of productivity that marked the US in the early part of this century.

Only two things are preventing this phenomenon. One is the particularly rigid and totalitarian form communism has taken in the two countries. The other is the lack of crucial technology 'catalysts' in sufficient quantity. The fact that the US recognised the importance of the catalysts themselves is inherent in the Cocom set up itself. The fact that quantity is almost as critical as availability, is recognised in several of the US fallback positions for the 1954 negotiations, which speak of substituting 'quota' arrangements for an absolute embargo. Given Peter Thorneycroft's remark that the Soviet Union could easily supply its copper requirements from its own resources, and given the level of information on the Soviet economy available to the US, their insistence on maintaining copper on the list, misunderstood by the UK as a negotiating tactic, was actually aimed at exercising control over the Belgian-controlled copper in the Congo, and the UK-controlled copper in Zambia. In practice, existing world markets for copper in 1954 and subsequently were pretty well fixed. No surge in consumption was likely while the US remained the major user. No decontrolling surge was likely so long as the two major potential world economies stayed trapped by their adopted ideologies, and without wide-spread access to the technology 'catalysts' on a scale commensurate with the needs inside their respective economic structures.

But this is an economic argument, not a military one. What is worse, the effects of the implementation of this policy have, in fact, been a military disaster, which may yet turn into a catastrophe for the West. And that is without even considering the industrial disaster that has actually occurred in Europe as a result of accepting US domination of COCOM. Over time, even the most secret of policies stand revealed, not by the discovery of documents relating to their formulation or implementation, but by their effects. If COCOM was meant to keep the Soviet Union in the military boondocks, then the US needs to explain four things:

THE PAST
1 The Soviet Union put the first man-made object into space, four months ahead of the US.
2 The Soviet Union put the first man into space, ten months ahead of the US.

[37]

3 The Soviet Union has had a manned space station in orbit for the past two years. The US/European space station is not due until the 1990s.

4 The Soviet Union has maintained space teams in orbit for more than ten times as long as the longest US mission.

THE PRESENT

1 By the time this book is in print the first manned mission to the inner planets will be in an advanced stage of planning. It will be a Soviet mission. At the time of writing the Soviet Union has a rocket with a 200 ton payload on the launch pad at Baiknur. There are three or four more such vehicles in preparation. The president of the European Space Agency, speaking to the author in the House of Commons in summer 1985, said he knew of the existence of the rockets, but did not know what they were for. To give some idea of the scale of what the Soviet Union is about to embark on, it is worth remembering that a Jumbo 747 with its full passenger load, weighs only 370 tons. What the Soviet Union is planning to do is put the equivalent of two jumbos into space, and fly the equivalent of one of them, containing two men and one woman, off on an eighteen month mission. They will be a lot more comfortable and have a lot more space to run around in than anyone on the ship in which Christopher Columbus discovered America.

2 The Soviet Union has test-flown a shuttle vehicle that is almost twice the size of the American *Columbus* vehicle, though this has not been reported in the Western media. Similarly, the Soviet Union is testing a small shuttle vehicle, similar to *Columbus*, again almost unreported in the West.

3 There are a series of other technical developments including a working fusion motor, which are far ahead of any likely development in the West, this side of 1990.

INNER SPACE

1 The Soviet Union has built a submarine weighing 25,000 tons with a titanium hull. The largest American nuclear submarine is 18,000 tons and titanium, with vital, 'low sound', and other characteristics, has defeated the best efforts of the West for twenty years to use it for submarine hulls.

2 The Soviet Union, according to *Jane's Fighting Ships*, has deployed six submarines, presumably of the hunter killer type, which can travel at 42 knots at 3,500 feet with a new propulsion system

[38]

which virtually eliminates propeller noise. There are no similar submarines in Western navies. Some US submarines are alleged to be able to reach 3,000 feet but unable to maintain high speed at that depth.

SUPERCOMPUTERS

1 In the computer industry, as in the car industry, there are family saloons and Formula 1 racing cars. The family saloons are the mainframe and mini-computers to be found in almost every Western business today. The Ferraris of the computer industry are known as supercomputers. At the time of writing there are still less than one hundred such machines in the Western world, even though the first such machine was produced in the early sixties. Only two men, Dr Gene Amdahl and Dr Seymour Cray, both Americans, have shown any aptitude for designing or building such machines. Dr Amdahl's backers, the multinational computer corporation IBM, lost heart in the sixties, such were the perceived difficulties of building and marketing these machines. But Dr Cray is still the world's leading designer/builder of such machines. He has created on the back of his devices a series of companies, each of which continues to be heavily reliant on his work and blueprints. All the manufacturing of supercomputers, which are used to model nuclear explosions, whole weather systems and so on, was, until two years ago, done in the United States. Suddenly, in 1984, there were five supercomputer companies in the world. The three newcomers were all Japanese.

Supercomputers are rated according to the number of floating point arithmetic operations they can do each second. The Cray 1, introduced in 1978, going flat out on a straight addition problem, the equivalent to running on a straight road with no bends and no wind against it, peaks at 2,000 million additions per second. On an ordinary calculation or problem, the average speed is between 20 and 30 per cent of that. At the moment, the Cray 3, due for delivery in 1987, is scheduled to peak at 10,000 million 'additions' per second.

The secret of a supercomputer lies not in either the technology or the electronics but in the architecture, that blending of brain power and arrangement of components which is the true frontier of high technology today.

The Soviet Union and Supercomputers

The Soviet Union, it is now becoming clear, focused its own extraordinary wealth of mathematical talent and that of the Hungarian maths institute in Budapest, on to supercomputers at least twenty years ago.

[39]

There appears to have been a deliberate decision in a technology appendix to a five-year plan in the early sixties which gave precedence to supercomputers and placed on a back burner the widespread introduction of data processing machines such as the United States has made the dominant computer technology in the West.

The result appears to be one of the best kept secrets in the Soviet Union, despite very occasional leaks. According to the fragmentary evidence available, the USSR has at least three, possibly more, supercomputer complexes. Nothing is known about the machines, their architecture or technology. All that is known is that they were used progressively to solve the titanium hull and deep diving problem for the Soviet navy. They provided the plans and calculations for the Soviet space effort, and largely explain why so little electronic technology appears aboard Soviet spacecraft. The handling of Soviet space telemetry and of space mission control is in the hands of daughter computers, designed as part of the solution to the space problem, in the big complexes themselves. According to the best estimates available, just one of those supercomputer complexes delivers 50,000 million to 70,000 million floating point operations per second. If that is true, then the US lead in the far less significant technology of data processing machines is more than compensated for by the two-generation lead in supercomputer technology that the Soviet Union possesses.

In passing, it is worth noting that Europe possesses no supercomputer building capacity and no independent mainframe manufacturing capacity.

The price of forty-one years of voluntary sacrifice by the NATO Alliance of its independence in technology is to find its main adversary in possession of a significant tactical advantage in three key areas of technology: in outer space, in inner space and finally in the very heart of computer technology. It is not only time that the wholly American policy which lay behind the situation was exposed. It is also time that the citizens of the United States asked their elected representatives to get an accounting for this prolonged error of judgment, which began as opportunism mixed with greed and which has, in its senile phase, led the West into a blind alley from which escape can only be purchased at immense cost, if at all. Had Peter Thorneycroft succeeded in persuading British bureaucracy to see through the policy he and Churchill endorsed and agreed in 1953 and 1954, it is just possible – but only just– that the UK, and possibly France, might still possess strategic foundation industries in high technology.

They do not, but no lesson has been learned from the debacle. No

[40]

lesson has been learned because to do so, as Enoch Powell has often noted, would force the UK Civil Service to question their unjustified faith in the US on the one hand and their day to day inability to succeed in negotiations with US representatives, on the other. Fear permeates the higher reaches of the UK Civil Service. Fear of the US, fear of the light of day, fear of discovery, compounded by a total and utter lack of faith in democracy, even in its elected representatives when they form the government. These statements are not merely polemical. They are the outcome of five years of dealing with the Civil Service, of watching ministers make fools of themselves in public because they have not been briefed properly, or of discovering that what the media imagines is policy is very often the result of the Permanent Secretary's perusal of that morning's copy of *The Times*.

If these statements are true, they should reveal that policy and its presentation show a total lack of analysis of the nature of technology, its origin, its foundations, its content and its framework. And it does, particularly in relation to the huge success of US high technology companies whose crucial development phases are all militarily (or publicly) funded in the United States. They should also reveal a failure to implement policy, particularly in relation to negotiations with the US. In fact, in extremis, they should reveal a dependence in detail on policy as formulated in the United States. The next chapter will show how the debacle of 1954 was repeated, almost word for word and action by action, in 1984. It will also show, not only UK policy being drafted in the United States, but UK law as well.

---

[1] This document was circulated as follows: Foreign Office; War Registry, Admiralty; Message Control, War Office; Registry Telegrams, Air Ministry; Mr P. H. Dean; Mr R. S. Crawford, F.C.; Director J.I.B.; Mr H. Crosswell.

CHAPTER 3

The Coordinating Committee

COCOM IS FORMALLY DESCRIBED as the extra-legal, non-treaty-based, informal body through which, it is claimed, the non-communist states, including most NATO nations, meet to agree unilaterally what trade shall be done with the nations of the communist world, including Cuba and the People's Republic of China.

Historically, as the previous chapter showed, Cocom was the recipient of instructions, issued by the US, the UK and France, to its other members. Between 1949 and 1974, Cocom had no independent determining power over the contents of the three key lists of goods emanating from it: the Nuclear List, the Munitions List and the Industrial List. Cocom still has no independent determining power but, as this chapter, based entirely on material openly available in the United States will show, the orders are issued from one source only – the US. And, as the same material clearly demonstrates, it is not the US government, or even the President, who is attempting to impose total control over all Western trade, within the West itself. It is the United States Department of Defence, or the Pentagon as it is more popularly known.

When a short examination and comparison is made between the US demands for Cocom as expressed in the Pentagon review of 1984, the US regulations and, finally, the United Kingdom law, they demonstrate a common drafting source.

It seemed appropriate in the spring of 1985, and especially in the wake of an uncharacteristic failure by the *Guardian* to find the Cocom HQ,[1] to go and make a personal search for the place. Something of a valedictory tour one might say, now that most of the Cocom machinations were out in the open, and now that we were assured of a debate in the House of Commons on the issue (see page 168). And, with my journalistic career coming to a temporary halt, it seemed appropriate to go back to first base in journalism, to put on, as it were, the grubby mac and the dirty fedora and go there myself. But first of all, to throw the hounds off the trail, and confuse my bugged phones, I had to find a nice, anonymous way to France. Easy: a friend booked me onto the overnight coach to Paris one Friday night. No name was asked for and no name was given. On the phone I booked myself a seat on an Air France flight and a room in the George V, neither of which I used. At the passport checkpoints on either side of the Channel I did not even have to open my passport. In Paris I booked into a single room in a hotel in the Rue Henri Monnier, for thirty-seven francs a night. No one asked for my name, but simply gave me a preprinted receipt with Prix 37f written on it. The wallpaper peeled off the bedroom walls in long curling lengths, along which I imagined fleas marching, before they began their regular para drop on to my body. The lavatory was down a dank corridor and the odours coming through the door plainly indicated that it should be used in emergencies only. The blankets were handed over with the receipt. Aid issue for the victims of an earthquake in Agadir it appeared from a very faint label on one of them.

On the Saturday morning, from a call box in the Gare Du Nord, I rang a very pretty girl photographer, Phillipa, I had met at an exhibition in 1982.

'Will Pierre let me borrow you for today? I want to commit a little espionage against our cousins across the pond, and I want you to photograph it for free.'

Pierre was now Jacques, it appeared, and she thought it was a hoot. I could hear her shouting, 'Hurry up Jacques, I must work today. It is the *Sunday Times* of New York.'

Oh well, if ships of passage use the Liberian flag, why not?

Her willingness to join me more or less immediately threw up the first problem. I had no actual plan, other than to try to find the annexe to the American Embassy, and then to try to find out if that actually was the Cocom HQ. It seemed more than premature to engage a photographer before I had established the facts. But it appeared I had.

There was also Regis Debray. Debray is now the president of the Council of State for France, the body which examines French law and administration for accuracy in relation to the Constitution. Once upon a time, he was the companion hero to Che Guevara, and could easily be confused in the musical *Evita* with the Guevara figure. After all, it was Che who died shooting and Debray who lived to ask all the awkward questions. He had published a book in the spring of 1985 in which he dealt with the problem of Europe versus the Empires of both the United States and the Soviet Union. I had made contact with him, and

[43]

he had expressed an interest in having sight of some of the material Paddy and I had. But that had to be delivered to the doorkeeper of the Council D'Etat, since Mr Debray was away in the country for the weekend.

Phillipa and I agreed to meet at the Crillon. 'I,' she said, 'will bring the lunch.'

Inspiration that was too. The day was fine and she decided, greetings and meetings completed, that we would desport ourselves and our Cahors, on a park bench just behind the Gendarmerie bus from which the guard on the annexe was being mounted.

'They will have to check that we are not planting a bomb,' Phillipa said, 'and maybe they will talk to us.'

She was absolutely right and following the acceptance of a courtesy mug of wine with us we managed to establish that indeed we had found Cocom. Not only that, but in a misundestanding, during which they assumed that we were going to Cocom too, the gendarmes told us that some of the delegations, the British and Portuguese they thought, had already arrived, and others were expected for some kind of reception. The rest of the day was spent in the vicinity of the annexe and in the bars, east, south, north and west of the place. But the best of all was the Crillon. By the time we got there, I had promised Phillipa, on the back of what we had established, which included most of the agenda for the coming meeting, that I would take her to dinner at the Deux Magots in Montmartre if she would face an hour in the Crillon. It was a good hour. A group of Americans were discussing what eventually transpired was the final day's negotiations in 1984. I was only sufficiently sober to get one full quote down:

'Godammit,' the big American said. 'The Brits bought the whole damn package. They just lay on their backs, put their feet in the air and bought the whole thing, the works. Well f . . k me, I could've died, after all that pissing about.'

But we left for Montmartre with Phillipa in possession of all the photographs we needed and me with a good guide to the negotiations then in progress. By the time I'd dropped off a very tiddly Phillipa and got back to my garret, neither the smell nor the fleas bothered me. Only one scream woke me that night. For the rest, oblivion that would have kept me out cold had I been sleeping on broken glass.

I got back to England, undetected. Was it worth it? I think so. Second hand evidence is not accepted in English courts and should not be acceptable in an English book. Nonetheless, the evidence in this case needed corroboration. It rested substantially on material already carefully gathered, mostly in London, starting in 1983, particularly in the wake of the Root resignation.

It became clear during the course of 1983 that some major deadlock had occurred in Cocom. There were two items which regularly surfaced off the record with DTI officials, and one which ministers, under pressure, referred to in Parliament. The off the record references were always to 'the computer item' and to US efforts to get a military committee added to the Cocom structure. The institution of a military committee has been a long term US goal, alongside the more recent demand for an increase in the staff and facilities at the annexe. The most implacable foe of both these proposals has long been the British Prime Minister, Margaret Thatcher. In one notable period of high tension between the UK and the US towards the end of 1983 an official in the Foreign Office actually quoted to me one of her remarks. 'The Prime Minister,' he said, 'has told the Americans that the right place for the military is back home in their own capitals.' I was told the quote could be used if I did not name the source.

What was revealed, of course, was what has always been the case, ie, that Cocom is a matter that has preoccupied prime ministers ever since the foundation of the organisation. Policy for Cocom is decided by the prime minister of the day, even if the decision is based on represent- ation from other ministers. In fact, the lead up to the 1983 crisis has so many similarities with 1954 that it is uncanny. Once more the key dispute focuses on an American attempt to expand the international lists, and a UK attempt to limit the lists. For the latter opinion we have Paul Channon's statement in the House of Commons debate on 13 April 1984. 'We want,' he said, 'a short, policeable list.' Just so, and a verbatim repeat of what Peter Thorneycroft was telling Churchill in 1954.

But the dispute over the computer item was radical, indeed terminal, for Cocom in one sense. To understand just what the computer dispute was about, it is necessary to have a look at two things. The first is the computer industry itself, the second is the more recent sequence of Cocom negotiations and their implementation.

In 1954, the period which was such a crucial one for Cocom and the clash of UK and US interests, the computer industry consisted of a handful of computer installations worldwide. In 1984 the computer industry and the semiconductor industry on which it is based and which did not emerge until the 1960s, together had worldwide outputs valued at 115 thousand million pounds. Semiconductors and computers together accounted for 14.1 per cent of world trade in manufactured goods. Unlike most manufactured goods, computers have characteris-

[45]

tics which very few economists have grasped.

It is very easy to draw comparisons between the speed at which computers have entered industrial life, and the speed at which the automobile penetrated our economic life. It is easy, but misleading. Cars, trucks, even railways and aircraft are outputs from the industrial infrastructure. Computers are a key component now, and will become *the* key component in the industrial infrastructure of the future. They are not consumer goods in the sense that cars, trains and planes are, and they never will be. The first point to make is that 90 per cent of all productivity gains in every single sphere of industrial and economic activity in the future will relate directly to the use of computers or robots, which are simply physically active computers. Computers do not generate, directly, the kind of incremental economic activity, such as road building, engineering and the oil industry, all of which sprung from the use to which the internal combustion engine was put. Far from generating incremental economic activity, computers have exactly the opposite effect on existing industrial and economic structures.

Properly applied, computers have a massive impact on the use of energy, people and finally raw materials. The net economic effect of widespread computer usage is an ending to growth in energy, employment and marginal raw material utilisation. For instance, all three major computer projects for which the author had responsibility, in the oil and the computer industries, resulted in significant job losses which were not in any way compensated for by new jobs created in the resulting computer installations. New jobs can only be created by new economic activity, new businesses if you will, they are never created even on a compensating basis by technology itself. In many ways this explains the intransigence of the UK unemployment 'mountain'. There is not enough marginal disposal income available to justify new economic activity whereas in the United States there is, which goes some way to explaining how the United States has at least maintained some momentum in job creation and the UK has not.

Now let us look at computers themselves. The net material and factory overhead costs in the production of a computer are extraordinarily low, and deeply distorted in relation to traditional relationships between manufacturing costs and end user prices. Computers are fundamentally priced at what the user will pay and the larger systems are in effect carrying a huge overhead that relates, much more directly than is normal, to continuous expansion based on intensive marketing expenditure. And that distorted relationship between traditional manufacturing overheads and the low cost of building a computer

[46]

are set to intensify dramatically as growth in chip size all but eliminates what few non-silicon components are still left in the computer box.

Now something else is set to contract in growth, and indeed probably disappear altogether by the end of the century. This is the phenomenon of the data processing department. For much of the first thirty years of the computer era, the installation of a computer meant the creation of a data processing department to service the machine, or more accurately, the shortcomings in its operating system, and the further shortcomings in the languages that were being used to adopt user systems so that they could run on the computer. This went some way to compensate for lost jobs in user departments, but won't for much longer. This is not because of any true gains in operating systems, or indeed in computer languages. What has happened is that productivity has demanded that users buy ready made systems for their user departments and cease to build their own. Even the maintenance crew is disappearing. The user system is maintained by the vendor, the machine is monitored remotely by the manufacturer and the mean time between failures in the machine itself is stretching into years rather than months. The overheads inside the computer industry, when they are not being generated to fund expansion, lie in just this area: in research and development, design finalisation and finally in production set up. Design technology is undergoing productivity gains of hundreds of per cent per annum, again based on the application of computers. Production technology is subject to much slower productivity gains and in the US in particular research and development seem to be in a situation of stasis, particularly in the big corporations.

The area has proved the least amenable to any meaningful gains from the application of computer technology is armaments. There are those who argue that the problem for the US in particular is that the procurement process makes the introduction of technology so slow that whole technology generations go by before the military see anything in the form of end user products. Indeed both Richard Perle, the US Assistant Secretary for Defence and International Security Policy and the US Secretary for Defence Caspar Weinberger have advanced the absurd argument that the Russians are able to adapt stolen US technology into their weapon system with much greater rapidity than the US itself. There is no evidence for this, and the evidence offered is highly selective and only stands up in the Western media because of the wholly incomplete and inadequate reporting of what is actually available about technology in the USSR.

In particular, Perle is very fond of saying that the Soviet shuttle is a copy of the American shuttle. The question to Perle should be: which Soviet shuttle? As he well knows, there are two: the small, crew-only vehicle, which is fairly similar to the US shuttle; and the machine known as Big Bird in the Western space community. Big Bird is about twice the size of the US shuttle, has no engines and a lift to weight ratio plus new design characteristics which will enable it to glide back to Siberia from an entry point anywhere in the planet's stratosphere. This is a matter which this book will address later in more depth, when dealing with the problem of Richard Perle, but it is necessary here to puncture some of the exaggerated claims being made for the technological failure in military systems.

The book, *The Threat*, by Andrew Coburn, shows how both US and Soviet military systems have had similar problems in adapting technology, though one could argue that it has taken the USSR until the 1980s to find out that high technology warfare cannot beat low technology insurgency (as in Afghanistan). In fact, one could argue that neither the US nor the USSR have learned anything from Vietnam. The US has not adapted its weapon systems to the tactical lessons of the war, and the Soviet Union has not adapted its strategic activities to the strategic lessons of Vietnam. The second book to read is *The Button*, by David A. Ford. This is a painstaking account of the huge shortcomings in the present US military command and control system. The system uses ancient computers, of the wrong type, throughout the North American Air Defence Command System. Those computers regularly malfunction and regularly raise false attack alarms. The recent answer was to replace the old computers with new ones of the same type from the same company.

So what we have facing us right now, in the free world, is a critical economic dislocation, computer introduced, which will intensify. The consequences will be of catastrophic proportions in the areas of unemployment, energy and finally raw material costs. As the dole queues grow and as productivity increases, so will demand for oil drop and, following on, the price of raw materials will drop. Unemployment costs will distort national economic structures in the West. An oil price collapse will render marginal the North Sea oil fields, but will also destroy the Arab re-input of petro dollars into the international banking system; in fact, will force most of the Arab producers out of surplus into deficit and into reborrowings from the system. The collapse of raw material prices will destroy even the most notional probability that third world countries will ever be able to repay their huge debts to the Western banks. And the banking system faces the very real possibility

[48]

of becoming the victim of massive fraud, fraud on an inconceivable scale which could, in a matter of days, perhaps weeks, put the whole system beyond any form of rescue simply on a liquidity basis.

Again, the fraud will be computer related and could only be perpetrated within a system which had adapted computers well ahead of restructuring banking procedures and controls to cope with the velocity that computers introduce into the system. For that is the real threat. That a good old fashioned rip off can now be accelerated and multiplied at computer speed, so that one or two major banks wake up during the afternoon reconciliations that are now mandatory in New York to find they are no longer solvent. It hasn't happened . . . yet.

Now, you may ask, where has all this led us? It has led us to some strategic facts which the US would much prefer that the West were ignorant of or at least silent about.

First of all, it leads us to Europe which as we have noted, no longer builds mainframe computers, has no supercomputer manufacturing capability, buys all bar one single chip design from the US and makes most of the others in American or Japanese factories here in Europe. Indeed, as market research shows, Europe buys 85 per cent of all its computers from the United States, and exports almost none at all. To put not too fine a point on it, Europe is now buying all future productivity gains from a monopoly supplier who also insists on controlling the use and movement of those machines throughout Europe. At the price charged by the US corporations for their machines Europe is in fact paying away a substantial percentage of future productivity gains and at the same time funding the expansion of American domination and control of the key element of all future industrial systems.

It should now be quite clear why the 'computer item' led to the 1983 crisis in Cocom, and why only blackmail of the most basic kind applied with utter ruthlessness, secured the US position and US control of all Europe's computer sector. What is not clear is when US policy makers first spotted that the European computer industry was vulnerable.

It is arguable that the US corporations, particularly IBM, Burroughs, DEC, Honeywell and Sperry, had between them created an unstoppable cartel as early as 1962, or were in the process of creating one, given the underlying restrictions they were imposing on would-be re-exporters within Europe. European cynics argue that the European computer industry destroyed itself by building the wrong machines, for the wrong price, and then failing to look after the end user, which is IBM's real strength. The accusation is partly true, but it is very hard to imagine any industry in Europe succeeding, when it was faced by a

[49]

series of competitors being R&D funded by the Pentagon at one end and guaranteed sales at the other, irrespective of how appropriate the systems were for the tasks assigned them, and on a scale in excess of the entire market in Europe.

To this central fact must be added the effects of the underlying Cocom and US constraints. The mixture was potent poison for small European manufacturers, and it worked. Europe is now totally dependent on the US for computers. It does not have the marginal excess value in the economic system to create jobs faster than they are being lost, and it faces an effective producers' cartel, with armament type restraints laid on the goods.

Having established the major underlying elements in the situation, it is now necessary to go back and explore the lead up to the most serious public crisis ever to surface out of Cocom.

In 1974, in the wake of a very contentious settlement of the Cocom lists, which struggled into law in the UK six years later, the Pentagon decided to alter drastically the main International List. A series of studies was initiated, of which the most important was the Bucy Report.[2] However, at the time it was produced, 4 February 1976, it set in motion the violent anti-Soviet, indeed xenophobic, policies which are the hallmark of the Reagan administration. It also gave Richard Perle, fresh from his victory in persuading Senator Scoop Jackson to introduce the Jackson-amendment to the 1974 Trade Bill, a new crusade to embark on.

The man who chaired the Task Force which reported to the Chairman of the Defense Science Board was J. Fred Bucy, the chairman of Texas Instruments. His company is a major producer of micro computer microchips, electronics instruments and a major defence and weapons contractor to the Pentagon. His letter to the boss of the Defense Science Board is notable for three things.

He recommended that the Pentagon should be given the policy formulation and control responsibility for all key technology exports. He recommended that the focus should be on design and manufacturing know-how and that the end products of technology should be ignored unless they are of direct military relevance. He defined the overall goal of technology export controls as 'the maintenance of US technological superiority', and he added that 'compared to this [goal] all other considerations are secondary'. He omitted to say over whom they should have technological superiority, and the entire report is in fact ambiguous to the point of being flawed because of this.

In the opening statement, Bucy says that deterrents such as end user

[50]

statements and safeguards for protection against diversion should not be relied upon or used. In other words, direct inspection, with its implied breach of other nations' sovereignty, is to be the *modus oper-andi*. A little later he pays lip service to Cocom, which is logical, since this was to be a public document. But then, once more, xenophobia strikes: 'However, for the most critical technologies, the US should not release know-how beyond its borders and then depend upon Cocom agreement for absolute control.' Here then was the intellectual foundation stone upon which the US came to depend totally for its new policy towards Cocom in the 1974/82/84 period.

The Bucy Report makes no acknowledgement of any priorities other than those of the US. It effectively moves all key high technology into the sphere of the military and it proposes a draconian approach to ensuring that US objectives are met. 'In the future the US should impose a sanction upon any Cocom country that fails to control a specific technology, by restricting the flow of know-how in that technology, to the offending country.' Which is exactly what the US did to the UK and West Germany in the run up to Cocom agreement in July 1984. Both countries were accused of allowing the re-export of computers by the DEC Corporation (US) to the Eastern Bloc. For almost nine months the flow of DEC computers to West Germany was virtually halted. Computers produced by DEC are used by many of West Germany's banks, manufacturers, government agencies and the military. That year became yet another year of 25 per cent plus growth for Nixdorf, one of DEC's main rivals in West Germany.

In the UK the halt to supplies lasted only four months and was hardly commented upon, even though the UK industrial infrastructure is even more dependent on DEC computers than is that of West Germany. Meanwhile, there was no word of a halt in supplies to DEC's distributor in Yugoslavia. While investigating the matter a spokesman for DEC UK informed me not once, but twice, that during the period of detente between the US and the USSR in the 1970s, DEC had legally shipped about 10 per cent of all its production of one particular type of computer, the PDP/11, to the Eastern Bloc. In the Bucy Report the neutral countries, particularly Sweden, Switzerland and Austria, were to be given only such technology as the US was prepared to ship to the Eastern Bloc.

By the time Richard Perle got behind this policy, the US was at least in public prepared to ship no high technology to the Eastern Bloc. Certainly that was the face he successively presented to each of those countries, as he attempted to force them, successfully in the case of

Austria, into passing Cocom-style laws. Indeed, in Austria's case, it is very doubtful if the law, enacted under the most primitive duress upon the Austrian government by the US Department of Defence, would stand up to constitutional scrutiny. It purports to make the laws of the US applicable in Austria. In principle, a sovereign parliament can do this. But Austria has a written constitution which guarantees the human and civil rights of each of its citizens. Any Austrian prosecuted under the re-export law would be entitled to argue that his parliament could not bind him or her to observe laws made in a foreign country, subject to arbitrary and non-notifiable change by the foreign state. Under those circumstances it is quite clear that what the Austrian parliament has done is undermine the connection between the citizens and the legislature of the state by seeking to insert between the citizen and Austrian law, the law of the United States.

However, while it was clear throughout 1983 that COCOM was in total deadlock over the computer item, it was not clear what the US was going to do about it. On 23 September 1983, however, every single allegation about America's intentions, activities and proposals at Cocom suddenly became highly public.

William Root, the head of the US team at COCOM for over fifteen years, who had resigned eight days earlier, sent an open letter to the President of the United States and both Houses of Congress. The reason he put his thoughts on paper was quite simple. Richard Perle, Assistant Secretary for Defence and International Security Policy, had put around the idea that Root had resigned because he was not doing the job right. The full text of the letter is as follows:

The arrogance of the United States Government is rapidly eroding the effectiveness of controls on the export of strategic equipment and technology. Those who proclaim the loudest the need to strengthen these controls are doing the most to weaken them.

In his television speech following the Korean Airlines 007 incident, the President stressed the need to 'redouble our efforts with our Allies to end the flow of military and strategic items to the Soviet Union'. Since that time we have, instead, been redoubling our efforts to convey to our Allies that their views do not count, that we know best, and that they had better shape up. This is no way to obtain cooperation. It most certainly does not constitute efforts 'with' our Allies.

Corrective action is needed immediately. We have set a time

bomb in COCOM, the Coordinating Committee where NATO nations and Japan coordinate such controls. It is set to go off on October 17.

The most significant COCOM control in terms of number of cases reviewed is the computer item. The COCOM computer definition is obsolete, having been last revised on the basis of 1974 proposals. COCOM has been unable to reach agreement on a revised definition during the past five years of negotiations because of US insistence that the Allies simply accept US proposals. The Allies have been receptive to a wide range of US strengthening proposals for both hardware and software. But they have also submitted many constructive proposals of their own which would make the controls more effective.

During many months of negotiations over the past year a composite draft reflecting everyone's views was hammered out. COCOM accepted the US proposal that a session to reach final decisions on differences not yet resolved begin on October 17. The United States is not prepared to negotiate at that session.

On September 14, on the eve of the September 15 deadline for submission of comments on the composite draft, Defence advised State and Commerce of its views that (1) COCOM was an inadequate forum to negotiate the important computer item; (2) the United States should not deviate from its pre-composite draft proposals at the October meeting: and (3) the real negotiations should take place later in an unspecified forum at which a senior Defence Official would represent the United States.

The clear (though unstated) Defence objectives are to demonstrate that (a) COCOM as it is now constituted is ineffective and should be replaced by a military committee and (b) Defence should replace State as the agency responsible to conduct the negotiations. But we have no alternative but to proceed on the basis of the existing COCOM framework and the existing statutory authorisation for State to conduct negotiations until one or both are changed.

If the United States cannot get its act together, our Allies will conclude that they must use their national discretion to decide what to license and what not to license. Indeed, this has already happened in several important cases as a result of frustrations from the already protracted negotiations. The fundamental objective of COCOM is to avoid diverse actions taken at national discretion by coordinating the national export control decisions of the member governments.

[53]

On October 17 there will be a major, justified explosion of Allied resentment of US contempt for the COCOM process.

US arrogance stems directly from the kind of thinking which led to Section 10(g) of the Export Administration Act. This section requires the President to report to the Congress any US export control case for which the recommendation of the Defence Department is not followed. Although it does not literally apply to differences between State and Defence on COCOM negotiations, a spin-off effect has eliminated the kind of cooperation between those two Departments which is essential for such negotiations.

The president has never over-ruled Defence on an export control case and probably never will as long as Section 10(g) is on the books. The required report to the Congress would indicate that the Commander-in-Chief was not master in his own house. Defence personnel know that their views have prevailed on several occasions when it was generally believed that the President held different views. Accordingly, they see no reason to listen to the views of other agencies or of other governments. They are no doubt sincere in believing that they are thereby protecting the nation's security. However, the end result is a situation in which it is impossible to conduct negotiations with our Allies. Effective controls depend upon negotiations, because the United States is not a unique supplier of most strategic items.

The issue is whether to have ineffective unilateral controls (the result of rigid adherence to US proposals) or effective multilateral controls (which can be achieved through cooperative negotiations).

Our perverse efforts have been in the strategically less significant oil and gas sites as well as in the computer area. Much attention has been given recently to recommendations to put our oil and gas proposals to COCOM under unilateral security controls and to deny a pending $40 million case for submersible pumps. The US oil and gas proposals now before COCOM are the subject of on-going negotiations. The Allies have been extraordinarily cooperative in helping to find well-justified and clearly defined oil and gas related items which should be put under multilateral control. But it is apparent that substantial revision in our original proposals will be necessary to further our common objective as the next scheduled meeting on this subject in January. Any stiffening of our unilateral licensing policy based on the original proposals would greatly damage the cooperative atmosphere. This atmosphere was re-established with much difficulty after the 1982 pipeline controls controversy. Without it there can be no strengthening of multilateral controls in this area.

What should be done? The Administration should (1) negotiate the computer item on October 17 on the basis of the composite draft and (2) revise the US oil and gas proposals to take into account the constructive suggestions of our Allies. The Congress should repeal Section 10(g) of the Export Administration Act when renewing this Act (which expires on September 30).

Sincerely
Wm. A. Root

Director, Office of East West Trade, Department of State until his resignation in protest concerning the above on September 15.

In his prediction that the Allies would walk out of Cocom on 17 October, William Root was wrong. Such were the pressures applied within the Western democracies by their own defence departments that the meeting took place, albeit with a new US head of delegation. What Root had sought, and what did happen was this: the new head of delegation reaffirmed to the Cocom delegates that the US would stick to the statutory guidelines. The US would continue to be represented at Cocom by the State department. The allies for their part, while welcoming the continuity, managed to have shelved, until the French resolved the matter, the issue of a military committee. That went on the backburner. The computer item did not.

Bill Root is an accomplished diplomat and was giving away no state secrets, at least he thought he was not. But in fact few outside Cocom circles themselves knew to what extent the Pentagon had moved on the issue. People like myself who were becoming seasoned watchers were unaware that the Pentagon had engaged in an all out bid to take over a committee that was already under American control. In fact the Pentagon, working specifically under Richard Perle's direction, were treating Cocom as just another piece of Washington 'turf' to be fought over like any other piece of 'turf' in that city. It never seems to have dawned on Perle that there are laws and constitutions governing the behaviour of his nation like any other. Without a change in the law, perhaps in the US constitution itself, the Pentagon could not have become the US

[55]

representative at Cocom, as Congressman Don Bonker was to point out to Perle, in public, a little over a year later.

However, neither parliament nor people in any of the Allied nations, much less the UK, were made aware that the United States was attempting to militarise the entire computer and electronics industry in the West. It sounds preposterous. It *is* preposterous; worse, it is a crime against the civilians who create and run the high technology industries of the West. It may seem fortunate that Perle did not get his way. It was not. It was the duty of every civil servant faced with the Pentagon's position to ring every alarm bell at their command. It was, and remains, a bounden duty on every elected government in the West to warn their parliaments that the United States was getting into an essentially illegal position. However, it is clear from the nature of the attitudes expressed in Garvey's memo[3] that the average UK civil servant owes loyalty to neither the elected nor the electorate. Owing to this lack of loyalty, there was no chance that Western governments would be warned adequately. In fact, Root's resignation was something of a contradiction. Though claiming to be resigning because of the threat to Allied unity, the real pressures he faced were those on his position as a State Department official. Perle, of necessity, had to get rid of the opposition in his own front yard first. And that meant removing Root. In fact, Root removed himself and in doing so did serious damage to Perle's plans, although Root himself had little faith in the long term value of what he did. Stephen Fay, *The Sunday Times* correspondent who later interviewed him, wrote on 2 October 1983, 'Root's message is an important one, though as we drove away in a taxi from Capitol Hill it was already clear that it was not exactly echoing through Congress.'

How could it? The Pentagon's actions in this matter are the brutal and unacceptable face of the American military industrial complex suddenly revealed by Root's letter. It also appears that Root only published his letter after Perle and other Pentagon officials had denied what every Allied negotiator knew to be true, even if very few of those negotiators had chosen to take the same stand as Root. Fay described Root as an uncommonly lonely figure in Washington. He was even more lonely in Europe, where many of those who are paid to serve the public thought more of their salaries than the safety of Europe. The manoeuvre over the computer item was neither more nor less than a Pentagon coup d'etat, aimed at putting every programmer in Europe into uniform, and ultimately under Pentagon control. Of this we can be totally sure. In late July 1984 the three exhausted Department of Trade officials who represented the UN at the Cocom negotiations admitted the truth: 'The United States representatives had hung out until the eleventh hour of the final day, with a demand that the UK (and presumably all the other Cocom members) should impose a movement restriction on computer programmers.'

What the Pentagon tried to do was have the UK authorities licence every person in the UK who could programme an Apple II or equivalent computer system. Had they succeeded, about 400,000 people would have needed a licence to travel out of the country. Their number would have included school children, school teachers, computer enthusiasts, shopkeepers and many other categories outside the relatively small corpus of people who make up the computer profession in the UK. This was the Pentagon's aim and they came within one hour of success, according to the UK delegation, who were not, from either their haggard appearance or the clearly perceptible bitterness in their voices, speaking metaphorically. The great pity was that, though we headlined what amounted to an analytical story, our headline in that first issue of *Computer News*, 'US military threatens European high tech trade', was only half the truth. Our journalistic fervour for 'the facts' obscured the reality. We got halfway there, which was almost worse than never even setting out at all. The rush of events, the demands, the effort required to get out a new paper, should never have obscured from us, even then, the fact that we had in front of us the evidence of a real conspiracy against the free world. We were so busy chasing individual facts and sets of facts to fit our stories that we never stopped to put them all together and see what really lay before us. The only small consolation was that we were the only ones out on the slopes at all. Everyone else was in the trees on the wrong side of the river.

Root had laid it all out in his letter. In fact the most dangerous revelation of all concerns not the fate of individual freedom for the citizens of the UK but the integrity of the US presidency itself. The veiled reference to the Pentagon over-ruling the US President should be read explicitly. Indeed, it is intended explicitly and contains the most profound implications for America and for its constitution. Having over-ruled the President, the Pentagon begins to assume the powers inherent in that office, but without exposure to any of the checks, balances or supervision which the American Constitution gives the people to protect them from an Imperial presidency. Indeed, what Root reveals, though it has immense consequences for the alliance, has even more profound ones for America. He has, in paragraph 11, exposed what many have long sensed but been unable to prove; that the American government is being exposed to a gradual coup d'etat by the military.

[57]

And, more important, Root reveals that the coup, long in progress behind the scenes, is now confident enough to risk exposure and not care about the consequences.

Stephen Fay, in the Root interview, wrote of an 'unapologetic Pentagon' and a 'silent, embarrassed State Department'. He forgot to mention President Ronald Reagan, who ignored the event – which he had to, or risk the inevitable explosion from the Pentagon. But so did America's elected representatives. They conspired with a power on the verge of entering the Imperium, against the people, just as the governments of the alliance entered a similar conspiracy of silence against their own people. De Juvenel has written that strong governments never fall to revolutionary mobs, only weak ones. He omitted to continue his analysis and note that strong democracies never fall victim to coups, only weak ones. If the elected representatives of the American people, in whose hands Congress vests the real truth of the American Constitution, were so weak of intellect as to fail to see where Root was pointing, and so weak of will that they forbore to take legal action against so obvious and palpable an evil, then the secret power that has already stolen half their authority well deserves the rest.

But we in Europe do not have to follow the American people into that deadly embrace in which they are already half locked. We can break free, recreate from the sands of our own shores and the brains of our own people, the technology that we have had stolen from us by the treachery of our civil servants and the predatory activities of the American industrial military complex. We can begin to slow the job losses. We can begin to look at ways to adjust to the inevitable attrition that technology imposes on older industries. But we cannot do that while we have no control over the technology that is stripping those industries of their jobs, reducing their energy demands and diminishing the need for the raw materials which are the only resource the third world has.

What might be mistaken here for an impassioned plea on behalf of European nationalism is not that at all. It is more a plea for enlightened self interest on everyone's part, particularly in the United States. In the past unbridled greed, for power, for loot, for domination, has destroyed families, states and nations. Unchecked greed at this juncture in humanity's history will destroy the world. And, just as victims often stare transfixed at their assailants, so are the European states staring transfixed at the United States and their own dissolution. The ideal solution is a resurgence of radical democracy, constitutionally based, on both sides of the Atlantic. The probability is that America is long past the point of no return, but Europe has not even entered its proper, and hopefully inevitable, phase of pre-federal constitutional radicalism.

[1] The Cocom secretariat is in Rue De La Botie, at the end of an alleyway showing only a dentist's nameplate.
[2] A report of the Defense Science Board Task Force on Export of US Technology, Chairman J. Fred Bucy, Chairman, Texas Instruments.
[3] See appendix one.

CHAPTER 4

Enter the MP for Yeovil

As I BECAME MORE DEEPLY involved with the subject, I began to make unrealistic assessments of what could be achieved by taking the story beyond *Computer News*, into the national media, including television; or, perhaps, to the House of Commons.

I have yet to talk to even the humblest worker in the computer industry without getting an instant appreciation of the implications of the second sentence of the IBM letter. On the other hand, a significant proportion of the bureaucracy, 'the permanent state whose objective is to survive all changes in government and every legal attempt to curb their powers', were faced with an appalling dilemma: no civil servant could afford to pretend not to be upset by the letter; none ever did. On the other hand, that letter contains implications of a legal nature which, in certain circumstances, amount to evidence of a serious infraction of the UK constitution and of UK sovereignty.

Not many civil servants who, upon seeing the text and pretending shock, failed to spot, immediately, the wider implication. This lent a quality of real sincerity to the many expressions of anger I heard in the Department of Trade and Industry in early 1984, when I circulated the letter. Unfortunately it did not lead to any effort by the DTI to get the staff at either the American Embassy or at IBM to provide an escape clause, a public relations fudge that would suppress the glaring illegality in the letter. Those endeavours failed as totally as Tebbit's did in the United States. There were two reasons for this. In the first place, neither the Embassy nor IBM were prepared to alter a procedure which, though of doubtful reality, had been in place and sanctioned by the UK civil servants, for years. There was no inclination on the part of the Embassy to alter long established bridgeheads within the British state, just because a noisy Irishman on an unknown trade newspaper, was making a fuss. And the Civil Service was seriously compromised, which made their negotiating position with the Americans, never very strong at the best of times, a great deal weaker.

To really move the staff at the Embassy the Department of Trade and Industry would have needed a full scale ministerial delegation, accompanied by the law officers of the Crown, armed with, and indicating clearly that they would use, the powers at their disposal. No such approach was ever made to the American Embassy. Indeed there is evidence that the Department of Trade and Industry failed to notify the Attorney General or any of the other legal officers of the Crown, of the letter, or its implications. Whatever the detailed reasons for this were, it is fair to surmise that the over-riding reason was the potential fallout should a full examination ever be made into the situation behind the letter and the continual dereliction of duty by various civil servants that would then be revealed. And that dereliction of duty, containing as it does implications of passive treachery, exists at two levels.

In the first place there is the directly evidenced breach of UK sovereignty. In the second place, there is the more mundane, but financially and commercially significant breaches of the Treaty of Rome, which Parliament authorised and undertook to implement and uphold in a true and rare reflection of the will of the people of the UK as expressed in the referendum of 1973. Governments, by and large, will do what they have to do, especially when legal obligations can be invoked to make them act. Governments will often act when advised to do so, especially by the Civil Service. In this case the question has to be posed: did the Civil Service ever advise the government of the continuing breach of sovereignty, or of the failure to uphold the Treaty of Rome? The answer is a probable no.

Although I did not have the IBM letter until January 1984, I was already certain about the situation, otherwise the 11 November story could never have been written. The question, back in October 1983, was: where would the story go, once it had been written? Parliament was the obvious answer. To the ordinary British citizen it may seem wrong that a journalist who lives in London, can simply hop in a cab and career down to the House of Commons with some certainty of being seen by an MP. In principle it may not be fair, but in practice it often represents a very real way of voicing a public interest or protest. And an individual MP, particularly on the opposition benches, has little power to bring pressure to bear on the government without some media support. Publicity, far from being the motive of most conscientious MPs, is the reward for work done in the public interest and it is the only way to bring meaningful pressure to bear on the government. Media

[61]

mentions, for all their transient value, have little or none in the long term, to any MP seriously interested in the public good and in decent government. And there are some who are so interested.

Unaware of the weakness in my situation, a lack of the kind of evidence IBM was later to provide, my first forays into the House of Commons proved fruitless, frustrating for me and time wasting for those I approached. Bound by a journalistic convention which says that having taken the views of the government departments you have the government view, I proceeded in search of the official opposition. But, given that there was a shortage of hard evidence, though no shortage of interesting headlines, even if they were all from *Computer News*, this proved more difficult and less rewarding than I might have thought. Unaware of this, at first, that autumn I began a series of preparatory phone calls in search of the Labour front bench spokesman on Trade and Industry . . . who never seemed to be available. I began to think I would have to look elsewhere . . .

The General Election of 1983 had returned the Conservative party to power as the government of the United Kingdom with an increased majority in the House of Commons. Margaret Thatcher's triumph was singular in many ways, but did allow for the odd anomaly.

In the safe Conservative seat of Yeovil a Liberal was returned as MP. A Tory majority of 11,500 became a Liberal majority of 3,500, a significant swing against the trend. I asked my sister, who once lived in this constituency, how this had been achieved. 'Paddy Ashdown did it, vote by vote,' she said. Before I knew this and as I walked along Victoria Embankment, to the Old Scotland Yard building which houses the overflow of MPs from the House of Commons, in the first week of January 1984, I had time to wonder if this issue was going to become a case of those outside the Government shouting at those within, from minor headlines in obscure papers.

On the ground floor of Normanshaw North, I walked past David Owen leader of the SDP. Michael Foot, the former leader of the Labour party, walked past me. I rode the lift, at least as far as the second floor, with Cecil Parkinson, former Tory Minister for Trade and Industry. It was heady stuff for, familiar though even trade journalists are with the famous, that was quite an encounter, all within two minutes. It ill prepared me for the neat office and bright enthusiasm of Paddy Ashdown. Most men of power, certainly the ones I had passed so recently, possess a second persona with which they face the world. It is often characterised by a hooded, cautious stare, a glazed and distant look, and

[62]

an easy flow of words whose content is so difficult to specify or remember.

None of that in Ashdown.

The coffee he offered, he had made himself. He asked me what my visit was all about and I handed him the IBM letter.

As ever, the effect was instantaneous. 'This,' he said, 'is monstrous'.

He asked me what had been done about it and I said very little, which was why I was in his office. We discussed the implications of the letter. At that stage the 4th or 5th January 1984, I was able to tell him that *The Sunday Times* was interested in the story and had a copy of the letter. He said that would help, but he also gave me a commitment that he would take the issue to the floor of the House of Commons and beyond, to wherever else was necessary.

The first castle to tackle was, of course, the Department of Trade and Industry. Paddy shortly wrote the first of many letters to Her Majesty's ministers, various and ill–assorted. The man who emerged in opposition to him was not the one who would have been predicted for the role. One of the little known but highly successful appointments by the first Thatcher government was Kenneth Baker as Minister of Information Technology. A man who combined a flair for industry and for spending, with an irresistible ability to avoid public banana skins, he made an immense impression on the encircled and poorly funded computer and electronics industry in the UK. Logically, Paddy's letter of complaint to Tebbit should have been passed to Baker. It wasn't: it wound up on Paul Channon's desk. There is now a rumour that Baker's department re-routed the letter to Channon on the grounds that it was legal and trade, both within Channon's remit. Whatever the reason, the hapless Channon was to bear the brunt of Paddy's assault throughout the next two years, while the Brylcreamed Baker slid away and went on, in 1985, to greater things and ever greater spending at the Department of the Environment, and on to the Cabinet in 1986, as Education Minister.

But before the letters, the media.

When Philip Beresford at *The Sunday Times* decided to pursue the story, we lacked a direct response from Tebbit. The Department of Trade and Industry press office had duly expressed gratitude for the letter, but were being mute and diffuse in terms of reportable comment. On the Wednesday, with Phil in full cry, it suddenly dawned on me that we could actually get to Tebbit himself. On my desk was an invitation to a press conference to be held by Hewlett Packard, a major US defence contractor and computer company, in a Kensington hotel about five miles from Gray's Inn Road. I hurled a visiting journalist from *Elec-*

tronics Weekly, Della Bradshaw, into a taxi alongside Phil and off we went, hoping that we would get a chance to field a question to Tebbit. We did.

The Hewlett Packard announcement of a new Research and Development centre at Bristol was made by David Baldwin, the company's UK managing director. During the question period which followed his speech I got my chance. I asked him whose laws would prevail over the movement of this technology. As he began his answer, Norman Tebbit rose, politely removed the microphone from David Baldwin, and said, 'What happens in the UK is governed by UK law.'

Most of the audience missed the implications of the exchange, not a difficult thing to do since the issue was still fairly unknown. To me it was significant that Tebbit spotted the question. The speed with which he answered, and the incontrovertible fashion in which he presented the answer were also impressive. It told me clearly that the issue was on Tebbit's desk, that he knew about it and that the government, even if it didn't have a policy, certainly had an attitude on the situation. Phil was able to use the quote in his piece on that Sunday, but it remained to find someone to go after the matter in Parliament.

The someone was Paddy Ashdown. Paddy has never struck me as academically or indeed technically minded. He is very conscious of the value of technology; his office contains a microcomputer linked to another in his constituency; all his letters are filed on a computer. But the inner workings of technology were something else.

By the end of my session with Paddy in January 1984 he felt convinced enough of the importance of the matter to commit himself in public on the issue to Phil, and that too went in *The Sunday Times* piece. My discussion with Paddy had covered a fairly wide range of topics, in a situation which was quite new to me. I had never been in an MP's office before, and had only visited the House of Commons on two previous occasions. I knew a good deal about democracy, particularly democracy under fire, but very little about the inner workings of the mother of parliaments, but I was about to find out.

Paddy felt that the best way to try to get the matter before the government was by letter. I saw no reason to doubt this, and Paul Channon's replies generally confirmed the central correctness of Paddy's approach, though not so those from Norman Tebbit which tended to be terse, limited and generally avoided answering the questions he was asked. At that stage, Paddy was uncertain how parliamentary questions could be framed so as to elicit information, given that the information initiative lay outside government. It seemed that a cam-

[64]

paign in the trade press, the affected constituency, was the answer. Though I could guarantee support in our own paper, something Paddy never asked for, this was not something I could promise on behalf of anyone else. On the other hand, the issue was so important, the damage so great and the future threat so onerous to the computer industry, that I felt the story would be taken up elsewhere, as indeed it was. My friends, rivals and colleagues in the rest of the trade press, did not let me down on this one.

At this point it is worth mentioning the manner in which newspapers work, and the way the issue began to have a place, sometimes in one news cycle, and sometimes in several.

A paper like *The Sunday Times* begins its news cycle on a Tuesday, with the aim of having the main stories identified and under way by Wednesday morning, with a view to completion by Friday night. As the week unfolds it becomes progressively more difficult to enter a story in the news cycle, which is always aimed at producing either new stories or exclusive angles on existing material for Sunday, with a virtual shut out of material by about noon on Saturday. Around five or six o'clock on Saturday afternoon *The Observer* and *The Sunday Times* swap their first editions and each paper's news editor will then decide whether to remake the front page of either the main paper, or of the business sections. Only reporters affected by the remake will be on station at the paper after about 5.30 pm. By eight o'clock both papers are virtually bereft of staff and the first editions can be bought at the respective back doors.

In the autumn of 1983 and the spring of 1984 the main paper of *The Sunday Times* was conceivably one of the unhappiest industrial organisations in London. The distress was palpable across the road in number 99 Gray's Inn Road. In part the situation was a hangover from the traumatic departure of Harry Evans. His successor, Frank Giles, had done little to change the organisation he had inherited. Had Harry Evans not left such an eclectic team behind, perhaps Frank Giles might have had an easier time. Had Frank made a real effort to reshape the paper, perhaps Andrew Neil might not, at second hand, have inherited an organisation just waiting to fragment into the inevitable end of a great journalistic enterprise. Rancour spread throughout the gossip columns of its rivals and most significantly into the ultimate sixth form magazine for Fleet Street, *Private Eye*.

The first part of *The Sunday Times* to fall apart after the departure of Harry Evans was the Insight team, once the very heart of the paper's reputation for investigative and campaigning journalism. Although

[65]

well distanced from Gray's Inn Road during my two years in Sutton, that disintegration twice impinged directly on the very early development of the trade war issue. Bruce Page, the one time Insight editor, applied for the editorship of *Computer Weekly*. I opposed this candidacy, on the grounds that he might do to *Computer Weekly* what Frank Giles was not doing at *The Sunday Times*, that is, he might attempt to reshape the paper in the traditional way of Fleet Street. Sudden inkbath and many departures. My intervention had, in the vernacular, about as much impact on the IPC selection process as that of a gnat pissing in the Irish Sea.

However, the second appearance of the Insight team in the life of the issue had a very different outcome. When I pinned the dirty tricks operation against UK membership of the International Institute for Applied Systems Analysis in Vienna on the White House in Washington, I immediately got in touch with Linda Malvern and Nick Anning on the Insight team. That first encounter led nowhere except to a night's drinking in the Blue Lion, an omen if ever there was one. But we did agree to stay in touch, and the next occasion for a few jars at the back of the Blue Lion was the last big Insight piece to appear in *The Sunday Times*. This appeared on 14 November 1982 and dealt at length with the case of Geoffrey Prime, the spy who is alleged to have sold Russia some of the most vital intelligence secrets in the Western world, having first stolen them from Britain's main signals intelligence centre in Cheltenham. As I read the piece I saw significant links between some of the information it contained, and our White House story. For a start, much of the technical data was wrong, but wrong in exactly the same way the CIA-supplied material in *Parade* had been wrong. The primary claims were physically impossible. For instance, the piece quoted American sources saying that Prime, and by implication the UK security services, who had failed to detect his activity, had permitted America's most critical satellite set up to be disclosed to the USSR. This set up is the Rhyolite surveillance system run by the National Reconnaissance office, a 'black' or 'undisclosed' department within the Pentagon. According to those American sources the Rhyolite system could read the number-plates of cars in Moscow, intercept all key Soviet military microwave transmissions, watch missile silos twenty-four hours a day and do innumerable other amazing things. Beginning with the assertion that Prime had betrayed the system, every single American assertion was, and remains, untrue, inaccurate or physically impossible. For instance, the Rhyolite system and every competent and relevant detail concerning the satellites and their communication facilities, including access

[66]

codes, had been comprehensively sold to the Russians years before by two Americans.

With the data from Christopher Boyce and Daulton Lee and a series of fly-past inspections, combined with radar and infrared interrogation from the ground, there was almost nothing, excepting the serial numbers of internal components, that the Russians did not know about Rhyolite by the time Geoffrey Prime started to produce his stolen material for the Soviets. The Rhyolite system is wrongly stationed to pick up the overshoot from Soviet military microwave systems and it is physically impossible to read line of sight microwave transmissions from an angle of 180° and a distance of 20,000 miles. The Soviet Union is under general cloud cover for about 60 per cent of the year and again, the laws of optics make the reading of number plates at a distance of 20,000 miles highly improbable if not downright impossible.

More significantly still, the information provided to *The Sunday Times* seemed to have exactly the same objective as that which appeared in *Parade*. Both tended to throw maximum discredit on the UK security services. In the case of Prime, of course, there had been the most monumental cockup by the security system. But then, if you employ 7,000 people, many of them civilians, in what is claimed to be a top secret military establishment, and you expect absolute secrecy, you have to be not only living in cloud cuckoo land, but one of the birds as well. In fact, such are the dimensions of the GCHQ operation, that short of a spy at the top or at director level the best way to get a real grip on the place is by careful external examination of the characteristics of the place, both the physical and the electronic. You record the variety and type of signals, the type of antennae, buildings and staff movement. Elementary stuff, long ago gathered for the USSR by any number of visitors to Cheltenham race course and the airport at Staverton, no doubt.

What became clear when, as diplomatically as possible, I presented this material to Linda, was that, while American sources that could only be assumed to be authoritative, had indeed opened up to *The Sunday Times*, the paper had been more or less refused even the most limited guidance in the UK. Faced with the undoubted quality and level of the US sources, the fact that there had been a truly unbelievable lapse in elementary security in the UK, I would have done the same as Linda. Journalism is not an exact science, the US is supposed to be our ally and no one in the UK was talking, ready though *The Sunday Times* were to listen. If the UK security services wish to behave like that, they must have something to conceal and the US material could only have been

[67]

successfully sorted out by a strategic analyst with a technical background. So *The Sunday Times* printed a reasonable general account of the background to the Prime case.

But the questions which the information provided to *Parade* and *The Sunday Times* pose are these: how far can the CIA be trusted by the UK at any level? They were the source, in the end, of both sets of briefings. What were they trying to achieve and, more importantly, is lying to the Allied media the way to go about it? Plainly, the exaggerated and absurd technical claims made for American technology are intended to impress two audiences, the Soviet military and the Allied population. In fact, the claims, because they are so absurd, help to persuade the Soviet Union that most of the Western media is the gullible tool of the CIA. They also persuade the people of the Allied countries that the armies of the West possess capabilities which they all too plainly do *not* possess.

One American analyst put it to me that one ought not to be so critical of the CIA. 'The object of the technical claims is to drive the Soviets into building hugely expensive land line communications systems, which help to bankrupt their economy.'

The problem is that the Soviet Union has done just that, though not for the reasons the American analyst suggested. Yes, the US had periodically been able to prove to the USSR that it was picking up some microwave transmission. The Soviet Union could not be sure how this was being achieved, but could be sure that the laws of physics were not being bypassed. But, taken with another problem, that of the virtual certainty of the collapse of all over ground and airborne communications systems, as the first effect of a nuclear strike on the USSR, the military reasons for going underground are fairly compelling. Again, we had come to Linda too late on that one, but she was interested.

When *Computer News* opened its doors at 99 Gray's Inn Road, Linda Malvern was in the final stages of detaching herself from *The Sunday Times*. Behind our doors lay my private files, which I had collected in the hours between 6.30 pm and 4 am, after the day's work is well and truly done. Dipping into these files in the autumn of 1983, Linda was able to gather new material on the issue of high technology smuggling to the Eastern Bloc. In return, she gave me access to her files, and an introduction to Magnus Linklater, who had moved from *The Sunday Times* to *The Observer* as its news editor. In the meantime, Linda had gone to the United States and obtained on a viciously short deadline, an advance for what eventually became *Technobandits*.

Now, to get back to basic news cycles. *Computer News* also had a weekly cycle, but one which clashed badly with a journalist's first professional duty, which is to his own paper. *The Sunday Times*, naturally, comes out on Sunday. We came out on Thursday. We could not expect that paper to simply follow our material, unless it was of exceptional importance, as was the case with the IBM letter. On the other hand, we benefited from more than usual good luck in that it was the Business Section, with a strong tradition of interest in the technology sector, which showed the most interest in our stories, as the issue developed. The Business Section of the paper had survived all the traumas of the post-Harry Evans era relatively unscathed. We were dealing with a stable, disciplined newspaper office, insofar as any newspaper office is that. Sometimes we were lucky and had material which was too general for *Computer News*, but which was valuable to *The Sunday Times*. At this point it is worth noting that our true rival, and a paper that grabbed not a few scoops on this issue, was the *Financial Times*. It is a daily paper, unique in quality, thoroughness and total professionalism. Its quality is slightly hidden to the every day world because it is assumed to be a paper solely for the financial community. In fact, for many journalists it is their own paper of preference and reference.

The FT has carried stories relating to this issue, sometimes as frequently as three or four times a week. On the other hand, the paper has not campaigned on the issue, nor done major investigative pieces. The failure of either the technology community or the government to collect and assess the material appearing in the FT is an interesting reflection on the manner in which daily news reporting is perceived by readers and the very different impact that a single story in a Sunday newspaper can have. Philip Beresford's piece on Sunday, 8 January certainly had plenty of impact. As a direct result of Phil's piece Paddy was drawn much further into both the issue and the computer industry, as the first of a flood of letters began to reach him. But the first parliamentary reaction was to place me in something of a quandary.

Roger Stott, the Labour MP I had been in touch with prior to going, via Ian Wrigglesworth, to Paddy, got in touch with me. He asked me to come down to the Commons and showed me a letter he had just written to John Butcher, the Parliamentary Under-Secretary of State for Industry. In it he raised the IBM letter as presented by *The Sunday Times*. This was interesting, as I'd been trying to tell his party about the issue since at least the beginning of November 1983, but no matter.

Roger Stott told Butcher, a likeable and well informed MP, that 'he found it extremely disturbing that any British company who own a mainframe IBM computer will in future have to seek permission from the American Embassy in London or the Department of Commerce in Washington if there is to be a change of ownership or a change of use . . .'

Butcher corrected Stott on the mistaken idea that this was something new. 'It appears that the arrangement set out in the IBM letter has been going on for some time without creating major practical problems.'

Too true, it had. But to infer that the situation was acceptable because it had created no major problems is rather like saying that because not many people are being injured in bank raids, the police are happy that the practical problems are manageable.

Stott's letter went on to ask what the government's position was on the matter.

'Our position on this issue is quite clear,' Butcher replied. 'If the Americans maintain that their Export Administration Regulations control the movement of equipment between companies within the UK this is a wholly unwarranted encroachment on UK jurisdiction.'

But then the possibility emerges that the Minister was being badly and incompetently advised, 'We understand,' he continued, 'that IBM do not regard the regulations as applying to the movement of computers within one company.' IBM's apparently mitigating view is hogwash and should never have been repeated in government correspondence. It fully maintains the illegal imposition of American law in the United Kingdom. Worse than that, by preparing to offer a relaxation on internal movement inside a company, IBM would appear to be misleading the UK government and succeeding to the extent that a minister wrongly uses this information to try to give the impression that things are not as bad as they seem. In fact, it is quite likely that the Minister was misinformed as to the reality of the situation by his own officials recounting IBM's interpretation of the situation.

We already know that IBM had prevailed over the US Embassy as to the correctness of its narrower interpretation of the regulations. To say that the regulations do not affect the movement or use of Advanced Computer Systems within one company is an incorrect understanding of the regulations. They do. There is no release from the regulations just because they are signed for by one part of a company enabling them to be shipped to another part of the same company. American officials in both the Commerce Department and the Pentagon are quite clear about this, and in general IBM has always taken the narrowest and most rigid interpretation of the rules. The error most likely lay in the Minister's own department, though that is no excuse for the despatch of a letter which apparently condones a major infringement of UK sovereignty.

The letter is also notable for its failure to realise that there was a glaring infringement of the Treaty of Rome and a compromising of the UK government's duties under that Treaty to enforce the various trade regulations, in the imposition of the regulations referred to in the IBM letter. Those points too were ones for an alert opposition to seize upon to harry the government with. And, if Norman Tebbit was in the business of giving hostages, so were his ministers on his behalf.

Butcher wrote to Stott that: 'During his visit to the USA this month, the Secretary of State will be raising the whole question of US Extraterritoriality with the US Commerce Secretary, Mr Baldridge and other top Administration figures. He will certainly raise the IBM letter and hopes to be assured that it is the result of a mistaken interpretation of the territorial scope of US laws.'

In fairness to Mr Tebbit, he did raise those matters. Indeed he did so several times. On the matter of the IBM letter, however, he was told, in no uncertain terms, that it was a correct interpretation of US law, and that the United States expected IBM UK to continue to comply with US laws. Presumably the tone of Butcher's letter was meant to imply a degree of optimism on the part of the Department of Trade and Industry that the US would behave reasonably on this issue. If so, it was a very seriously misplaced optimism.

While Roger Stott was waiting for his reply from Butcher, he also decided to write to Neil Kinnock, the Labour Party leader, also due to visit the United States. In a letter dated 2 February 1984 he told Kinnock:

> Over the last few weeks I have been in touch with a number of journalists who have been deep throating me regarding the extent of the American involvement in extra-territorial interference in British trade.
>
> My own belief is that the IBM scenario is merely the tip of the iceberg. I have been following very closely a series of articles that have been written in *Computer News* by Mr Kevin Cahill, indicating that the European computer industry is under threat as the United States military attempt to take unilateral control of East/West trade in technology. I must confess that this is an exceedingly worrying trend whereby the United States can have total control over the movement of these computers and use their high technology dominance together with their licensing

[71]

agreements in order to further the foreign policy aims of the Reagan administration.

Quite clearly, the reasoning behind the strict monitoring of the movements of these high technology computers is to prevent them from eventually ending up behind the Iron Curtain, something of course which we do not necessarily disagree with, but most European mainframe computer manufacturers have to import certain specialist parts from the United States. ICL for example, Britain's only wholly-owned computer company, uses specialist parts provided by American companies and even if they only use one per cent of the parts which are required for a mainframe computer, if that computer was to be moved anywhere within the United Kingdom or anywhere within Europe, then the United States Department of Commerce would have to be told and the company concerned would have got the appropriate licence. In my recent discussions with ICL I posed the question to them that if they were to tell the American administration to get stuffed, what would be the repercussions. In their view they would be quite severe. The United States would not allow any further export of computer parts to ICL and the company would be put on the denial list. A somewhat similar exercise occurred a few years ago regarding the Soviet Gas Pipeline, where British companies were prevented from supplying the Soviet Union with vital equipment because of the American administration's attitude towards the position in Poland.

I have also included a letter which I have received from IBM dated 27 January explaining to me that the position as has been outlined in the press is inaccurate and confusing and that these export licences have in fact been in operation for some time. If that is the case, why have British companies suddenly been put under so much pressure and I must confess I am singularly unconvinced by the explanation of IBM and I am coming round to the view that there is a clearly designed covert operation on behalf of the American administration to get control of the movement of these computers through their licensing system.

I hope you find this information useful to you and I hope that you have an interesting and successful trip.

From this letter it will be seen that despite the difficulty I had in contacting people in Her Majesty's official opposition, Roger Stott at least

[72]

had clearly identified the main issues and had also made the correct deductions. His efforts plainly left me in a quandary. Obviously, like Paddy, he was deeply interested in the issue, and was prepared to have a go at it. But there seemed to be more personal and practical reasons for sticking with Paddy. For one thing, I had been a Liberal for years. Paddy and I shared both an Irish and a military background, as well as homes in the West Country. There were other things: his enthusiasm, his complete openness, personally and officially, his willingness to trust people. It was a heady mixture indeed, one I found irresistible.

There was also a matter of absolute practicality. Dominating though this issue was, I had a full day's work to do besides. Every Wednesday a page or two of company and financial news had to be completed for *Computer News*, as well as a feature or two and five or six new stories each week. There were press conferences to attend on a daily basis, regular meetings of the British Computer Society, then on the verge of its Royal Charter. The difficulty I had had in contacting Labour MPs, fruitful though it was when it finally happened, had made me a bit chary of them. I could not afford the time. Paddy, on the other hand, was easy to reach, always returned calls, and could be reached at weekends in less than an hour's drive from my home near Exeter.

Practical considerations prevailed. I effectively joined Paddy, and then sought to steer any other journalist who was interested in the issue towards Roger Stott. Joining is of course a relative term. What I was actually doing was relying, as my distinguished mentor across the road had done in the Thalidomide case, on an MP to lead the parliamentary battle, while I tried to lead in the media. It was never as clear cut as that in early 1984, though.

About a week before Roger Stott wrote to Norman Tebbit, Paddy had also written him a lengthy letter. He showed me a draft, from which I took a copy on 16 January. We had talked about the draft during the previous week and I made no effort to find out if he had made any alterations before he sent it. This was one of the worst mistakes I was to make with Paddy. It gave me a rare opportunity to find out how tolerant he could be of mistakes and how essential it was to double check all material for publication.

In the draft, Paddy had asked Tebbit to ban the delivery of all big machines from the US until the issue was resolved. In the version he sent to Tebbit he had deleted this sentence.

On Thursday we came out with the banner headline: 'MP calls on government to ban big US machines.' In the office we had sight of the paper on Wednesday and I rushed back to Paddy in total panic having,

[73]

in the mean time, seen the final draft of his letter. He suggested that if there was flak, he would divert all callers to me, and I would explain the error. We never considered the no reaction option, though I did tell him that within three months I expected other calls for such a ban to be made. 'You can then point out that you were there first,' I told him.

There were a number of new and important elements in the story however. Based on *The Sunday Times* article, a number of companies had written to Paddy or phoned to complain about unusual problems they had encountered in attempting to ship UK manufactures' high technology abroad.

The most interesting of these was Plasma Technology, a small company based near Bristol which manufactures equipment used in the chip-making industry. The Managing Director, David Carr, had been trying to obtain licences to exhibit and sell his equipment in China, since the summer of 1983, without luck and with the maximum of non-assistance from the Department of Trade and Industry. He had become totally outraged when he discovered that his American rival, shipping through a subsidiary in Sweden, had been able to bypass the system of controls agreed in Cocom, and display and sell its system in Beijing.

'The UK is still playing by the rule book,' he raged. 'The lifting of restrictions on the import of high technology goods to China made in November 1983 and for which many of our US competitors appear to have had advance notice, has not been passed on to the UK.'

Had David known the full extent of American duplicity over China, he would probably have had apoplexy. But in the end the lies, obstructions and threats of officialdom, tend to silence even a David Carr – though not before he had done a lot to shake the living daylights out of more than one civil servant.

But that comes later.

When the contents of Paddy's letter were put to the DTI press office they refused to comment until Tebbit answered, but under considerable pressure they did say that, 'We take a serious view of extra-territoriality'. Considerable pressure in this case meant an argument on the phone that lasted over twenty-five minutes, and ended with a further denial, the fourth or fifth, of any knowledge of the unilateral action over China by the US in November 1983. The Foreign Office, also for the third or fourth time of asking, similarly denied any knowledge of the US action. (This is discussed more fully in chapter 6.)

From Manchester, unharried by direct questions from the press in London, the ubiquitous Ken Baker was coming as close to the issue as he was ever willing to get in public: 'If we are dependent on the Americans or the Japanese, they (the computers) may not be here tomorrow.' There was a note in the story to the effect that the UK is ninety per cent dependent on the US for its computers and electronic components.

In the US the news broke that IBM was seeking to put the IBM personal micro-computer under roughly the same kind of restrictions as the bigger machines. As usual, the UK announcement was made in totally misleading terms. The Department of Defence (the Pentagon) had started this particular hare, designed to place under US control the most popular and widely used micro-computer in the world. According to the Pentagon, in off the record briefings – that is to say, unauthorised, unattributable and deeply suspect oral statements, the IBM PC would be of military significance if it fell into the hands of the Eastern Bloc. It needed to be controlled. At this point, January 1984, IBM PCs were entering China, almost certainly from the US, at the rate of about 1,500 a month. What the Pentagon really meant was that the machines, each and every one, should be made subject to US control throughout the Western world.

And there was a far more sinister idea behind the Pentagon move than the simply objectionable one of attempting to restrict or control trade in IBM machines in Europe. At about the time of the statements about the IBM PC by Pentagon officials, Sir Clive Sinclair, the UK's most flamboyant computer entrepreneur, was just introducing a new computer, based on an American chip. Quite correctly the Sinclair organisation sensed the thrust and detected the intent in the move. A spokesman told me, 'There have always been constraints on importing to the Eastern Bloc. But the idea of controlling imports to other European countries would concern us greatly.'

Just so, and that was precisely the Pentagon's intent. But the truth of the matter was that by looking for a direct Pentagon effort to get at Sinclair, or indeed any other UK company, we were all looking in the wrong direction. The secret enemy in our midst was no further west than Ashdown House in Victoria Street, London, the home of the Department of Trade and Industry. It was among the thousands of ill-informed and technically uneducated officials in this Department that the Pentagon would look to see its wishes carried out, however indirectly. It is in the DTI that licence applications to ship ancient technology to the Eastern Bloc, technology in daily and regular supply from the US, are delayed for years or denied.

[75]

CHAPTER 5

'Unwarranted Encroachments on UK Jurisdiction'

WHILE OUTRAGE WAS STRONG upon us, and when it became clear that Norman Tebbit was not going to take any action over the imposition of US law in the UK, it became equally clear that Paddy would have to engage in battle with the law officers of the Crown and the government. What Ron Condon and I had in mind was that somewhere along the line we would (as Harry Evans warned me we would have to) go to the High Court and sue the Attorney General. We never discussed this in detail with Paddy, though I did mention it to him once or twice. The problem was money. Though we might be able to draft the statements and provide the evidence, there was no way we could afford the fees of leading Counsel, which would start at several thousand pounds and, if the government contested the writ which we had decided, not necessarily correctly, should be *mandamus*, then we could find ourselves facing costs of £20,000 plus. Not something the board of The Publishing Company, the owners of *Computer News*, were likely to be happy about. I was very keen to try to find the money, however. Apart from the fact that our campaign was unprecedented in the computer industry, to sue the government on this issue would show that we had bite as well as bark. It also struck me that the national media would certainly find our actions interesting, which would add further to the pressures on the government. But how were we to do it?

I told a friend from the *Financial Times* that we were seriously considering going to court. He promptly remarked that, 'The spirit of Harry Evans hasn't left Gray's Inn Road. It's just moved to the other side of the street.' It was just the kind of encouragement we needed. But from whence the money?

While we were squaring up to this problem, I began to draft a series of letters for Paddy. Those drafts quickly showed that the real issue was a constitutional one. In fact, it is the issue of sovereignty which alone

[76]

makes this whole story important and which gives an obscure trade wrangle with the United States dimensions which affect the very legitimacy of the UK government and the underpinnings of the State itself. To put it very simply, if the UK government cannot end the erosion of its jurisdictional authority and restore the rule of UK law here on the mainland, then it can no longer lay claim to the complete legitimacy it must have if it is to continue as the government of the United Kingdom. At that point, in the late spring of 1984, Paddy was inclined to focus on the ministry on the other side of the ring from him. Trade and Industry. He recognised, quite clearly, the constitutional issue, but dealing with it or at least getting some measure of the government's thinking, was very important. So, we worked on the drafts.

If you are going to pursue a constitutional issue in the UK, the best place to be born is somewhere else, preferably somewhere with a written constitution. The 'unwritten' nature of the British constitution makes for a national woolliness about just what the constitution actually contains and a further woolliness in the legal profession about the nature of certain constitutional principles such as sovereignty. It is commonly held that sovereignty in the UK rests with the Crown in Parliament. By contrast, the Irish constitution holds that sovereignty devolves to the state from God and in America sovereignty arises from the people. Of the three proposals the better by far is the one held in the United States, since it implies that the people are the arbiters of the constitution and can unmake and change what they have made.

By contrast, the UK position implies a continuing governing role for the sovereign that is not simply symbolic and provides for no arbiter of principle separate from Parliament, which means, in effect, the government of the day. Almost alone amongst modern states, the UK provides no ultimate defence for the citizens against a wayward governmental power. And it is only by the narrowest of conventions, based on a principle seldom made explicit in British politics, that Paddy Ashdown was able to proceed against the heart of legal power in the UK in search of a remedy for the jurisdictional intrusions of the US into the country. Paddy's first instinct, after the early letter exchanges and debates, was to go to the Lord Chancellor on the constitutional issue. By tradition the Chancellor's department deals with constitutional matters. The first move, however, was to get a draft letter together, get it vetted by the lawyers and in the course of the exercise try to find out who it should be sent to.

Initially I suggested a relatively short letter, focusing as narrowly as

[77]

possible on the sovereignty issue as evidenced in the IBM letter, and on the fining of ICL. Paddy thought we could go further, though he resisted the idea of raising the issue of the ministerial oath of office at that juncture. He felt strongly that illegalities were occurring all around the country and the government was doing nothing to stop them, and that getting them stopped was the first priority. That would be the object of the letter, not politically assaulting ministers. On the other hand, I had excessive expectations as to the outcome of the correspondence.

As we prepared our drafts, we started to encounter the problem of the lack of constitutional understanding in the UK. First, there are very few lawyers in Britain who understand constitutional principles as opposed to constitutional practice. Written constitutions, particularly modern ones, tend to reflect fairly clearly the basics of constitutionality; that is, jurisdiction is defined, usually coincidental with the national territory. The precise relationship between the various organs of state, beginning with the head of state, is usually stated, as is the source of sovereignty, ie God, the people, or whatever. In the UK, very little is explicit in that way. Almost everything is a matter of either precedent or legislation – in other words, much of the British constitution can be found in statute law, whereas the real purpose of a constitution is to separate the ordinary work of government, which is the creation of legislation, from a set of protective principles, which should only be alterable by direct intervention of the real source of sovereignty, which is the people. In fact, despite the extraordinary – not to say totalitarian – potential this places at the disposal of the party with a majority in the House of Commons there is actually reserved for the government, within the conventions of the British constitution, a power defined as the Royal Prerogative. In summary this piece of constitutional malpractice that the UK government, as heir to monarchs who once reigned absolutely, has inherited, is their arbitrary capacity to act without restraint. It places the government, at least in law, beyond the reach even of its own party in the Commons.

The importance of the Royal Prerogative in this story is the manner in which a number of lawyers suggested that the government would use it to block my more extravagant suggestions, including suing the Attorney General. But there is another side to this coin: whereas the government might, in certain situations, be prepared to use this procedure, it would in so doing usurp the notion that sovereignty rests with the Crown in Parliament. Both principles, that of the locus of sovereignty, and that of the government's reserve power of arbitrary rule are,

[78]

like much else in the constitution, a matter of some imprecision. They are also a matter of balance and expediency. The expedient thing to do in relation to the IBM letter was to invoke the Protection of Trade Act, which is a minor bill of sovereignty in heavy disguise. This was the law which enabled Prime Minister Thatcher to order the companies in the Siberian gas pipeline to proceed with their contracts after President Reagan had tried to impose US law, and stop them doing so. Again, it is worth noting that so overwhelming were the pressures being applied to the British government over the computer item, that this option has never been used despite the fact that the infringement of sovereignty is far more intensive than it was in the case of the Siberian gas pipeline. On the other hand, to use the Royal Prerogative to halt a bid to end the infringement, would involve the government in an attempt to sanction activity within the country by the United States and would by so doing focus attention on both the infringement itself and on the contradiction between Parliament's assumed absolute rights where the matter of sovereignty is involved, and the dubious powers reserved for the executive under the Royal Prerogative. It was a move I was convinced the government would not make, but I failed to convince the lawyers.

For almost twelve months, until May Day 1985, drafts circulated to various legal authorities, including the House of Lords. Tim Clement Jones, the chairman of the Liberal Party's legal panel, was a major contributor to the internal debate about just what should be in the first attack. It was his decision in the end that directed the letter to Sir Michael Havers, not in terms of his title, but in terms of the functions he discharges. These, among others, include 'Guardian of the Public Interest,' senior legal advisor to the Crown and legal advisor to the House of Commons.

In this case the public interest was as clear as the public reaction to the IBM letter. Public interest, of course, does not mean what it appears to mean. Depending which constitutional viewpoint you take, it means both public policy, which is in effect government policy; and, in a much more diffuse manner, it means those matters of public concern for which specific legislation has not been made and in which the government ought to have an interest, lest its standing with the public is damaged. Taken together it is simply another power conferred on government to ensure that its more diffuse and non-specific interests are protected.

The argument behind addressing Sir Michael on the point of the public interest is that the American intrusion offended not one public policy, but several. In the first place, it is public policy to uphold the various commonly agreed principles of international law. In this case, the American position most certainly contradicted the nationality principle. This principle states that nationality does not follow goods and is lost as soon as the goods leave their original jurisdiction. The American legislation also imposes movement controls, in the form of licences to travel, on persons having any data in their heads, which is made licensable by the legislation. This conflicts with both constitutional freedoms and public policy in the UK. The technical position on this item is very complex, but in general UK legislation is deemed only to restrict personal freedoms for specific reasons, which are usually based on national security considerations, or which are enacted in an emergency, such as war. In general, UK public policy, best exemplified in the lack of the identity card system which is mandatory in most continental countries, refrains from any formal attempt to impose movement controls on individuals on a generalised basis.

The more obvious examples of US intrusion into UK jurisdiction related to hardware, to physical entities and was, as such, not too difficult to understand. But the same legislation, since it extends to computer programs and all technical data of US origin, would, if exercised, cover about eighty per cent of the technical staff associated with computers in the UK, say 400,000 people in all. In theory, no one in that category could leave the UK for destinations such as Sweden, Austria or Switzerland, not to mention the Eastern Bloc, without obtaining an American export licence for the data in their heads. As a matter of practicality there was no way the US could enforce this absurd piece of legislation on a wide scale. But, in practice, they had imposed this legislation throughout Europe in relation to hardware, and were certainly capable of imposing it in relation to the operating systems and advanced software used on the kinds of machines mentioned in the IBM letter. No legislation exists in the UK to protect people from this kind of thing. Paddy accepted that, if it came to court action, the various contradictions of public policy could be convincingly enunciated.

In general, Paddy's view, based on practicalities, was that court action should only commence when all the means of persuading the competent public official to do his duty had failed. That included a full enunciation of where his duty lay and why action should be undertaken. By addressing the Attorney General in his capacity as guardian of the public interest, we at least ensured ourselves a whole range of arguments, should the matter ever come to court. Again, it

[80]

would obviously be much better if parliamentary pressure, rather than action in the courts, produced the remedy we sought. Paddy, as an MP, had a vested interest in seeing that action in the House of Commons produced results.

Our final letter addressed Sir Michael in two other capacities, for very specific reasons. As senior legal advisor to the Crown he would, under the constitution, be bound to advise the Queen if there were a serious infringement of her writ, anywhere in the kingdom. When it comes to the processes of law, only the Queen's signature makes lists passed by Parliament into effective law. Thus known usurpations of her writ, apart from other considerations, should be reported to the sovereign by her senior advisor, who is the Attorney General. In this particular case there is no evidence that the Queen has been advised. The obligations on the Attorney General are more moral than legal, and as such either avoidable or, more likely, fudgeable. It is just possible that somewhere at the bottom of some memo between the Law Courts and the Crown, there is a footnote to the effect that there is a 'minor problem about computers', and probably adds that the matter is being dealt with. Together, enough to get Sir Michael off the narrower hook of dereliction of duty, though not in our view off the alternative hook of failing to truly fulfil his role, to the fullest possible extent, to Crown, Parliament and people.

The final address, in anticipation of future legal action, was to Sir Michael as the legal advisor to the House of Commons. Were it to be supposed that we were wrong in both the other two points, this one at least focused the issue exactly. Precisely because of the weakness, previously identified, which enables the House of Commons to create the effective constitution by legislative action, the American intrusion is a direct challenge to its authority in every sphere. And particularly so because its effect is so extensive in the country.

So in tne first three lines of his letter Paddy Ashdown paved the way for a series of writs of *mandamus* on points of public policy against the Attorney General. In addition, he prepared the ground for questions about how the Attorney General was carrying out his duties as the senior legal advisor to the Crown. Finally, from a political point of view, he opened the way for a parliamentary examination of the conduct of its own senior advisor, in relation to a challenge to the very foundation stone of its authority. But whether any of those steps could be taken rested entirely on the quality of the evidence. This evidence, all verified by affidavit, was as follows:

[81]

Dear Sir Michael

I am writing to you in your several capacities, as 'guardian of the public interest', senior legal advisor to the Crown and advisor to the House of Commons.

In the course of last and this year, it has become clear that the US Department of Commerce, through its office of Export and Administration, claims jurisdiction over firms and persons in this country. This is achieved via US Export Regulations, made under the Export Administration Act of 1979, not only in respect of the export from the US of certain 'advanced' computer systems as specified, but also in respect of any subsequent dealing whether within the country of original destination or otherwise.

Letters confirming this are sent as a matter of course to purchasers of this equipment notifying them of this fact. I enclose a copy of the standard letter used by IBM to its leasing customers, applying also to all users of those machines, about 1400, in the UK.

Paragraph four was inserted upon advice. It was the only paragraph I disagreed with. It contradicts the point made by the British government in their memorandum to the US in the wake of the Siberian gas pipeline affair, that attempts to introduce US legislation in the form of terms in commercial contracts is unacceptable. Given the arguments of principle made in this chapter, paragraph four does not make sense, since it clearly appears to accept a back door method of extra-territorial entry for US law. In fact, given the way the US legislation is written against the US companies themselves, in that it makes them responsible for events and goods beyond their legal control, the paragraph is in support of that position too, which was not the intention.

You will note that the letter does not simply purport to make observance of the US Export Regulations a contractual commitment, with an obligation to indemnify the original supplier in the event of breach. This would in my view be perfectly legitimate.

The heart of the next four paragraphs is a demonstration, backed by evidence, that the US will act and that it can and does enforce its jurisdiction in the UK. The ICL item is particularly interesting.

In 1978 ICL, for many years a target of US hostility for its business

[82]

in the Eastern Bloc, sold a large computer to South Africa. The computer was made in the UK and was exported with valid UK export licences. But the system contained two discs, part of the computer's memory system, that were built by CDC Corporation of the US. No US re-export licences had been applied for in the case of these 'memory' units, which constituted less than five per cent of the value of the whole shipment. According to several sources, one of ICL's numerous American rivals eventually informed the Commerce Department that the two disc units were in South Africa. The Commerce Department checked its files and found that no application for a re-export licence from the UK had been made by ICL.

Now, two CDC disc units were but a drop in the ocean of American computer supplies reaching South Africa. All the major American computer manufacturers were there, including IBM. At least in theory all those companies refused to sell to the South African military or police, something they were prevented from doing by a foreign policy decision of the US President Jimmy Carter. Despite the prohibition, the original source for most computer technology in use by the South African apartheid administration is the United States. The reasons for going after ICL were wholly political and the South African offence was seized with glee by the US government for two reasons. In the first place it finally gave them a chance to impose controls on ICL, controls that were ultimately aimed at destroying its business in Eastern Europe and which have, to a large extent, succeeded.

The second reason for going after ICL on the South Africa pretext was the prevalence in the UK of a very high level of antipathy to the apartheid regime. If the US claimed that ICL was supplying the proponents of apartheid with computers to help in imposing the pass laws, there would be little sympathy for the company and no inclination on the company's part to go public on the affair. The American government, advised closely by the US Embassy in Pretoria and in London, moved against ICL in May 1982. But the official notice of the $15,000 fine omitted ninety per cent of the real facts. Caught in the wake of a near terminal cash flow crisis, in the middle of a major restructuring with ambitious plans for American expansion, ICL had no real choice but to comply with the US enforcement penalty, of which the fine was the most minor part.

The full penalty included the submission to Department of Commerce control of all ICL's major computer exports from the United Kingdom. Indeed, members of the US Embassy staff in London complained in March 1984 at a breakfast meeting in the Ambassador's residence, that

ICL was not in full compliance with its undertakings to the US Government.

'The Company,' an official said, 'should be getting US export licences for all its movements of computers, including those from its Manchester factory, to its customers *within* the UK.'

Among those present at that meeting was Lord Weinstock, the Chairman of GEC. It is not clear if he heard that particular remark, but he was certainly aware that US extra-territoriality was the issue of that meeting, even though it was nine more months before the imposition of the controls became public.

ICL did not sit idly by during the period of investigation. The company commissioned a report from a team of American lawyers which made a comprehensive and damaging examination of the many anti-free trade practices prevalent in the US. The report, along with a request for help over the South African affair, was made to the UK government in late '81 or early '82. ICL got no help. This was partly because the government was engaged throughout most of 1981 and 1982 in trying to prevent first, the complete collapse of ICL and secondly a ruinous American takeover. In order to accomplish the first objective, the government was forced to do a partial U-turn on its 'no money for lame ducks' policy and provide huge guarantees to the banks which put up the rescue package. It is impossible not to feel some sympathy for those in the DTI who were working long hours just to keep ICL afloat.

Unfortunately, mending a breach in sovereignty should come before the rescue of one ailing company, because it affects the legal status of the government itself. Someone, somewhere, left the government vulnerable to serious charges of neglect of duty when they failed to move to stop the American action. The main charge was the failure to uphold the Treaty of Rome as undertaken by the government in Article 40 of that Treaty. This is a serious charge and could involve the government in huge compensation payments to aggrieved shareholders and others. The prevailing argument in the DTI was that ICL was so dependent on supplies from the US that it could not afford to lose them, which is what the United States was threatening. The US was also threatening to seize ICL's factory in Utica, New York State, if the company did not comply. Final compliance has forced ICL to spend up to $150,000 per annum and wait months for licences, as well as keeping two senior legal executives almost permanently in Washington. It has also persuaded the company to reduce the level of US-supplied components from about forty per cent of the total make-up of the computer to an insignificant amount worth less than $50. In the end, US policy will create the very

[84]

independence and competition it was trying to stifle. When the first drafts of the letter were being prepared we did not know these latter facts, which only became available in December 1984.

The Systime problem, mentioned in the draft which continues below, is dealt with in chapter 10.

'In the event of breach of the regulations by the non US national in their own country the US Department of Commerce has imposed heavy fines and additional conditions.

'As the enclosed extract of the 1982 Report of the Export Administration shows clearly, fines have been levied on non US companies, including a fine of $15,000 on the UK company ICL. Currently a Leeds based company called Systime Limited faces fines of $400,000, despite its compliance with UK export regulations. Attached to the fines are conditions, which, in ICL's case, include a requirement to obtain the consent of the Office of Export Administration for import sales transactions involving the relevant computer systems.

If the fine is not paid and the conditions are not met, orders are made, and names entered on the US Export Denials list.

I enclose a copy of a letter received by a UK based distributor from the UK from lawyers (sic) acting for a US based firm informing him of an order to this effect.

'One result of the actions of the Department of Commerce is to give an unfair commercial advantage to US companies, and I have in correspondence with government ministers cited examples whereupon orders having been made to prevent exports by a UK based company, a US company has subsequently been allowed to supply.

The matter in paragraph 10 encompasses irregular activity in the UK by various agencies of the US government. Among the departments of the US government which undertook surveillance (CIA) inspection (US Customs) enforcement (US State Department officials from the Embassy in London) and investigations (State and CIA) perhaps the most reprehensible of all were the UK Customs themselves.

In 1980 and 1981, under the auspices of the Combined Customs Agreement of 1953, units of the US Customs service were based at the US Embassy in London and at the headquarters of UK Customs in King's Beam House, London. A number of UK Customs officials were sent to the United States, for training in operations relating to high

[85]

technology smuggling to the Eastern Bloc. The outcome was a series of extravagant prosecutions, undertaken at great cost, resulting in the jailing of a number of UK citizens for what amounted to trying to compete with the United States in supplying the Eastern Bloc with old and dated technology. This extraordinary situation is more fully dealt with in chapter 10 but Paddy's intention was to ensure that the apparent block put on the US intrusions in January 1984 by the Foreign Secretary was actually being observed.

> In order to establish breaches of US Export Regulations it appears that agents of the Department of Commerce have conducted investigations in the UK. It does not appear that they have received the permission of the UK government to do so. In addition, they appear to have adopted illegal methods in order to obtain access to evidence. I enclose a copy of my letter to the Prime Minister on this subject.

In the next paragraph (eleven) Paddy was much more diplomatic than I advised him to be. I felt, and I think that Paddy now agrees, that the principle of Cocom, already under serious threat from the abuses the US was perpetrating there, was totally undermined by the alternative extra-territorial controls operated by the US under the Export Administration Act. But Paddy felt that this letter was not the place to make that argument. Also, much of the material available in chapters 7 and 10 was not available in May 1985.

> It must be understood that these controls imposed by the US government are not the result of any treaty obligation on the UK negotiated through the Co-ordinating Committee (COCOM), the body which is responsible for co-ordinating controls on militarily sensitive equipment. The enclosed letter from the residing Director of the Office of East West Trade at the Department of State makes this clear. (Root's letter, page 52).

Paragraph twelve was a minor reference to the EEC. Even then Paddy had in mind an approach to the Commission, but in 1984 we had no idea how we were going to make that approach. It was enough simply to draw Sir Michael's attention to the fact that there was an EEC dimension to the problem. For that too reflected a key feature in Paddy Ashdown's approach. He never once, to my knowledge, sought to raise

[86]

an issue for the publicity it would give him. Quite the opposite. After his launch into the Liberal leadership stakes by the bored media entourage at the Liberal Assembly in 1984, he had all the publicity he could ever need and some to spare. It is an accepted convention that an MP may write a letter to a minister and publish it without waiting for a reply, if he or she thinks the issue important enough. Inevitably, such a course of action will constrain a minister's reply, but that too is part of the liturgy of Parliament. Paddy's practice is to await a reply, unless it is an ongoing issue where ministerial response has been either inadequate or evasive. In the case of the EEC reference, Paddy was going a step further. In this his first letter to the Attorney General, foreshadowing, as it might, future legal action, he felt it only fair that he should raise all the issues with Sir Michael and his staff. There could then be no shadow of a suggestion that he was simply scoring political points. Which he was not interested in doing. The letter, when it went, had been a year in the legal mill. Much midnight oil had been burned over it and if the advice had been paid for it would have been well into five figures. Political point scoring comes cheaper than that.

The ideal outcome, from Paddy's point of view, would have been just two things: the immediate proscription of the American intrusions and a reference to the EEC. On every side and in all its many dimensions, the tempo of Paddy's life was stepping up. In his constituency, which is the heart and soul of his political life, the main employer, Westland Helicopters, were going into serious cash flow and empty order book trauma. Paddy himself is a former Westland employee; about ninety per cent of all the employment in Yeovil, taking sub-contractors into account, is based on Westland. His mail often exceeds one hundred letters a day – good practice for when he inherits Ashdown House, I like to rib him. He has two secretaries, not to mention his staff of five or six fully occupied part timers like me. On this issue alone his files now run to over 1,400 documents and he has been an MP only since 1983.

The letter itself had closed, after a summary of ministerial statements and inactivity, with a reference to precedent. This is probably one of the most effective steps to take with the Civil Service establishment which is always more inclined to advise action if precedent exists. No one could say that the homework had not been done.

The EEC Commission is, I understand, investigating whether EEC based companies are in breach of EEC law by complying with these fines and conditions.
    During the course of last year I made representations to the

Secretary of State for Trade and Industry, asking him to seek to lift the effect of these unilateral regulations on UK based companies. Although I believe that negotiations have been conducted by the Secretary of State for Trade and Industry, with the imposition of a fine of this magnitude on Systime, it is clear that the US Department of Commerce remains unmoved and continues to make the same assumptions of jurisdiction.

In a *Today* programme on the BBC on 20 January last year Mr Tebbit described the actions of the Department of Commerce as 'contrary to international law'.

I believe that this is indeed the case and that the actions of the US Department of Commerce amount to a major breach of UK sovereignty.

You will recall that your predecessor, Mr Silkin, intervened in the Westinghouse Uranium Contracts case on the basis that the US Justice Department was attempting to extend its anti-trust investigating procedures to include the activities of UK companies which took place outside United States territory.

The current imposition of fines on a UK resident company and the method by which evidence was obtained, appears to be an even more flagrant violation of UK sovereignty. In the Westinghouse case Viscount Dilhorne said that the Attorney General's intervention 'was . . . not only his right but also his duty to make, on the grounds, despite the representations made by Her Majesty's Government, that the sovereignty of this country has been prejudiced and that there has been an "excess of sovereignty or an excess of jurisdiction" on the part of the United States'.

Although there are no current court proceedings in which you can intervene, it seems clear that in your role as guardian of the public interest you have a duty to consider these issues as a matter of urgency and to take action on behalf of the Crown, whether before the International Court or otherwise.

It may be that in another role you have already advised the Department of Trade or the Prime Minister on the implications of the US Department of Commerce's actions. If so, I would ask you without delay to seek their permission to the publication of your advice.

If this is not the case I would ask you as a matter of urgency to give your opinion to the House of Commons.

I believe that the effect of the exercise of US Export

Regulations has far reaching implications for the sovereignty of the United Kingdom. I urge you to take the necessary action without delay.

Yours sincerely
Paddy Ashdown

While we waited for Sir Michael to respond, how happy we would have been had we known the true extent to which we had forced the most senior levels of the Civil Service to engage with the complaint. The letter was studied by most of Sir Michael's staff, who held extensive consultations with the Lord Chancellor's department. In turn, the issue was taken to the legal advisors to the Foreign Office, the Department of Trade and Industry and No. 10 Downing Street, and the matter was placed on ministerial agendas. I sensed that the letter was causing mayhem, but could get no bearing on its progress. Paddy was not approached by anybody, though it is highly likely that the American Embassy was informed of its contents. Certainly the Embassy's friends within the system who might, under Section 2 of the Official Secrets Act be described as spies, would know of the consternation in the main government law offices. The Foreign Office probably stepped up the tempo of enquiry to the Embassy and in Washington the British Embassy probably did the same to the State Department.

On 3 July the Attorney General replied. The letter is extraordinary from two points of view, neither of which were anticipated by us. Paragraph four says all we wanted to hear: Yes, the situation is illegal. Yes, it is an infringement of UK sovereignty. The Attorney General made specific reference to the IBM letter. But the rest of the letter is one long crawl away from any attempt to end the infringement, or deal with the illegality.

One former Cabinet Minister who later saw the letter said, 'If one of my civil servants had let a letter like that out of my ministry, I'd have throttled him'.

It takes a minister to recognise a political and legal disaster when he sees one. That minister was also a barrister, and the general view in the UK legal profession and in the Irish and Belgian legal communities, was that the letter was 'impossible'.

It identifies and recognises one of the most serious crimes a government can face, short of armed insurrection, and the Attorney General proposes to seek a remedy at least in part, by discussing the matter with the legal profession of the 'criminal' state. The text now follows:

[89]

I refer to your letters of 1 May and 25 June about US claims to extra-territorial jurisdiction and about the Export Administration Act.

US claims to extra-territorial jurisdiction have been a continuing source of friction for many years. Although these matters are primarily the concern of the Secretary of State for Trade and Industry and the Foreign Secretary, I have for some time been watching this closely and have been playing a part in trying to increase US awareness of the United Kingdom's view of their assertion of jurisdiction and in seeking to persuade the Americans to moderate their claims.

Two years ago I was invited to address the International Law and Practice Section of the American Bar Association in Atlanta and I took the opportunity to speak on this subject to US lawyers on their home ground. That speech was published in the *International Lawyer* and I enclose a copy of it. In particular you will see that on pages 792 to 794 I explained our objections to the Export Administration Act and suggested ways of curbing excesses in extra-territorial jurisdiction.

Thus you will see that I entirely share the views of the Secretary of State for Trade and Industry that claims by the United States government to control the export of goods from the UK and, as illustrated by the IBM letter, the more extravagant claim to control the sale of certain advanced computers within this country, are unwarranted encroachments on UK jurisdiction and are contrary to international law.

Similarly I share your view that the US has no right to impose fines or take other punitive action against firms in the United Kingdom which have 'violated' US re-export controls. Although US claims to extra-territorial jurisdiction are offensive it is only realistic to recognise that we cannot in practice compel the US to stop making such claims and seeking to enforce them. We have, of course, in the Protection of Trading Interests Act the means of making it unlawful for British firms and individuals to comply with such US action. This offers a means of safeguarding UK sovereignty, but it is necessary to consider in a particular case whether its use is likely on balance to benefit UK trading and commercial interests. The government's judgment has been that in these difficult circumstances UK firms and individuals should generally be allowed to make a commercial judgment about whether to comply with US licensing requirements and any subsequent enforcement action. The government are, however, always prepared to see what can be done to assist British companies experiencing difficulties.

You also suggest that the US has been operating its export rules to the advantage of its own companies. Such allegations are made from time to time but I understand that none has yet been substantiated. If satisfactory evidence were to be found, however, it is a matter which the government would take very seriously indeed and which I would expect to be taken up with the US authorities in the strongest terms.

As to the activities of US officials in the UK, there are no formal restrictions on their visiting British companies provided they keep within British law. It has been made quite clear to the US authorities, however, that their officials should not visit British firms to investigate possible breaches of US law without obtaining the agreement of the appropriate UK government department.

You mention activity by the EC Commission. It is certainly true that the Community as a whole shares our opposition to US extra-territorial claims and that a number of representations have been made to the US on the matter. I am not aware, however, of any investigation of the sort you mention, and it is not immediately obvious to me how that payment of fines by EC-based companies could be a breach of existing EC law.

You suggest that the issue should be before the International Court of Justice. Even if the Court had jurisdiction in the case – and I think it likely that the US would contest their jurisdiction – recource to litigation is not always the best method of dealing with differences between States. The Government view is that the most productive approach to US extra-territoriality is to concentrate on managing the practical problems to which it gives rise. We have maintained this approach in talks between the two countries which led to the arrangement on export controls announced by the Minister for Trade in November last year.

The practical approach of course does not imply any weakening of our position on the principle. In appropriate cases the UK has submitted representations to the US government and *amicus curiae* briefs to US courts on important points of principle; and with other Western Allies, has continued to lobby the US on the need for legislative change.

For as long as the US claims extra-territorial jurisdiction, there will be an ever-present threat of disputes arising from US efforts

[91]

to enforce these claims. There have been some limited signs, however, that continued representations by the UK and like-minded countries (no doubt coupled with growing awareness of the damage to US commercial interests of some of its policies) have led the US authorities to show rather more sensitivity about the application of US controls. The most recent example, I think, is the efforts made to avoid claims to extra-territorial application in US regulations prohibiting trade with Nicaragua. Our immediate aim must be to increase such sensitivity.

I think that to achieve this we have to work on the Americans and I believe that this is more likely to have an effect than a statement by me in the House of Commons. Later this month many lawyers from the American Bar Association will be coming to London for this year's Annual Conference. That will provide a further opportunity for discussion of these issues with the Americans.

This is an important matter and I hope that, sharing your concern as I do, I have been able to bring some influence to bear on American thinking on this and will continue to do so.

Yours ever
Michael

Before making a quick examination of the key elements of the letter it is worth remembering that the sum of the letter is a lot more than its parts. So weak a response to an admitted illegality, coming from the major legal figure in the UK and knowing how many hands were up to their wrists in Sir Michael's draft, means that he must have been facing some insurmountable barrier to action. I have no real idea what that barrier is, it is my belief that the clues lie in the telegram and Shotgun Diplomacy note reproduced in Appendix 2. It is highly likely, taking the hard evidence presented in this book, that the United States stepped up the pressure by some intolerable measure. The US has countless opportunities to do this, so beholden has the UK become to it, in computers, weapons, intelligence and the other hard foundations for state power in the modern era.

But to return to the letter itself: paragraph four is more than Paddy could ever have anticipated. The Attorney General agreed with him. Most people would have said 'enough, and thank the Lord'. In any normal circumstances the declaration would have been followed by either a number of guarded paragraphs hinting that the minister would act but not committing him to any specific course of action. That would have been neat. It would have given Paddy a small hostage to fortune, a quick headline, and then a long haul trying to find out what action the government would take, and when it would take it.

The first serious error in the letter is in paragraph five. It is true that the UK cannot stop the US making illegal claims to jurisdiction within Britain, but not true that the US cannot be stopped from seeking to enforce such claims. There is the Protection of Trade Act, which was very successfully used to stop such enforcement activity just three years before. In the next two sentences the Attorney General confirms this view but tries to avoid taking action on the grounds of 'reasonableness'. This on the one hand overlooks the recourse the UK has to the Treaty of Rome, which provides an umbrella of generality to cover individual cases. Put bluntly, if the EEC slammed the anchors on the offending companies and refused them permission to import from the US, IBM would be into a cash flow crisis within twenty weeks, and DEC, the second largest computer company in the world, would be in trouble even earlier.

It is a game of bluff, but dealing 'reasonable' cards to the trickiest player in the international trade game gets you nowhere. In general trade the US is just as vulnerable as Europe, but on this issue its vulnerability is much greater. The EEC is the buyer, the US is the vendor; and one great thing about computers is that once they are in, they can be run for quite a long time before key items from the United States become necessary. Meanwhile, the huge manufacturing base in the US eats up money and will be in crisis long before a crisis of equal proportions hits Europe.

In his second to last sentence in paragraph five Sir Michael yet again abdicates upon a central point of principle that binds reasonable men and women to their government. It is this: Sir Michael essentially says that the UK government will stand idly by while a powerful foreign government, acting as state power, picks off UK companies one at a time. There is an obvious response to this: 'If you cannot protect me in my country, in my castle, from a foreign power, why should I pay your taxes and why should I obey your government?'

This is neither a rhetorical nor an unfair question. To defend sovereignty is the first duty and the first self interest of any government, since upon a successful defence of sovereignty rests the integrity of the state and the legitimacy of that government.

In paragraph six Sir Michael is simply repeating bad advice, prob-

[93]

ably sourced only in his own department. The Department of Trade and Industry have long known all that needs to be known about the situation in China, the Soviet Union and the Eastern Bloc. There is massive evidence in the Cocom files of US trading that does not seem to appear in either the OECD figures, or the US figures for licences issued for sales to the East Bloc.

Paragraph seven is quite normal. The UK would expect the same facilities in the United States. The key is the last sentence. Jack Lacy, the head of Customs at the US Embassy in London, had for some time considered himself free to visit and 'check out' any British company trying to buy US technology. He did so on many occasions without contacting anyone in the UK government. *Newsweek*, in its main feature article on 11 November 1985, tried to imply that Lacy had been unfairly treated by the UK press. 'Jack Lacy, Chief US Customs Officer in London, was portrayed as a brutal vigilante in the British press after he questioned two British businessmen.' In fact Lacy, though unobjectionable on a personal level, would have been declared *persona non grata* in any country whose government had a modicum of spunk.

Before he questioned anyone, Lacy usually implied, if he didn't actually state, that unless he was allowed on the company's premises, no US technology would be delivered to it. This he did to Plasma Technology near Bristol in 1984 and to SAL, another West of England company, earlier the same year. For companies critically dependent on US supplies, Lacy's terms for a visit amounted to coercion. The fact that he was operating like this, from the US Embassy, was an extraordinary breach of diplomatic protocol. He had no one but himself to blame for the fact that he wound up 'locked up in the Embassy' as one of his colleagues put it.

. In paragraph nine, Sir Michael says that the government view is to try and manage the problems as they arise rather than challenging the US in the courts. This statement is absurd since there is a sovereignty problem for the British government in at least 2,000 or more computer sites around the country. There is a breach of sovereignty occurring every time a computer is exported from the UK with a US export licence superseding the UK export licence. This is a daily occurrence. In short, the practical approach to which Sir Michael refers is nowhere in operation, and the UK is doing nothing to restore the principle at stake, which is sovereignty. Nice though Sir Michael plainly wants to be, the American Bar Association is not an appropriate body with which to discuss the sovereignty of the UK, particularly when that sovereignty has been breached. In fact, it is not a topic which the United States

[94]

should even raise, under the normal international conventions, as the Foreign Office legal advisors should have told Sir Michael. It seems highly improper for the British government to discuss the issue of sovereignty with the United States while it is in breach by that country.

Sir Michael's reply got a certain amount of publicity, but this chapter has tried to show that the waters into which the United States has driven the UK are deep indeed. Computer industry trade papers are not about constitutional laws. The national media should be, but *The Sunday Times* could not find space for it, so the *Financial Times* carried the story on 15 July 1985. There was a follow up on the legal pages a little later written by the legal correspondent, Mr H. Hermann. Apart from that, the issue has once more, perhaps happily from Paddy's point of view, sunk into media obscurity.

Not so for his advisors. Responding to Sir Michael produced a neat divide between Tim Clement Jones, who wished to proceed interrogatively, and myself. I wanted to go for the constitutional issue bald headed. Our compromise letter, as amended and rewritten by Paddy, follows. I liked his questions and felt that they would certainly assure the issue the undivided attention of the Lord Chancellor's department as well as Sir Michael's.

Dear Sir Michael
re US Claims to Extra-territorial Jurisdiction
   Thank you for your letter of 3 July. I am grateful to you for your considered reply.
   I am very encouraged by the view you express, that in conjunction with the Secretary of State for Trade and Industry you consider the cases highlighted in my letter do indeed constitute an unwarranted encroachment of UK jurisdiction and are contrary to international law.
   I am however very far from encouraged by the outcome of the representations which you describe yourself and the Secretary of State as having made to the US government. I cannot accept your assertions on page three of your letter that faced with the current situation the most productive approach is to 'concentrate' on managing the practical problems to which it gives rise'. It does indeed seem to me that without strong representations at the highest level and legal counter-action, this carries all the risk of compromising on both the principle of sovereignty and of international law by permitting the situation to persist.

[95]

In your position as guardian of the public interest I do not believe that it is open to you to do other than advise the Prime Minister herself to take this up at the highest level and pursue all remedies available to the United Kingdom government. Failing such action it is clear that British companies such as ICL remain outside the protection of the British legal system in respect of their export activities.

From my own reading of the proceedings of the American Bar Association discussions on the subject of extra-territoriality they may be showing sensitivity to the issues involved but arguing as American lawyers have done on occasion that there are no accepted rules of international law in this respect, they appear hardly in the mood to concede to reasonable argument.

It is clear that if our high technology exports are not to suffer, the issue of infringement of UK sovereignty must be taken up with the US government by the Prime Minister at the highest level. In this light I would put to you the following questions:

1 Do you accept that you have a continuing duty to parliament to take all possible steps to stop the infringement of UK jurisdiction by the US government?

2 Will you ensure that the Prime Minister places this as a matter of priority on the agenda the next time she meets President Reagan?

3 Evidence that the US is operating these regulations to its own trade advantage is readily available with the Department of Trade. Will you undertake to carry out the necessary enquiry into their records?

4 Despite what you say about the way in which visits by US officials should be conducted, this is not what is actually happening on the ground. US officials continue to visit US subsidiaries in this country without informing either the DTI or anyone else. In May such a visit took place to a company called Masscomp near Reading. You will also note that the US officials are determined to carry out audits. Will you investigate the circumstances of those visits?

5 I note your statements regarding the EEC. The kind of investigation I have in mind was being undertaken by the Industry Commissioner Viscount D'Avignon and is, so far as I know, continuing under his successor Willie De Clerq. Fines are but one of the issues. The conditions imposed alongside the fines are what I see as a breach of EEC law. Will you actively

[96]

explore joint action with our EEC partners in order to ensure that the US changes its Export Regulations, and desists from such practices?

In the meantime can you also please inform me what the government does in fact propose to do for those British companies who have paid US fines and agreed illegal US trading conditions, in the light of your statement that the government is prepared to see what can be done for them?

To date and for the past two years or so it is clear that you and your governmental colleagues have sought to deal with this matter by representation at ministerial level. I would suggest to you that it is now a matter of legal and national principle that the issue is raised at heads of government and international level.

Yours sincerely
Paddy Ashdown MP

In fact, with the constitutional issue muted in the preamble, the strength of the letter lay in the questions, and the first question certainly puts the Attorney General on the spot.

As we awaited the outcome of this letter, Tim and I mused, at infrequent meetings, over the final outcome. Never one to ignore fundamentals, my commonest comment was that eventually, the Prime Minister would have to act, or resign. 'Eventually', I know, is a long time in English politics. Tim, much more experienced than me in such matters, was taking what in law is known as the practical approach. To my mind, 'practical' in English politics means never doing anything as a matter of principle. But here, with Tim and Paddy, was the forgotten joy of radical liberalism. In moving a great issue, one that affected the liberty of many, the integrity of the constitution and the relationship between the UK and the US, we could afford a variety of approaches, and find a common way to put them which left all that was positive in each approach intact. The heart of my argument was this:

The government, as the executive body of Parliament, does not possess authority through the Royal Prerogative or any other constitutional device whereby it can waive or dilute Parliament's absolute right to seamless jurisdiction throughout the realm inherent in the core of our sovereignty as represented by the Crown in Parliament. Acts of Parliament, such as those which give temporary local jurisdiction to visiting forces commanders over their own nationals, or which link us to the

[97]

EEC, are acts proper to a sovereign authority, since they are made by Parliament as a whole, and ultimate jurisdiction is reserved. But the power to make those arrangements is not devolved to the executive.

In any case, after Sir Michael's reply, the boot would be on the other foot, relative to the Prime Minister's position as I saw it. We, and Paddy in particular, would almost certainly have to act. I saw room for maybe one more round of correspondence, perhaps a raising of the issue in the Lords. After that, and in concert with actions in the EEC, the crisis would be all too visible; too visible, I hoped, to ignore.

CHAPTER 6

Debates in the House

JANUARY 1984 HAD BEEN AN extraordinary month in terms of news on the issue. The IBM letter had set the pace, but the focus was definitely moving to Parliament as further confirmation arrived that the US negotiations in Geneva had offered the entire Cocom list to the Russians in return for an arms deal. The information came from a very senior UK official in the Foreign Office and was indirectly confirmed by the State Department in Washington. At *Computer News* we originally treated the story with some caution despite the fact that the international media had left no one in any doubt that Ronald Reagan was desperate for an arms deal with the Russians in order to improve his chances for a second bid for the presidency in November. Had I known then what I know now, we could not only have run the story, we might even have been able to anticipate it.

The Cocom list has always been a bargaining chip for American negotiations in Geneva. In whole or in part, the list has been offered on a number of occasions to the USSR or to selected countries in the Eastern Bloc, depending on the whims of the US President or administration at any one time. In fact, in 1981 the US licensed $130m worth of nuclear technology to Romania. Despite Romania's moderate, independent foreign policy, the country is a full and active member of the Warsaw Pact. The assumption too is that the 1981 licence was the last in a series and not the first, meaning that the US had sold a complete nuclear facility to a Warsaw Pact state. It can be assumed that the information made public on the issue is either untrue or misleading or both. No matter how low key a nuclear installation and no matter how often inspected by international officials, the possession of a large reactor immediately gives the possessor country a nuclear weapon making capability. This much was clear after the illegal Israeli bombing of the Osirak reactor in Baghdad.

The question about Romania, which was also a massive recipient of US computer and electronics technology in the period 1978–83, is why? The most probable answer, given that the licences were issued well into the Reagan presidency and given the same administration's willingness to supply nuclear technology to China, is that by nuclear arming potential defector nations within the enemy camp, you decrease the options for successful coercion and increase the opportunities for defection and for dissent. Machiavelli is but an amateur compared with modern American administrations.

The Allies were not informed in advance of the US decision to place 'its' technology on the table at Geneva, though history should have taught both the Foreign Office and the Ministry of Defence to anticipate such a move. No doubt the information passed to me was 'grudge' based, as are many key items coming out of such meetings. The Foreign Office had been reminded of my interest in the issue on a weekly basis, as I tried to find out just what the Allies had been told about the unilateral American move to relax the rules in relation to China in November 1983. Indeed when I was told that the Cocom lists were on offer to the Russians at Geneva, I had again raised the point and I was again told that the US had not officially informed the UK of any such move and that the UK knew nothing about it.

Another of my sources, this time in Japan, and close to the Prime Minister's office, perhaps came closer to the mark. He told me that efforts to find out what effect the US move would have on controlled technology were being stonewalled by the American Embassy. But this was only part of the picture. The various embassies in China would have known, with some clarity, what was going on because it is Chinese practice, in a very discreet way, to play one would-be supplier off against another, and in the process reveal a good deal about the propositions being made by various countries. Japan had been stepping up its supplies of technology to China since the late 1970s, to a point where it is probably the dominant supplier in the field of office equipment, micro and minicomputers and other low and medium level computer technology. Japan had kept clear of problems at Cocom, largely by taking advantage in precisely the same way the US did, of the inadequate and out of date classifications in use by the OECD to conceal quite advanced computers as office machinery.

The Japanese had learnt a sharp lesson in 1981 when Hitachi and Fujitsu tried to ship one large computer each to Beijing. Despite the fact that the US was allowing similar machines into China from a variety of US corporations, the US vetoed the applications in Cocom on

[100]

the grounds that the customers, a trade ministry sub-division and an industry ministry sub-division, were connected with the Chinese military. This was an ingenious line of reasoning, since most the key ministries in Beijing are connected with the Red Army, as suppliers just as most key contractors in the US, are connected with the Pentagon. In practice, as the Japanese discovered, it was a blocking tactic designed to give a number of American computer corporations an opportunity to set up and implement large scale deals, including manufacturing plants in China.

As January ran its course, so the first opportunity to air the issue on the floor of the House of Commons hove into sight. Ever since he had seen the IBM letter, Paddy had been trying to get an adjournment debate on the issue. An adjournment debate is usually a half-hour period at the end of the day's business in the House of Commons when an individual may raise a topic, usually without a motion other than the motion for the adjournment. Paddy had not been specifically blocked by the Speaker's office – his grasp of essential procedure is sharp and he is respected for this – but pressure on parliamentary time is intense, although this is not always obvious from the content of speeches made in the Chamber. The Speaker must do his best to ensure that individual MPs have a chance to speak and to raise topics, as well as ensuring that the relative strength of the parties is properly reflected in those chosen to address the House. The Speaker is the arbitrator of a series of interests that are often in conflict with each other, all the more so when the House of Commons is in a constitutional quandary because one party has an overwhelming majority. This would enable it to operate as a dictatorship, unless there was rigid enforcement of ancient rituals and devices giving opposition MPs the opportunity to raise issues and air topics of public interest.

Against that backdrop, a lone opposition MP has some difficulty getting his voice heard. The first chance to be heard and to put the IBM letter centrally on the menu, came on 17 February 1984. Don Dixon, the Labour MP for Jarrow, put down a motion calling on the government to present the House with new and relevant proposals to prevent any further decline of the UK as an industrial nation. This was in the specific content of the new technologies. Paddy got a reasonable indication from the Speaker, who took the debate, that if he attended, he would be called. Because of his status as a front bench spokesman, Paddy was able to speak for about twenty minutes, thirty at the outside, remembering that he had to address the main topics of his speakership, as well as the narrower one of his 'urgent topic' during that time.

[101]

The debate was good natured, as are most debates in the House of Commons, but suffered from two fundamental flaws, which in turn are central to the poor quality of much of the work of the House, and consequently to its public image, which determines the level of support that people are willing to give to the democratic institutions of the state, the cornerstone of which is the House of Commons. The first of these flaws emerged in Don Dixon's speech, but bore more than an accidental relationship to the fact that Labour, in advance, had obviously decided not to go for a vote at the end of the debate. Without the discipline of a threatened division, attendance was inevitably poor. Given that the new technologies are the very heart of future prosperity, not only for the UK but for the whole world, and given their parlous state in Britain, it was disgraceful that between 10.30 am and 2.30 pm when the debate adjourned, fewer than thirty MPs, less than five per cent of the House, attended. Only fourteen MPs spoke, though this is more an indication of time available and how it is allocated than a lack of interest, a lack which was demonstrated both on members' benches and in the press gallery, where less than six of the 150 lobby correspondents showed up throughout the morning.

Dixon's speech ranged over many things, including the construction of his own home 'with these horny hands of the soil' as he put it. But he lacked focus or sharp research. One of his key points was that there was a £1 billion deficit in Information Technology imports, admitted by the government in 1982. In February 1984 that deficit had risen to £2.3 billion and authoritative sources were forecasting a deficit in the late 1980s of between £4 billion and £6 billion. Targeted research in this area would have quickly produced those figures for Don Dixon. Indeed, almost any computer trade journalist could have produced them. But what chance has an MP to produce decent research which results in an informed speech, when the total allocation of secretarial desk space for 654 MPs is 450 desks? MPs are allowed £12,000 a year for all secretarial expenses, which includes any help they may have in their constituencies. This extraordinary situation, apart from often producing out-of-date information for major speeches, such as Don Dixon's, makes it very difficult for those elected to represent the people, and to protect them from the excesses of those who run the state machine, to function efficiently in those roles.

In effect, there is no budget at all for the kind of research work that went into Paddy Ashdown's speech, much less for the kind of general examination of the state's behaviour which alone can make MPs effective in their protective role. This gap has enabled American uni-

[102]

versities to flood the House of Commons with young students who, as unpaid researchers, can add greatly to the administrative capability of an MP while obtaining for themselves a free college course credit. There has been a sharp reaction to the scale of the American student presence, mostly from the Conservative benches. It is noticeable, however, that the opponents of free, intelligent labour have not come up with any solution to the 200 'missing' desks or to additional allowances for MPs, that might enable them more properly to fulfil those tasks for which they were elected. It is also noticeable that these opponents of free help for the democratic representatives are usually independently wealthy, or have lucrative directorships which enable them to treat the House of Commons as a club of amateur status whose main function is to maintain in office the establishment that has held power in England since the Reformation.

So, Don Dixon ranged wide, and he ranged so widely out of focus that no conclusion could be drawn from his speech, other than that he, as a member of the opposition, opposed the government. On the critical point of the way foreign governments, particularly the United States, use the military budget to fund essentially civilian development, Mr Dixon had almost nothing to say. He noted that according to the OECD the West German government spent fifty per cent more on R&D than the UK government. The Japanese government spends twice as much as the UK on R&D. He failed to mention that, as a proportion of the UK's expenditure, that which goes to the military is fifty per cent more than in any other Western country. Whether this is normally right or wrong is one matter, but there is mounting evidence, much of it developed by Congressional researchers in the United States, which shows that military R&D expenditures are both economically unproductive in terms of spin offs, and a serious inhibitor on the rate of output in the civilian R&D sectors. Indeed, a number of recent Congressional studies have argued that much of Japan's high tech success can be attributed to the low percentage of R&D devoted to military research. Instead of a series of vague statements which did not prove anything, least of all that the government was particularly wrong in its approach to basic investment in the nation's high technology future, Mr Dixon might instead have focused his precious thirty minutes more clearly on what really is wrong with the government's approach to R&D. To do this would have required a week or two of intense full-time research, something which neither his allowances nor the House of Commons structure provide for.

Don Dixon was followed by a much more narrowly argued case from

[103]

Ian Lloyd, the MP for Havant, in whose constituency resides IBM's major manufacturing and information centre in the UK. Mr Lloyd raced his favourite hares: he wanted the government to appoint a minister for science, but he did agree with Mr Dixon that the new technologies were badly catered for, in terms of money from the government, interest from members of the House or proper interest on the part of the media. By 11.20, when Paddy finally got to his feet, most of the key problems had been raised, by both sides, without too much party point scoring. But none of the points raised, or analyses suggested, went beyond a need for more government money as the ultimate remedy to the situation. In fairness, there was a passing reference by Mr Doug Hoyle, a Labour MP, to the fact that in the lifetime of the Conservative government over £12billion, that might have been invested in the UK had been invested abroad. There is a substantial truth in this, though this is not the book in which to elaborate it.

Paddy began his speech, which had probably taken thirty or forty hours to prepare, and a tenth of that to write, by carefully seeking to separate government rhetoric from government actions. He sought even-handedness by congratulating the Prime Minister on some of her initiatives and by gently getting to the shortcomings of most of the government projects, without at the same time condemning the projects themselves.

'The Alvey programme shows the government's concern about moving into the fifth generation in an appropriate fashion,' he said, then cited the problem, quoting a small computer manufacturer, Nigel Smith. 'We will be left with the crumbs. There is nothing in it for the small man. Alvey is a beautiful instrument for large companies to obtain low cost R&D.'

From this gentle beginning Paddy moved, with a much more significant set of figures, towards the crunch point in his speech.

'In 1975 the European Community had an information trade technology surplus of £1.7billion. In 1983 that surplus had turned into a deficit of £5.3billion. In 1985 that deficit is predicted to reach £9.7billion. The speed at which the deficit is building up is itself as alarming as the overall size of the imbalance, most of it with the United States of America.'

In pursuit of this point he noted, 'For many years, our high technology industry has suffered because of the inability of the Department of Trade and Industry to stand up to the United States in particular. I refer to the disgraceful case of the IBM letter sent to its United Kingdom customers. I do not blame IBM for sending that letter,

[104]

because I understand that it was under great pressure from the American government to do so. I should like Honourable Members to take particular note of the fact that the IBM letter required all those companies owning American computers in Britain to ask the American government for an export licence whenever they wish to move those computers.'

Much of what Paddy said there, and the comments he made, were widely felt and held by other members of the House of Commons, including some members of the government. By deliberately putting his finger on the US-built computers in government and defence, he was throwing down the gauntlet, but inside the sacrosanct fence of government itself. It was clear, when Paddy was preparing his speech, that Tebbit's appalling catastrophe in the US over the IBM letter meant that the wider issue of extra-territoriality would be avoided by government ministers. The new mileage would come from forcing the government to admit, and hopefully do something about, the fact that lots of their own computers, so widely bought under the much more open competitive regulations introduced by the Conservative government, were in fact subject to extra-territorial jurisdiction. Here indeed was a spot between a rock and a hard place.

It would be a fair and practical assumption that the Inland Revenue were not complying with the terms of the IBM letter in relation to the big 3081 they had bought in the early 1980s, and which was installed in Haywards Heath. It would be an equally reasonable assumption that IBM was doing the complying on their behalf. However, the trap for ministers was to admit that conditions that were unacceptable for their machines could, by some twisted logic, be acceptable when applied to the rest of the country. When he told the computer community throughout the UK to look after their own commercial interests, Norman Tebbit jumped headlong off more than one legal pier. The obvious one was sovereignty. The less obvious one was equity. The minister was overwhelmingly wrong, under the legal principle of equity, to suppose that he could make that distinction between the civilian parts of government and the computer using community in the rest of the country. From the moment he announced the 'look after yourselves' policy, Norman Tebbit had effectively forfeited a lot of the credibility of his Department's legal position. Especially it meant placing one group of people in the country under the protection of the Crown and excluding others from that protection. Paddy went on:

'The IBM letter states: "As you are aware, transactions within the United Kingdom involving 'Advance Systems' are also subject to the

[105]

obtaining of United States export licence approval."

'I shall not dwell on the infringement of our national sovereignty entailed in that action, nor on the larger point of extra-territoriality. The Americans have been seeking to impose their laws on us. Recently the Secretary of State has said that what happens in the United Kingdom is the subject of United Kingdom law alone. The matter of extra-territoriality is a larger subject.

'Despite what the Government are seeking to do, Britain remains ninety per cent dependent on United States' computers. Those computers are in government departments – Inland Revenue, the Ministry of Defence, and even in GCHQ. Therefore, any action could have the most disastrous and long-term consequences, perhaps even to the integrity of our defence system. That action is planned. The information has been published and has not been denied by the American administration. The United States Department of Commerce in Washington has said: "If any company tries to move licenced commodities within the United Kingdom without our permission, there will be big trouble. They will be subject to legal investigation and will suffer the consequences."

'Furthermore, a United States Department of Defence spokesman has said that a "complete embargo will be placed against any country which refused to comply with United States regulations".

'I am told on good authority that we have perhaps as little as three to six weeks' supply of spares for those American computers on which the government, the Ministry of Defence, perhaps even the GCHQ and the whole of our industry, depend. The United States government are threatening this action in a way that could do more damage in bringing GCHQ to a stop than the unions could ever do. This is a serious problem.

'I brought this matter to the attention of the Secretary of State for Trade and Industry before he left on his recent American trip. I wrote him a four or five page letter making those statements. I understood that the Secretary of State was to see the chairman of IBM and have high level discussions. I regret to say that, on the key issue of our national sovereignty and perhaps even the integrity of our defence system, the minister returned empty-handed. He returned with no reassurances for us on this serious matter. According to press reports of a press conference – I paraphrase what was said – the firm that had received letters requiring them to obtain United States export licences to move their goods within the United Kingdom should obey United Kingdom law but look after their commercial interests. If that is not a

[106]

Janus-faced attitude on the part of the Department of Trade and Industry, I do not know what is. The Department is saying that those firms must obey United Kingdom law, not United States law, and should look after their commercial interests – in other words, if a firm has an American computer, no doubt its commercial interests will point it in the opposite direction. I should have thought that the Department would have been prepared to take on its own back the burden of assuring British industry that it does not suffer from such interference. The Department should have the strength to say – I hope that the minister will comment on this point – that if there are repercussions for United Kingdom firms for not obeying the strictures of the American Government, they will be dealt with entirely by the Department.'

Perhaps the intensity of the misunderstanding of the two legal points at issue by the government side is best illustrated by the intervention in Paddy's speech at this point by Mr Ian Lloyd, the Conservative MP for Havant. Ian Lloyd is a decent, slightly old fashioned Tory, with one of those majorities that is weighed not counted. As IBM was one of the major employers in his constituency, he was only too well aware of the IBM letter, and had already discussed the matter with the company. Indeed, it was his idea, as Chairman of the Parliamentary Information Technology Committee, to summon the American ambassador to a PITCOM meeting in the House of Commons, to explain the implications of the letter.

Mr Lloyd's intervention ran as follows: I am following the hon. Gentleman's point with the greatest interest. He is implying that he would like to see the withdrawal of the instruction by the American Government through IBM. He mentioned that it was a threat to the integrity of United Kingdom defence systems. Does the problem not arise from the fact that there is a greater threat to the integrity of the defence of the West as a whole? If that letter were withdrawn, how would the hon. Gentleman advise the Americans to meet that threat, because we know that the transfer of this type of technology in multifarious ways and for many purposes significantly alters that balance?

To say that Ian Lloyd was uneasy about the letter was to put it mildly. IBM, presumably, had offered him no more comfort than they offered the American Embassy. As far as the company was concerned and is concerned to this day, the contents of the letter represent American law and that law will be obeyed. Nothing Ian Lloyd ever said to the company altered its stance. That he could see nothing ahead but a running political sore for the party of which he was a member, and a serious legal threat to a company which in every other respect was a

[107]

model local employer, was obvious. It was equally obvious that he wished to place the blame where it belonged, with the American government, while at the same time deflecting what was beginning to look like an anti-American diatribe on Paddy's part.

On the latter point he need not have worried, as Paddy's subsequent remarks will show. However, to try to suggest, as he was doing, that the defence of the West required a substantial peace time surrender of UK sovereignty in the area of commercial transactions, was being a bit disingenuous to say the least. Moreover, Mr Lloyd seemed to be implying that the US could not trust the UK to look after its own internal affairs. In general, neither position would seem to equate with my own knowledge of Ian Lloyd in private. The danger in the way he framed his intervention lay in the fact that he reproduced American arguments that are both fallacious in their logic and hugely wrong in law. And they are the kind of arguments which have been far too widely used in the UK by officials and company representatives in support of the American position, which is quite wrong in international law.

Paddy then continued with his speech. 'I am grateful to the Honourable Gentleman for that intervention because it brings me to my next point. I recognise that it is necessary to ensure that the export of technology to the eastern bloc should not be done in such a way as to weaken our defence system. It is right to have a structure within which that technology should operate. I leave it to the Honourable Gentleman and other Honourable Members to decide whether it is appropriate that the American government should treat one of its allies in this fashion in relation to internal movement. I believe that it is not right, and that it is a clear infringement of our sovereignty and something we should not expect from our allies.

'I turn to the question raised by the Honourable Gentleman about the structure by which we inhibit that trade – the Co-ordinating Committee Controlling East West Trade. COCOM is an old committee. I am told that it dates from 1949. I asked the Library of the House of Commons about its genesis, but the information was somewhat confused. The subject of COCOM has never come before the House. I hope that I shall demonstrate to Honourable Members that it has a severe restrictive capacity on our foreign trade in high technology. It is the mechanism through which that trade is regulated, and, supposedly, has sprung from the NATO agreement. In fact, COCOM does not include Iceland, but includes Japan. It is not listed under the NATO agreements. COCOM is now so out of date that it is, practically, ridiculous. I am afraid that it is now so much in the hands of the

[108]

American administration that it is being used as an instrument by which the Americans regulate their advantage. I am aware that that is a serious statement, but I hope that Honourable Members will follow me as I back it up with facts.

'The COCOM list of embargoed products is out of date. I am told that it springs from about 1976. It now includes a vast variety of items that are in common use. I am told that if people leave Heathrow airport wearing a digital watch, such as the one I am wearing, technically they are infringing the COCOM agreements, unless they have an export licence. The chips in the digital watch are on the COCOM list and an export licence is required to take them from this country. If a person leaves Heathrow airport wearing a certain brand of heart pacemaker, without an export licence, that person is technically infringing the COCOM agreements and the Export Control Order that springs from them. That shows how ridiculous the list is. I mentioned that in my letter to the Secretary of State and it was undenied. So ridiculous is the list and the interference, that the ZX80, a toy that we might give our children at Christmas – which was available for sale from W.H. Smith and Son Limited on the duty-free side of the barrier at Heathrow airport, was, on the insistence of the American Defence Department, not allowed to be sold from that side of the duty-free barrier without an export licence. I am ready to be contradicted if that statement is wrong.

'The present COCOM list is not just inadequate, it is out of date and practically unenforceable. Another list has been proposed by the American government. It contains no fewer than 400,000 items of new technology. It is, effectively, an inventory of the entire American technological warehouse. For us to agree that list in its entirety – I am aware that the government have made representations that we should not – would be an act of technological suicide. The list must be up to date and refined to the new technology that has defence implications and strategic value.

'I said that I believed that the Americans were now using COCOM to promote their trade against ours. In a recent confidential report from ICL, which I sent to the Minister, the company referred to the American attitude as nothing short of technological imperialism. Those are not my words.

'I will give some examples. The first is in relation to our trade with China. I have been in correspondence recently with Plasma Technologies, a firm in Bristol which is one of the few firms in Europe to produce chip making equipment. It has been seeking to sell to the Chinese for some time, and there is a good deal of Chinese interest in its products.

[109]

The firm was aware that American salesmen were in China seeking to sell goods which they knew were on the embargoed list. The firm had about £1 million of order interest from the Chinese. Without any reference to the Department of Trade and Industry, on 23 November, the American government unilaterally relaxed COCOM's regulations to allow the American firm to sell the goods that Plasma had been seeking to sell. The Chinese are still interested in Plasma's high technology equipment for making chips. The company knows that American salesmen are still in China seeking to sell goods that remain on the embargoed list. The company and I fear that when the high technology exhibition is opened in May by President Reagan in Peking, there will be further unilateral relaxation. Meanwhile, Plasma Technologies, despite letters to the Minister and the Prime Minister, has failed to obtain an export licence for its goods, and is told that the trade cannot continue.

'I mentioned that matter to the Minister and I will quote from his reply: "I have noted the views of certain UK companies about the COCOM rules as they apply to China. Let me assure you that American companies wishing to export embargoed goods to China must go through the same procedures as companies in the UK and other COCOM member states. Indeed, the US government has stated categorically that it will continue to submit exports to China for COCOM review as in the past . . . However we shall take every possible step to avoid the danger of the rules being manipulated to give unfair advantages to any one COCOM member state. My Department is in touch direct with John Hadland Ltd" – John Hadland suffered the same problems in relation to exports to China – "and Plasma Technologies Ltd whose letters to you on this subject you attached to your letter."

'I take that as some reassurance. However, in his reply to Plasma Technologies the Minister said that the United States wished to relax the COCOM rules further to speed up exports to China. He said, however, that the other COCOM countries were blocking that move. Who is doing that? Are the government blocking any further relaxations? I fear that once again a major and successful high technology firm will be blocked from exporting such goods to China that will help our trade and that the Americans will relax the rules unilaterally, move in and clean up.'

The case of Plasma, in fact, was lost as late as November 1985; the Department of Trade and Industry had failed to take Plasma's licence application to Cocom and so the order went to an American company and with it twenty-five jobs in the Bristol area. The imcompetence that

[110]

lay behind the DTI's decision is protected from civil legal action by Crown privilege, but the political penalty has to be paid, and a minister has to accept responsibility for what his department does. The DTI behaved with polite but calculated contempt towards David Carr's entrepreneurial drive. One senior figure in the DTI told him, at the end of a meeting, that it would have been much better for him if he had been born an American. Later, the same official threatened him with the loss of his government R&D grants if he didn't stop rocking the boat. The DTI's position would have been understandable if they had no way of knowing what American companies were doing in Beijing, which they implied they did not, by demanding that David Carr produce the evidence himself. But if the DTI did not know what was going on, then presumably the UK Embassy in Beijing didn't know either. If that were true, then they were on their own. Even the smallest embassy in Beijing knew what was going on in the electronics sector, and at the shows that David Carr was trying to get to. So did the commercial and scientific staff at several European embassies in Tokyo, as I subsequently discovered.

But the DTI staff who were dealing with David Carr, while being determinedly polite, placed every conceivable bureaucratic obstacle in his way – and some that were illegal. They refused to take his export licence to Cocom, even to test the waters with the Allies. They refused to investigate the matter through their representative in the UK embassy in Beijing. They did nothing about his evidence, when he produced it. When they did, with the utmost reluctance, offer an exhibitor's licence to him, they insisted, despite evidence that American competition was able to sell off the stand, that he bring the equipment straight back to the UK and presumably be refused a licence to re-export it, should the Chinese wish to buy it. What the DTI was apparently trying to do was to draw the teeth of the political hounds braying at their heels while at the same time blocking any attempt by Carr to achieve some export sales. The DTI behaved so badly in relation to David Carr that any attempt to analyse the reasons for the department's actions might suggest that logic, legality or equity were somewhat lacking. I wouldn't wish to convey such an idea, even inferentially, but it would appear that a bunch of people, paid from the public purse to protect our industry at home and our trading interests abroad, were not only failing to do so, but were actively damaging the public good on both counts.

The brevity of this narrative conveys no idea of the hours, days, weeks and possibly months that David Carr spent talking to the DTI, only to end up with his customers being supplied by an American company. He is owed substantial financial compensation for the time and profits lost, and the country is owed a reckoning for the export income and the jobs lost. But David Carr's case is neither unique nor uncommon. Just as the DTI press office tried to sell me misinformation, albeit at the specific direction of more senior civil servants, in the early days of the story, so do DTI officials daily fob off, misinform or delay any would-be exporter to any market on which the Americans have put a prohibition. The crawling obeisance to the US administration which seems to typify the outlook of the senior reaches of the DTI is not worthy of a dog, much less the civil servants of a once great country.

Paddy, however, continued to lay on the pain for the handful of MPs still in the Chamber.

'While the United Kingdom high technology exports to China remain blocked, it is interesting to note that United States computer business with China has increased dramatically. In 1981 United States high technology exports to China amounted to $71 million; in 1982 it was over $100 million and in 1983 it was $500 million. I am told those figures come from the Department of Trade. This is an extraordinary increase during a period when our exports were blocked by the COCOM rules and we were urged to take a strong stand in support of the United Kingdom high technology industry. The same thing is happening with the eastern European bloc.

'I believe that the Cocom rules are being manipulated. Honourable Members will remember the tremendous storm over the export of a VAX 11/782 computer from Sweden which was believed to be being smuggled to Eastern Europe.' That is precisely what the firm was doing. The VAX 11/782 was nothing more than two VAX 11/780s pinned together with an interface board between. The interface board is important but not essential. It is something that almost any computer technologist could fit. The Americans have six VAX 11/780s which are in Moscow hospitals. There are also British 11/782 computer programmers working in Moscow hospitals programming those VAX 11/780s which are earning £1000 a week. The Americans are raising enormous steam about the export of a piece of equipment that is already in Russian hands.

'Similarly, the export of a DEC PD11 computer, about which there has been considerable anxiety recently – I believe a court case involving a firm on the south coast which wished to export is pending and therefore one must be careful about what one says – is being blocked.

[112]

Meanwhile the Americans have an agency selling PD11s in Yugoslavia. According to DEC's figures they have already sold 30,000 machines to eastern bloc countries.

'At a time when the government have been asked by the American administration to withdraw a ZX80 toy computer from the other side of the duty-free barrier at Heathrow, the Americans have admitted selling 30,000 DEC PD11s to eastern bloc countries.

'Tasbian, a company in Plymouth that makes printed circuits boards for microcomputers has contacted me recently. It was a Racal-Redac system for computer-aided design. Some of its spare parts are British. Tasbian tells me that its Racal-Redac computer-aided design mechanism has recently broken down. The company has applied to the United States for a licence to re-export from America the British-made spare parts. The company has been waiting for two or three months for the export licence, which has been blocked. Yet there is evidence, which is available to me, that the United States is selling those same British-made parts to eastern bloc countries. So while United Kingdom firms cannot get British-made spare parts from the United States, the United States is selling those parts, in finished machinery, to the East. It cannot get the spare parts because that would require an export licence.

'I heard recently of a software house that was banned under the Cocom regulations from selling simple accounting software to Hungary. While the United Kingdom's high technology exports seem to be being blocked and while simple accounting technology has not been allowed to be sold to Hungary, United States exports of high technology goods to Hungary have leapt from £12 million in 1980 to £26 million in 1982. There are similar increases elsewhere. In Bulgaria, they have risen from £4 million to £8 million and in Czechoslovakia from £21 million to £27 million.

'The Honourable Member for Havant (Mr Lloyd) is a well-respected figure in this area. He said that we must be preeminent and paramount. Indeed, we must be. However, even if we were, such is the structure of the Cocom regulations, so out of date and manipulated are they, that they are being used against us so that any ascendancy that we have is quashed by those trade restrictions. I agree that we should have a tariff-free system for trade. When he returned from the United States, the Minister said that he wanted a free flow of technology and ideas. I wish that we had a free flow of trade. The problem is not so much that we should not have tariffs but that certain unfair trading systems appear to be operating against us.

'On the Minister's visit to the United States we hoped that he would

[113]

stand up for Britain, or, in the phraseology of the Prime Minister, bat for Britain. However, he has returned empty-handed – indeed slightly worse than that, as I shall try to reveal. He was proud of the agreements that he had arranged for technology transfer. I fear that unless the Department of Trade and Industry is prepared to stand up for the high technology industries in Britain, there will not just be a technology transfer system from America, but we shall be inferior and subservient to America. I ask for a free flow of trade. The Minister has missed his opportunity. I am aware that it is a brave man who will stand up and call the Minister wet but, in failing to stand up for Britain and British high technology exports, he is behaving in a manner that can only be described as wet.

'We have missed the opportunity to tell the United States that we shall no longer accept its manipulation of COCOM and other agreements so that British high technology exports are blocked and United States industry can move in and clean up. That is how things stood, but I am told that things are now worse than I imagined. I shall read the notes that I received from a well-respected journalist of a meeting that he held with Department of Trade and Industry officials earlier this week. He was informed that the United States was attempting to "embargo all computers over eight bit", "embargo all except the most obviously commercial software", "seeking to control the movement of individuals with software knowledge". That was put rather pleasantly in the euphemism of "intangible materials". The officials also said that the United States was "refusing entry to UK nationals to US computer related conferences. Attempting to control at source all academic and scientific developments in certain computer areas. . ."

'The officials acknowledged that the US had not notified the UK about the change in controls relating to China introduced on 23 November, 1983 and were continuing with attempts to impose US domestic licensing requirements on UK companies. In particular, the US had attempted directly to force ICL UK to use US licences for all computer sales, ie in the UK.

'I am also told that it was accepted at the meetings, and stated by the legal representative of Hewlett Packard, that the United States was attempting to force United Kingdom subsidiaries "to provide to the US a complete list of all customers including those in the UK in order to get new general export licences".

'I do not wish to plunge the House into a fit of anti-Americanism. It is important for us to realise that we are vitally dependent on our cousins on the other side of the Atlantic. However, it is unacceptable that we

[114]

should allow this to continue. It seems that the Department of Trade and Industry is prepared to lie down in front of the United States high technology industry and invite it to walk over us. Of course the Americans are only too happy to oblige, with enthusiasm. The major United Kingdom high technology industry is in severe danger of dying, because of its exports record. It remains the case that nine tenths of Britain's computers are American. The installations used by the major government departments are American.

'The Honourable Member for Havant asked whether the government are adequately equipped. They are, but with American, not British, computers. The major banks, the stock exchange, the Inland Revenue and the Ministry of Defence use United States computers. Yet it seems that we must ask the permission of the United States government to move them.

'The policy of the Department of Trade and Industry is moving Britain into permanent technological subservience to the United States, so that we are assuming the status of a technological satellite to the United States high technology industry. There is undoubtedly, as other Honourable Members have said, great potential in Britain. I congratulate the Minister on recognising that and pursuing it, but now is the time for the Department of Trade to stand up for the British high technology industry and give the encouragement and support to high technology exports that is needed so that the industry can survive and prosper and realise the potential that we know it has in abundance.'

While the Tory speakers chose to ignore the issue Paddy was addressing, Roger Stott, the Labour front bench spokesman on Information Technology, waded in in support of Paddy, as part of an obviously well researched speech.

'There is another matter upon which I should like to address the Minister. The Honourable Member for Yeovil (Mr Ashdown) has already mentioned it. The Minister will be aware that I wrote to him on 15 January on the points raised by the Honourable Member for Yeovil about the United States government's extra-territoriality. The Opposition are worried about that for the same reasons as the Member of Yeovil, I received a reply from the Under Secretary on 9 February. He said that the Secretary of State would raise the subject of the IBM letter and hoped to be assured that it was the result of a mistaken interpretation of the territorial scope of United States law. The Secretary of State returned with a dud cheque from the United States because nothing appears to have changed. He obtained no concessions from the United States government.

[115]

'It is completely unacceptable to the Opposition that an ally and friend should impose such conditions on the United Kingdom. I hope that today or in the future the Minister will rebut those suggestions and tell the United States administration that that is not the way to behave commercially and that they must not impinge upon UK sovereignty by instructing British firms what they can and cannot do with their computers. That matter worries the Opposition a great deal.'

But what impact did all this have on the ever polished, ever presentable Minister for Information, Ken Baker? His opening remarks are worth quoting because some of them are relevant to the overall framework of the story.

'The Honourable Member for Jarrow spoke from the long and worthy tradition of the common sense of the Labour movement. He comes from a traditional craft background – he referred to his horny hands – and from an area of the country which contributed to the wealth and prosperity of Britain in Victorian and Edwardian times through its strength in the traditional engineering, steel and coalmining industries. Nevertheless, the Honourable Gentleman has an instinctive, commonsense feeling that the future of our country and of the part of it that he represents will lie in other areas and that we should therefore debate and discuss these matters to try to agree a strategy which, I am glad to say, is remarkably non-political.

'It is one of the tragedies of debates in the House that we spend far too much time debating the problems of the past and not enough on the opportunities of the future. There has only to be threat of the closure of a shipyard, steelworks or coalmine for a debate to take place in prime time – and I understand that, in view of the worry and anxiety of the people working in the industry concerned. Nevertheless there are very few debates in prime time in which one can step back and consider the question that politicians of all parties must answer – what will happen to Britain when the oil runs out?'

The remainder of this speech was quite predictably a hymn of praise for all that the government, and his department in particular, had done for the information technology industry. He did not once refer to the internal ball and chain imposed on commercial traffic in computers in the UK by the United States. He did not once refer to the gross burden his government was even then contemplating for any would-be IT exporter under the Cocom rules. He did not once refer to the abandonment of sovereignty which Paddy had evidenced. No, Kenneth Baker can see a political banana skin at twenty miles on a foggy day and is adept at avoiding them. Roger Stott and several of the other Labour speakers had addressed the pending sale of the government-created chip maker Inmos. Baker addressed this

[116]

sensitive issue and disposed of it neatly, but the only way to dispose of Paddy's points, with any safety, was to ignore them. This he did. The debate ended without further reference to the matter.

However, less than sixteen months later, Cocom, which had never previously been debated by the House of Commons (it was mentioned during a debate in 1974) had been the subject of a standing committee debate one day, and the subject of more than sixty hostile references in a debate on China the following day. People were beginning to wake up, even if it was a slow and tortuous business.

When the new technology debate ended at 2.30 on 17 February 1984 without a vote on the resolution, the vast bulk of what had been said was lost forever. The opposition had said its pieces, the government had said its pieces. In relation to the new technologies, the government had been faced with no new information that would in any way compel it to change course. No imminent closures or frauds were revealed. The facts of the growing trade deficit were already available to ministers, who remained either unwilling or unable to do anything about them.

Only Paddy had introduced a dissonant note, but it had been heard, even if no one chose to acknowledge the fact. When I spoke to Ian Lloyd about the issue at a PITCOM meeting some days later he suggested that the American Ambassador should be invited to come and explain what was going on. I phoned the embassy and our normal contact in the press office suggested that we ought instead to accept Tim Deal the Economics Counsellor, who we were told knew all about the issue. Ian Lloyd readily accepted the idea, and a special meeting was set up for Monday, 19 March in Committee Room 10 of the House of Commons.

Before that event could take place, however, the computer leasing association had called a meeting of its own for 29 February to be held at a secluded country club in Surrey. That meeting was addressed by three people. Colin Moore, an official at the US Embassy, Des Lee a former President of the IBM Users' Association, the largest user group in the country, and myself. Because of the outspoken and blunt fashion in which Moore addressed that meeting, I at least was able to penetrate Deal's more obscure and diplomatic language at the later meeting.

But Moore did more than simply 'shoot from the hip' as the embassy later put it. He made a number of claims about the level of information available to the US authorities, the means they had used to get it and the use they were willing to make of it if anyone got out of line. In one way he merely repeated what the Pentagon had told me earlier in the year, but there was something extraordinary about a scene in which a junior official from a foreign embassy tells the chairmen and managing directors of some of the largest computer companies in the UK that they had better shape up and get in line under his country's laws. There were audible murmurs of 'treason', which was hardly surprising. In fact, Moore, who still stands commended for his brutal honesty, was quite lucky not to be physically assaulted, such was the effect of his talk on the audience. But because there is still reason to believe that CIA representatives attended the meeting, it will be dealt with in full in Chapter 9.

When Deal stood up beneath the huge biblical panel that dominates the western end of Committee Room 10, everyone thought he was going to pour oil over troubled waters.

But everyone, including peers, MPs and junior ministers, got a surprise. Deal, although using language a good deal less frank than Moore's, said much the same thing.

'The US asserts, and will continue to assert, its right to control technology of US origin, wherever it is.'

He then attempted to justify this position on the grounds that the US was entitled to do this in order to starve the USSR of Western technology. The US objective, he said, 'was the protection of its lead times over the Soviet Union in relation to technology with potential military uses'. He was angrily challenged by several MPs who reminded him that he was talking about a serious infringement of the sovereignty of the UK.

His reply to this was quite unique: 'Debates about general legal principles are not useful.'

In one sentence the rumoured deputy ambassador of the United States had both dismissed UK sovereignty and any attempt to defend it in discussion. There is no licence in this description: the MP's statements contained the word sovereignty. He knew what he was saying, and he was fully aware of where he was saying it and to whom. He was aware of the row over Moore's remarks, and had to deal with the parliamentary flak, mostly from Paddy, over them. When Roger Stott got up and told Deal that his position was unacceptable, he did not bat an eyelid, but merely repeated himself.

In retrospect someone should have grabbed Deal at that point, removed his trousers and thrown him out of the House of Commons, with the reminder that a few centuries ago he would have found himself either in the Tower of London or being challenged to a duel. Perhaps it was his pleasant manner that saved him, which was a pity, because he moved perilously close to the inaccurate statements he was later to tell in Cambridge when he denied that UK scientists had been thrown out of or denied access to conferences in the United States. In a thoroughly disingenuous fashion he asked that anyone who had such information

[118]

should let the embassy know. 'It is not US policy,' he said.

Well, it might not be US policy, but it was certainly Pentagon policy. At the time of his speaking, the UK government had details of eight conferences where the US had excluded foreigners, and the EEC Commission was busy gathering information on other conferences from which NATO scientists had been excluded.

Presumably what Deal really wanted to know was just how widely known the problem was, so that the embassy could put out more misinformation. On the other hand, he did, with obvious reluctance, admit that the Export Administration Act contained clauses relating to 'intangible data', in other words, data in people's heads. Those with sensitive information would be prevented from travelling to Eastern Europe and would, it seemed, need export licences to travel elsewhere.

If this account makes Deal seem like a man under exceptionally harsh cross-examination, then I am giving the wrong impression. Most of the exchanges passed off in a reasonably amiable way, partly because the implications of what Deal had said were swept along and hidden by the pace of delivery. Perhaps the one truly sharp exchange occurred when Lord Avebury pointed out that information which Deal had said the American companies would soon have to provide on their UK customers and which DEC had already supplied, would be illegal under the Data Protection Act. Deal winced at that one, but implicated all UK companies in DEC's problems over alleged shipments to the Eastern Bloc, by announcing that the other companies would not have to comply 'for at least a month' but making clear that eventually compliance would be mandatory.

Big deal indeed. Every claim Colin Moore had made about the extent of US information on computer sites in the UK and Europe, if it was not true when he made it, would certainly be true within a month if what Deal said was true. There are several appalling things about what Deal was saying, all of which have since happened, but the most basic one is that no such inventory of computer users is required by any UK law, or is even compiled voluntarily by the British government. The violence done to the UK by a singularly illegal administration in the US is absolutely extraordinary. But no one can claim that the UK government did not know. It did, and once again the question of why the government has done nothing, had to be raised. I did not get to speak to Ian Lloyd after the meeting, but it is hard to imagine that he left a happy man. Surprise, which had given way to dismay as Deal proceeded through his talk, was almost total.

But nothing happened, except the inevitable onward roll of United States law in the United Kingdom.

[119]

CHAPTER 7

Casey's Blacklist

THE FOLLOWING STATEMENT WAS MADE BY William J. Casey, Director of Central Intelligence, before the Commonwealth Club of California, Palo Alto, California, 3 April 1984:

'They (the Soviet Union) also use sophisticated international diversion operations. We have identified some 300 firms operating from more than thirty countries engaged in such diversion schemes. And there are probably many more that remain unidentified. Most diversions occur by way of Western Europe, which is why we have made such a strong effort to enlist the help of our European allies in combating illegal trade activities.'

In those few sentences William J. Casey, lawyer, man of honour and integrity, tells the result of the largest single CIA operation ever mounted inside the alliance nations, without the consent or knowledge of most of the governments concerned, with the possible exception of the UK government.

The list of 300 companies includes the names of almost all the major electronics and computer companies in Europe. It was compiled by the CIA team that began work in Europe in late 1980 and early 1981 and that at one time numbered over 200 people. They picked up their leads in trade papers and European government export publications and at East-West trade seminars. They pursued those leads in the European countries by attending export seminars, chatting up civil servants and talking in bars at sales and technology conferences. They pursued them in the Eastern Bloc countries at trade fairs by posing as staff, sales people and journalists associated with Western companies. They attended the 1981 Leipzig Fair in East Germany and the Brno Fair, in Moldavia, in 1982 in significant numbers. They photographed or noted every caller at Eastern Bloc stands in the 1982 and 1983 Hanover Fair, in West Germany. They persuaded a number of gullible Western

Intelligence agencies, including MI5, to make additional taps on Eastern Bloc trade mission phones, to note callers and attenders at Eastern Bloc commercial receptions, and generally to report on any East-West technology contacts. In the European states they posed as bankers, dealers, brokers and sales people, often under cover of some of the most prestigious American multinationals.

In the end, they produced Casey's list, which subsequently proved somewhat indigestible to most Western governments since, almost invariably, it contained the names of their most important electronics and computer companies, which were often also major defence contractors. The list was based on every technology company doing business with the Eastern Bloc and not just those trading illegally of which very few were detected.

Such was the naïvety and arrogance of Casey's team, or rather teams, that they assumed that any technology being sold to the Eastern Bloc without a US re-export licence had to be an illegal sale. In 1983 some of Europe's most prestigious NATO defence contractors suddenly found that spare parts from NATO defence systems that they had built and sent to the US for repair did not come back again. Shipments of high technology from the US destined for companies like Ferranti, Marconi and Nederland Telecommunicacions, were seized or detained by US Customs. Most of the companies thought that it was simply the US Customs suffering an excess of zeal under the Operation Exodus guidelines. In a way it was, but the zeal had a basis beyond the guidelines, and that was the CIA list.

Faced with Casey's absurd and illegally obtained list, you might have expected a robust European government or two to ask for Casey's head, pickled in sulphuric acid, perhaps, or a ton of gold reparations, followed by a few dozen exemplary expulsions. Not a bit of it. Elements of the UK and West German governments began a witch hunt of their own, based on the list. Thousands of man-hours were spent checking several years of export licences to the Eastern Bloc. Having cooperated with the CIA in gathering the data, it was going to look very odd if the same agencies then rejected the summation of that data. In general they did not, and for those few West European companies still in the East-West export business, the pressures and delays became nearly intolerable. Small companies stood no chance at all and most left the business. Meanwhile, in 1983, 15,000 IBM PCs went to China and by mid-1985 the volume of Cocom references for exports to the Eastern Bloc from the US had risen to over $1 billion, a 300 per cent rise on the 1980 total.

However reprehensible the CIA activity was – and it was not merely reprehensible, but both illegal (under the UK Official Secrets Act, section 2) and a breach of the NATO interagency intelligence guidelines, and the bilateral intelligence guidelines – it was nothing to the failure of Western Intelligence agencies adequately to warn the elected governments of the NATO countries; and subsequently the failure of those governments to take action to protect the companies, to end the delays in the United States, and to officially reject Casey's list.

In the UK the situation reached the point where the Prime Minister was forced to concede for the first time ever that the CIA were active in the UK. So universal had become the activity of American officials in the United Kingdom – of whatever agency – that I was receiving three or four calls a week, sometimes two a day, from UK computer companies complaining about visits from people claiming to be either US embassy officials or just US government officials. Sometimes the visits were by appointment, always they were accompanied by the threat, either implied or explicit, that if they did not provide access, they would get no more technology from the United States.

Naturally I passed these on to Paddy Ashdown, for two reasons. First, many of the incidents needed too much work to turn them into a story. Because the pages of company news and various other stories had to get done each week, there was simply not enough time to go to places as diverse as Bristol, Manchester and Cardiff to take verbatim statements, nor the hours it would take to make the embassy skip the lies and tell the truth. Secondly, enough public warnings had been given for the paper to feel that it had fulfilled its duties. Duty now lay in keeping the elected representative informed. This I did.

Paddy's early letters to the Prime Minister had always been answered by a private secretary. Suddenly, the response got slower, shorter, and signed by the Prime Minister herself. Now the Prime Minister would never lie to an MP, particularly in writing, but she could hardly be seen to announce that the CIA were indeed here, given that her Defence Minister in the Lords, Lord Trefgarne, was more or less simultaneously announcing that the agency had no role in the UK. But the evidence in Paddy's letter seems to have driven both the Prime Minister and her advisors into a corner. Admit the truth, order an investigation, or cover up. In the end the choice was the cover up, though it was well and competently done, and left the way open for the Prime Minister to change her stance, should we come up with more specific evidence, such as photographs or tapes. Given the 'map' of US interference, and the regularity with which it was being updated, this could have been

[122]

done, but that would not have served our wider purpose, which was to expose the overall grip on UK technology imposed by the United States of which the CIA operation was but a small, if significant, part. There was a huge part of the US control system that only the government, or sustained legal action, could have exposed. This was, and remains, the change of use, movement and re-export conditions imposed by all the US computer companies and subsidiaries and evidenced in the IBM and Texas Instruments' letter.

Within that system of control, and within the subsidiaries, lay the real heart of darkness, and it was through the subsidiaries that the real, long-term damage, the gutting of the European high technology industry, was done. Moreover, since the US assumes jurisdiction over the subsidiaries, based on their US parentage, that has not at the time of writing been contested in any court by any European government, it is only fair to assume that some of those subsidiaries, since they imposed the conditions, also acknowledged the jurisdiction. In that context, they would see no reason to inform the UK government or anyone else of police visits from the US, sanctioned by the parent company there. Certainly DEC in Reading has been ultra zealous in imposing the illegal constraints, particularly since the company was visited by US Commerce Department officials in 1984. In fact, the status of any US official involved in the high technology issue in the UK is open to serious question if not outright rejection in terms of the Attorney General's letter of 3 July 1985.

When the final credits had rolled on the *Today in Politics* programme in which Paddy had confronted Perle with just a few of the consequences of his actions in the UK, he had told Perle that the issue was rather a big one to be handled by Customs. Perle then said it was not being handled by Customs, but by intelligence. If he was telling the truth, then the so-called Customs team at the embassy may have been part of the original Casey operation. In fact, the assumption that Lacey and his group were CIA had a few other supports too. At least one of the team had recently (1982) returned from Angola, where he had, he said, been chasing gun runners. Hardly what one expects of US Customs. In addition, it was Lacey who was most in the habit of 'going down the country' without informing the UK Customs or the UK Department of Trade and Industry. This would not be the normal behaviour of a foreign civil servant on a visit to the UK. Indeed, Lacey seems to have avoided some of the more stupid mistakes in the List of 300. At least one request from Washington called for 'the turning over', ie the investigation of one of the largest arms contractors to the UK government. Apparently the request was ignored.

But Perle, Casey and the Prime Minister weren't the only ones offering proof, direct or otherwise, that the entire operation by 1984 was in the hands of the espionage gangs. At a seminar on US Export Controls held in London on 14 May 1985, Terence Roche Murphy, a US lawyer, twice warned of intelligence participation in the technology issue.

'But be aware the Exodus may *not* always tell the Freight forwarder when goods have been detained, particularly in counter-intelligence operations.' Later he added that 'not all investigations are aimed at the exporter; the investigator may really be interested in the consignee or even a third or fourth party for intelligence reasons.'

In a slightly less direct manner, Professor Heinrich Vogel, the director of the Federal West German Institute for East European Trade and International Studies, described the situation thus: 'Exaggeration of security concerns, denial of cooperation and exchange of information and rude practices of interference in other nations' R&D, licencing and procedures and exports . . . are bound . . . to damage cooperation in the Alliance.' Going back to Casey's speech, and remembering the second largest item of US electronics exports to the Soviet bloc, we find Casey demanding that 'most importantly, automatic test equipment which can alleviate acute Soviet deficiencies in military-related manufacturing areas, must be strictly controlled.'

Sure, Mr Casey, from everywhere except the US, which shall export all it wishes to wherever it wants, including to the alleged potential adversary.

While much of what Casey said has profound legal and security implications for most Western nations, the explanation he gives for how the information is collected has quite profound implications for Americans abroad, since he virtually hands to any foreign state the right to arrest or expel any US businessman or scientist.

According to Casey the CIA '. . . tap scientists and businessmen who roam the world in their professional capacities for the information that comes their way and for the insights and understanding they develop.'

Many people have said to me that there is nothing new about this. Everyone does it, so why not? Well, maybe everyone *does* do it. But they haven't been fingered, in public, by the head of MI5, or MI6, or of the KGB for doing it. And even if the head of one of the UK intelligence agencies did say something like that, it would not carry either the

[124]

weight or the legal implications it does coming from a senior member of the US government whose appointment has specific Congressional approval.

What Casey has done, unequivocally, is place the taint of espionage on every US businessman and scientist travelling abroad. And in a world which the United States itself is doing the most to polarise, that lacks even the most elementary sense of either prudence or responsibility. Any Eastern Bloc state could now give a degree of legitimacy to the arrest of a US businessman or scientist on the grounds that he or she might be gathering information for the CIA. In third world countries the position is even more dangerous, given that the CIA is in the business of active espionage and not passive intelligence gathering. Should a dictator assume that the most recent coup attempt was CIA-backed – and there has to be a fifty-fifty chance that it was, especially if he has Socialist leanings – then, given the nature of justice in most dictatorships, his chief of police would merely have to point to what Casey said and there would be a *prima facie* case for rounding up any American scientists or businessmen in the country.

What most states have learned long ago, and what the US appears not to have learned, is that if you declare most of your expatriate community to be an adjunct of your main espionage agency, you put them all under suspicion. You also severely limit their utility and in certain circumstances you place them in grave and unnecessary danger. It is a matter of intense alarm that Casey was not instantly fired for that remark (or for his remarks that the Japanese companies NEC, Hitachi and Fjuitsu were a threat to US national security).

US officials frequently claim that the object of much of what people like Casey and Perle say in public is to frighten the Europeans into behaving the way the US government wants them to behave. Aside from the fact that the United States has never been granted the role of Universal Aunt by the governments of Europe, the most alarming thing is that the US administration seems quite happy to tolerate very senior officials telling lies in public in order to promote policy objectives. The question about Casey's speech is: Is the claim, oft repeated subsequently in the US media, that the CIA has a 300 company list, a lie? The answer, according to the evidence separately compiled by myself and others, is that the claim is true. The CIA team was in Europe; much of the team's activity became so public that it was almost a matter of routine. And, under the most extraordinary duress, Paddy Ashdown extracted from the CIA an admission that some of the 300 companies were British.

[125]

On 8 April 1984 I was given a copy of Casey's speech which the US embassy denied was available from the United States Information Service. Our story in *Computer News* continued, as had Louise Kehoe's piece in the *Financial Times* on 5 April, to focus on the criticisms of the US–Japanese links. This was because, after IBM, Japan is the only other source in the Western world for a significant range of the workhorses of the computer world, mainframe computers. An assault on Japan by Casey, though it was ignored by most Western media except the *Financial Times*, was of no small import. But what I had not been able to do, given *Computer News'* limited resources that week, was find out whether there were any UK companies on the list, and if so which ones. In addition, there was also the question of whether the US government had passed the list to the UK government. It was clearly a case for across the road. As soon as *Computer News* had gone to bed on the Monday night, I phoned Phil Beresford at home and arranged to see him the following day.

Sitting in The Lamb in Lamb's Conduit Street the following day, we examined what Casey had said. I told Phil that I was sure there were UK companies on the list. That's fine, he said. But how do we prove it?

By Thursday we had still not discovered any way to establish just which companies were on the list. The CIA press office was utterly adamant. They were more or less refusing to even confirm that William Casey was their director, much less that he had spoken at Palo Alto, though there were near enough a hundred witnesses. Then Phil had a brainwave. 'They won't talk to journalists – maybe they'll talk to an MP.'

I got onto Paddy straight away and I explained the problem. He said he'd call that night at *The Sunday Times*, after he'd finished an early speaking engagement.

He arrived at about 9 o'clock, long after all except the mice had left the fifth floor of *The Sunday Times*. Phil took Paddy to the conference phone room at the back of the *Business News* office and we dialled Washington. Naturally CIA asked to phone back. Curses indeed. It wouldn't take them a moment to find out that they were on to *The Sunday Times*. Paddy was faster off his feet than Phil and I. He made an excuse about delays in getting the call through, gave them the House of Commons phone number and said to call him in thirty minutes, as he had to finish off a meeting. Then there was a frantic dash down to Gray's Inn Road for a taxi. As luck would have it, we were at Norman Shaw North in less than fifteen minutes. Quite promptly the call came through, a Mr Dale Peterson of the CIA Press Office on the line. Forty minutes later, he was still on the line. In a virtuoso performance of tenacity that would have done justice to the Watergate journalists, Paddy hung on and hung on, never letting his caller say goodbye, until finally he admitted there were British companies on the list. If ever the phrase 'gotcha' was justified, that was the moment.

Once again, Phil's piece led the *Business News*, and rightly too. It is a matter of the utmost seriousness if a foreign intelligence agency is spying on British firms. The Department of Trade and Industry denied, as the Prime Minister was to deny in answer to a parliamentary question, that the CIA had communicated the list of the UK. This is extremely odd. Here is the CIA, allegedly a friendly intelligence service, with a list of British companies which are, apparently, engaged in illegal diversions of technology to the Soviet Union, but the list, a year old at least at the time Casey mentioned it, has not been passed to the UK. At some much later stage, a version of the list was given to some allied governments. It still contained a number of unacceptable inclusions, but the bulk of the offenders had been whittled down to companies in just four countries, Sweden, Austria, Spain and Switzerland. In Sweden, both Datasaab and ASEA, the country's largest electronics and high technology companies, were on the list and it is upon such companies and their countries that the US has focused its pressure, or, not to put too fine a point on it, plain ordinary blackmail.

But why should such a list be mentioned, if they were not prepared to share it with friendly governments? The reason eventually emerged from a series of ever more reluctant officials. The mention of the list itself was intended as part of the overall pattern of intimidation of the European governments. Roughly translated, the European and allied governments were meant to understand that the US had such intensive information on illegal transfer of technology from their own countries that the US could break the back of any high technology industry in any European country by denying high technology to the named companies, in other words, to most European companies. There was a very interesting coincidence between this revelation about what was really going on, government to government, or rather government against government, and Moore's remark that the US had enough information on the companies to slap the irons on most of them. Here was Casey telling the Europeans that he had enough information on all of them to crush most of their high technology industries.

There was another odd coincidence: Casey made his speech on 3 April 1984. On that date two European countries were in the middle of what amounted to an embargo on certain computer supplies from the

[127]

US. The UK and West Germany were being denied any supplies of DEC computers or spare parts from the United States. In both West Germany and the UK DEC computers are used extensively in banking, government, defence and in universities and laboratories. For four months, from about mid-January 1984 to the end of May 1984, few, if any, DEC shipments reached the UK from the United States. What did arrive came from the DEC factory in Galway in the Irish Republic, and from depots on the continent. The stranglehold on Germany only ended in August and September. The US on this occasion hid behind a very carefully constructed camouflage operation. Enquiries from the trade departments of allied governments elicited only the fact that the US government was in deepest negotiations with DEC over a 'haemorrhage' of its products to the Eastern Bloc.

In the US later that month the President of DEC, Ken Olsen, told a financial analyst that the company had, or would, lose about a quarter's deliveries, as a result of the paranoia. Thus the allied governments were held to ransom and they scarcely even knew it, so cleverly was it done. The US was after all entitled in law to sort out its own companies. But the truth was radically different from anything the public, and perhaps several European governments, were allowed to know.

The US had forced the Austrians to pass the previously mentioned law, and the US had a stranglehold on Cocom. In Sweden as one Swedish Minister told me, 'even the diplomatic correspondence had sunk to naked blackmail'. The UK and West Germany were under an embargo for one of their most critical computer devices (supercomputers). Spain had its main electronics company Piher on the US Export Denials List. Now, into this scenario, comes Casey with his key list of European companies obtained from 'businessmen and scientists travelling the world'. And remember, as a US government spokesman was to tell the BBC, the US had teams of 'customs officers' in embassies in London, Rome, Bonn, Paris and several other European capitals too. The pressure was therefore being applied quite directly from the US embassies in the European capitals. More seriously, as the group of senior UK executives at the Ambassador's breakfast discovered, the pressure was also being applied indirectly, by insinuation and veiled threat. At this stage, no carrot was on offer, just threats. There was every reason to curse the national media, print and broadcast, and particularly the diplomatic correspondents. Here was a major US diplomatic offensive, underpinned by the CIA, and involving illegalities in every country in Europe, in full flight, and not a squeak from any serious commentator except in the *Financial Times*.

[128]

At this point, it is worth returning to Casey and his 'businessmen and scientists'. Far too late for my story, in about August 1984, details of the CIA operation that had produced the list, began to reach me. It then became clear that the mention of scientists and businessmen was a red herring. And the US government subsequently used this list to blackmail the allied governments into participating in a kamikazi mission against their own high technology companies, and their own trade with the Eastern Bloc. It was the crowning moment in the second largest commercial coup in history. (The United States elimination of Britain from the Middle East and the Far East was the first.)

But the ground had been well prepared for the operation. By Europe's failure to react to the continuance of US law within the computer and electronics industries, the US had been able to isolate and crush most of the major European high technology companies, but particularly the key computer companies.

By 1984, through the extended regulations attached to the Export Administration Act, the United States had been able to get hold of the customer lists of all the US subsidiaries, thus giving them the kind of information Colin Moore had referred to in his talk. All that was really missing by 1984 were some of the secondary movement records, those that would have become available automatically to the US if the European computer user base could be drawn into the same level of compliance with US law as the subsidiaries.

When the CIA got their marching orders for the high technology raid, they were not moving into unknown territory. Apart from the resident CIA stations throughout Europe, there are also the US subsidiaries, some with their long time 'deep' CIA moles, and managements always ready to do their patriotic duty in an emergency. But beyond that again is the US Western European Economic Database. Nothing wrong with that, you may feel, and under normal circumstances you would be right. But things haven't been normal in the US for quite some time. One of the major contributors to the Western European Economic Database is the active espionage arm of the US government, the CIA.

The Database itself is not a single file, but is distributed to computer memory systems at twenty-one government departments in Washington, after it has been compiled for the Economic Intelligence Com-

[129]

mittee of the US Intelligence Board, the major focus for all US intelligence, before the summaries are passed to the National Security Council, the President's own major intelligence committee. The organisation of economic information gathering is in the hands of the State Department, which oversees an effort generally called the Combined Economic Reporting Program. There is a companion intelligence gathering operation, run by the intelligence agencies themselves, and covering political, military and scientific questions, which is known as CIRL or Current Intelligence Reporting List. Generally, the questions on the Economic Alert List, as the CIA element of the programme is known, are classified confidential, but, unlike most confidential material, it is exempt from declassification, and no date has ever been set when it may be released. Until recently the answers to the questions sent out under the programme were coordinated by a small team in room 2640 at the CIA HQ building in Washington. A careful examination of Casey's own speech will show that there have been significant shifts in that the agencies no longer present a sanitised and homogenised view to the Intelligence Board, which in turn now presents the National Security Council with a best estimate, forecast or cause/outcome summary, with its sponsoring agency. This has had extraordinary repercussions in terms of the cohesiveness of the American administration, not least because Reagan is now presented with choices which were largely made for his predecessors by the process itself. The ageing President is also forced to make choices on the basis of summaries which often reflect agency bias rather than objective fact, and with equal frequency refer to data trends and framework assumptions of which he appears to be ignorant. The loss of discipline in the higher reaches of the US intelligence structure has fed on down into the information gathering operation itself, where there is enormous duplication of effort, and frequently irresolvable conflicts about the very data itself.

However, though the names have changed somewhat since the 1976 document, which was obtained in the United States and passed to Paddy from Canada by people who had followed the issue in the computer press, the process, apart from having become more fragmented, with each of the major intelligence agencies now having its own economic board, has changed little. An enlarged and much more detailed Economic Alert List is produced by the State Department, and updated about once a quarter. The Key Economic Questions (KIQs) are now originated monthly. The CIA which with its independent programme produces a parallel set of answers to those produced by the

[130]

State Department. These two agencies remain the main source of assessed data for the main databases. The raw data, the foundation stone for the whole file, is collected in a completely routine fashion by the following departments of the US government, (who also receive copies of the CIA reports), in the following order of importance, the Treasury, Energy (Nuclear) Commerce, Federal Reserve Board, Agriculture, Export Import Bank, International Trade Commission and finally Transportation. The Labour Department, Department of the Army and Interior and several other smaller government organisations such as the office of Management and Budgets, also have inputs, and receive copies of the CIA reports and assessments.

Sections of the 1976 Economic Alert List is reproduced in the Annexe. For 1985 it was only possible to obtain an outline of the questions, based on the CIA and not the State Department document. Those questions show that the technology transfer issue was dominant among questions asked about the UK, West Germany, France and Spain. Ireland, Denmark and Luxembourg had been added to the list of countries about which questions were being asked and again questions relating to how those countries would tolerate a further increase in the number and level of controls on high technology were prominent.

To find out what happens to all that data, it is necessary to go back in time to Chile, prior to the American financial coup against the elected left-wing president Salvador Allende in 1973. Allende had commissioned a very bright UK computer scientist called Stafford Beer to build him a computer system which would display, in a systematic way, all the major high aggregate flows in the Chilean economy. The object of Allende's experiment, which resulted in an economic control room in which all the raw facts could be displayed on a huge screen and made subject to 'what if?' and other analysis, was to identify bottlenecks in the existing structures and policy options for the future. Financed in part by the CIA, and in part by a $1 million subvention from the US multinational ITT – according to claims made before the Congressional Investigation began in 1974 – the Chilean military overthrew Allende, murdered him and about 14,000 of his followers. One of the last acts of the dying administration was to order the dynamiting of the Cyberstride project control room. It was a spectacular but totally ineffective act. Over eighty per cent of the project programmes, hardware and documentation, were handed over intact by the Chilean military to their CIA paymasters, one of whose major objectives in the coup had been the capture of the project.

Cyberstride was important in itself, but the CIA already had most of

[131]

the primary code and merely needed the control room to speed up the Cyberstride version they were already developing. The major programming for the project was done in London and the CIA had copies of all the tapes before they left for Chile. The relatively innocent purposes for which Allende wanted Cyberstride, the betterment of some of the poorest people in the world and the improvement of his government, were turned on their heads. By 1978 the CIA had its mini Cyberstride and the United States Intelligence Board had its full scale, fully operational, Cyberstride.

CHAPTER 8

The Lawful Rights of All Mankind
(including those of Europeans)

'THUS YOU WILL SEE THAT I entirely share the views of the Secretary of State for Trade and Industry that claims by the United States Government to control the export of goods from the UK and, as illustrated by the IBM letter, the more extravagant claim to control the sale of certain advanced computers within the country, are unwarranted encroachments on UK jurisdiction and are contrary to international law.' – Sir Michael Havers, Attorney General of the United Kingdom, to Paddy Ashdown, MP, 3 July 1985.

Welcome though Sir Michael's declaration in Paddy's favour was, it is and remains little beyond a re-affirmation of the position adopted by the UK government in its note of 18 October 1983 to the US government, rejecting that government's attempt to stop UK supplies for the Siberian gas pipeline project. And, powerful though that intervention may have been, because of the manner in which the UK government used its legal powers to ensure that UK deliveries to Siberia went ahead, the Attorney General on the occasion of Paddy's letter backed away from taking any action. However, both the EEC note of 12 August 1982 and the later UK note fell far short of describing the true position in international law.

Both notes took the issue at the respective levels of the two institutions most affected, the EEC Commission and the British government. Neither note took the issue to the higher level of the ultimate seat of sovereignty from which each of the two institutions derive their own legitimacy, authority and power. In the case of the EEC Commission, this is the Treaty of Rome. In the case of the UK government it is the Crown in Parliament. To do so would have paved the way for the real clash of powers, the clash that remains inevitable so long as the United States continues to seek judicial imperium throughout the world.

[133]

But there is another level, far more pertinent to the man in the street, or more specifically to the men and women in the high technology sector, or among those using high technology. In each of the countries of Western Europe, but more especially the UK, each of us, apart from the rights ancient and modern granted by our own laws and constitution, is protected by a higher set of laws adopted by our own Parliament, for our better protection and in accordance with our nation's historic struggles against tyranny, slavery and oppression. Collectively these higher laws, many of which now have the force of law in the international sphere, apart from their binding force on those who have adopted them, may be called the lawful rights of all mankind.

Those rights are enshrined in five main treaties or convenants, all of which have been signed, adopted and made valid in the United Kingdom. These are, the United Nations Charter and the accompanying Universal Declaration of Human Rights, the International Covenant on Civil and Political Rights, the International Covenant on Economic, Social and Cultural Rights and, perhaps most important from the point of view of this book, the European Convention for the Protection of Human Rights and Fundamental Freedoms. The fifth pertinent treaty is the European Social Charter.

At the global level there is the American declaration and the American convention. Like all other treaties affecting human rights, including the UN Universal Declaration of Human Rights, neither these nor any other such treaties have been signed by the United States of America. This makes the process of cataloguing American illegality, in relation to the manner in which the Export Administration Act reaches beyond the institutional concept of sovereignty, and seeks to limit the basic human rights of non-Americans, a little difficult, but not impossible.

Beginning with that one treaty which the US has signed, the United Nations Charter, let us have a look at Article 1, sections 2 and 3. (Section 1 is too vague though it too might be applicable.) Section 2 states: that the purposes of the United Nations (which include the United States) are: 'To develop friendly relations amongst nations based on respect for the principle of equal rights and self determination of peoples, and to take other appropriate measures to strengthen universal peace.'

The two key phrases are 'equal rights' and 'self determination'.

The American citizen, affected by the Export Administration Act, has redress before his or her local court, and local right of complaint through his or her local representative in the US legislature. Those two rights are absolute under the US constitution. A citizen of a foreign country possesses neither of those rights and even if he or she were granted such rights, which would require an amendment to the US Constitution, the argument of 'reasonable access' would still stand against the US. It is hardly reasonable that I, a citizen of Austria or the UK, should have either to travel to the United States or to hire lawyers in the United States to defend myself against alleged infringements of US law in my own country. Of course, the US could set up courts in its embassies, and perhaps that is what it eventually intends. But what is quite clear here is that American citizens have unequal rights under a law which the United States claims applies universally, ie to other citizens in other states.

On the point of self determination, the issue is simpler. Self determination means, at its most basic, the right of people to their own government, and simultaneously, to their own laws. If US law is to have, as it claims, universal jurisdiction, then self determination is everywhere impaired.

Section 3, of Article 1 of the United Nations Charter, says that the purposes of the United Nations (including the United States and the UK) are: 'To achieve international co-operation in solving international problems of an economic, social, cultural or humanitarian character, and in prompting and encouraging respect for human rights and for fundamental freedoms for all without distinction as to race, sex, language or religion . . .'

Here, the potential breach is less specific, since the intent of section 3 is put in very vague legal terms. The operative phrases governing section 3 are 'achieve', 'promote' and 'encourage'. Hardly the stuff of which definitive charges of law breaking can be made. Nonetheless, the US did sign the Charter, and must be assumed bound by it. On that basis we can fairly say that in attempting to extend unilaterally their jurisdiction to other peoples and other states, the US is demoting and discouraging international co-operation, as well as hindering any form of achievement in this area.

The vagueness of sections 2 and 3 of Article 1 is slightly reinforced by Article 55 of the UN Charter, which re-affirms that the parties to the Charter will 'promote' those stated objectives. But we are still left without a firm legal text which defines the substance of basic human rights. This gap has been filled by the Universal Declaration of Human Rights, which is an inherent part of the UN Charter, and which is generally considered to bind all parties to the Charter[1]. The United States of America, almost alone in the world, has never ratified the subsequent two Covenants which have the effect of making the contents of the Universal Declaration of Human Rights a binding legal obligation on all states which have signed them.

There is a very obvious reason for this, given the nature of certain American legislation. Article 2 of the Universal Declaration of Human Rights states the following: 'Everyone is entitled to all the rights and freedoms set forth in this Declaration, without distinction of any kind, such as race, colour, sex, language, religion, political or other opinion, national or social origin, property, birth or other status.' Furthermore, no distinction shall be made on the basis of the political, jurisdictional or international status of the country or territory to which a person belongs, whether it be independent, trust, non-self governing or under any other limitation of sovereignty.

You do not have to be a lawyer to see that, as far as the UK and European high technology workers are concerned, the US is in clear breach of Article 2 of the Universal Declaration of Human Rights. As we noted before, the USA has not adopted the two specific treaties which give specific legal effect to the Universal Declaration. Nevertheless, it was upon the UN Charter that the United States relied when it sought help from the International Court of Justice in freeing the US Embassy hostages in Iran. In its favourable judgment on behalf of the US, the Court used a reference to the Universal Declaration to support its judgment. In his book on the Lawful Rights of Mankind, Paul Sieghart in a few sentences states the position, in law, of the United States, in relation to the UN Charter.

'Once any state has become bound by such a treaty as the UN Charter, through ratification or accession of such a treaty, any violation of any relevant right for which it is responsible is no longer merely immoral, it is a breach by the Government currently in power in that state of its legal obligations under international law.'

As Sieghart notes, the two Covenants which make the Universal Declaration part of the legal obligations of states, have been signed by most countries who are members of the UN, with the notable exception of the USA. Worse still, the Helsinki Final Act, which some deem to be the international legal instrument that formally ended World War II, and which was signed by the thirty-five key states affected by World War II, and which appears to bind signatory states to a legal treaty, does not do so. Of the thirty-five states which signed the Helsinki Final Act, four – the USA, the Holy See, San Marino and Monaco – remain uncommitted in law to any global or regional human rights treaty. Despite this, Sieghart argues that:

[136]

'. . . if one takes the view that the provisions of the Universal Declaration are retrospectively incorporated into the UN Charter, then this is the case of all the members of the UN, whether or not they have adhered to the Covenants. And if one goes even further and says that the Universal Declaration is now part of customary international law, then it binds also those few remaining states which are not members of the UN.'

Though the force of convention, practice and orthodoxy stand behind Sieghart on this point, it has become customary for the representatives of the US government, under the Reagan administration, to reject all these aspects of international law. What is worse, perhaps, is that non-governmental American lawyers, some of them practising in Europe, have given advice to clients and others which often amounts to tacit support for the US position. By so doing they are rejecting the very principles of reciprocity and mutual respect for the law, upon which other states extend to them the right to practise in Europe and elsewhere. This has been particularly so in the case of American lawyers acting for US computer companies, or speaking at high technology conventions in Europe.

Because, and this is the bone cracker on this one, though the US may have signed nothing and may claim that it is bound by no international law, a lot of other states have signed the key treaties or covenants, and are bound by them. Where the United States has behaved in such a way that it abrogates or seeks to overturn any of the human rights in the Universal Declaration or its two Covenants, all of which have been fully adopted by the UK and many other European states, it places those states in breach of each of those treaties and in breach of the legal obligations each state has undertaken, to ensure, by law, that those rights are enshrined in the law of each state. For instance, all signatories of the covenants to the Universal Declaration, including the UK, have legally bound themselves as follows:

Article 2(1) (International Covenant on Civil and Political Rights)
'Each state party to the present Covenant undertakes to respect and to ensure to all individuals within its territory and subject to its jurisdiction the rights recognised in the present Covenant.'

Before dealing with the two Covenants, and the obligations the UK has assumed under them, it is worth examining which of the human rights in the Universal Declaration the US is in breach of by attempting to give itself universal legal control over all parties using US technology or data of US origin. We have already seen how the United States

[137]

breaches Article 2 by effectively giving to its own citizens prior and specialised rights, which are denied to all others, because the US presumes that they are subject to its legislation.

Article 5 of the Universal Declaration states that: 'Everyone has the right to recognition everywhere, as a person before the law.'

No doubt there are lawyers in the US who would construe this in their favour, saying 'sure, you are recognised before the law, our law everywhere'. To clarify this article, which was intended to be taken with the next five articles to create certain fundamental legal standards, applicable to all human beings, we have to fall back on the competent powers who signed the Charter, and these were sovereign states. Article 6 presumes that each of the sovereign states which belong to the UN is sovereign in its own territory. What Article 6 reinforces positively is the idea that persons from one state shall be treated as equal before the law in the state they happen to be in, even if it is not their own. Article 6 made no provision for, and did not envisage, one state attempting to effect its laws in another sovereign state. Article 5 is jeopardised, if not broken, in that it would seek to have the legally competent authorities in the UK recognise me as two legal persons, one of them is subject to UK law and one of whom is subject, separately, to the universal law or laws of the United States.

Article 7, based on the same presumption of territorial integrity, states that: 'All are equal before the law and are entitled without any discrimination to equal protection of the law. All are entitled to equal protection against any discrimination in isolation of this Declaration and against any incitement to such discrimination.'

At least the situation here is clear-cut. Because I live and work in the UK, I cannot be held equal with US citizens before a law of the United States, which claims effective universal jurisdiction, but which provides for tribunals only in the United States. Nor is the United Kingdom providing me with the protection of the law, if it permits my activities to be regulated by a law which it has not enacted, authorised and for which it has provided neither tribunal nor remedy. The UK is in very specific violation of this article, where it formally permits, with the full knowledge of its officials, which has certainly been the case for the past two years, the United States to impose penalties on UK corporations and persons, such as ICL, Systime and Brian Butcher, John Pridmore Smith, John Gow and many others.

Later in this chapter we shall consider what remedies are available to parties affected by US law. The next relevant article is Article 10, which states that, 'Everyone is entitled in full equality to a fair and public hearing by an independent and impartial tribunal, in the determination of his rights and obligations and of any criminal charges against him (or her).'

A trial in the United States cannot be considered fair or impartial if it is trying an offence allegedly committed in the UK by a United Kingdom citizen, on the basis of the law made in the US.

Perhaps it is in Article 11 that we find the most profound opposition to the US position: '1. Everyone charged with a penal offence has the right to be presumed innocent until proved guilty according to law in a public trial at which he (or she) has had all the guarantees necessary for his (or her) defence.'

Here there are two considerations. US law is not the same as European law on several important points, and is contrary to the spirit of this article in some of its assumptions. Secondly, a trial in the US for an alleged offence under US law committed in Europe by a European, cannot be considered a fair trial in law, under this article.

'2. No one shall be held guilty of any penal offence on account of any act or omission which did not constitute a penal offence under national or international law at the time it was committed.'

This article is utterly conclusive and quite rigid. The offences created under the Export Administration Act are not offences in any country other than the United States. They are not offences under British, Swedish, French, German or any other national legislation. And any government permitting the United States to introduce laws creating 'extra-territorial offences' is in absolute breach of this article. On the point of international law, the then member states of the EEC and the UK in 1982 separately claimed that the US actions, and the law on which they were based, are contrary to international law. But they have taken no effective action to end the role of US law as it affects the European employees of the US computer subsidiaries, and all those who have purchased or used US technology or data in Europe. Dozens of people have been prosecuted, companies fined and exports made subject to illegal constraints. The European governments have done nothing, or worse, have connived with the United States in this massive undermining of those legal obligations that the majority of European governments have undertaken. But the source of the undermining of human rights and the failure to react in Europe lies almost exclusively with the legal and foreign service civil servants in each state. Pinning down the effects of the US actions in law is a tricky operation and politicians are inevitably reliant on the civil servants for technical

[139]

advice. In the UK it is highly probable that the government was never advised that it was being placed in breach of a whole range of legal obligations by failing to end the US intrusion.

Insofar as the United States is procedurally bound by the Universal Declaration, through its membership of the UN, it is also in breach of Article 19 and also of Article 27.

Article 19 in part states that, 'Everyone has the right to seek, receive and impart information and ideas through any media and regardless of frontiers.'

The Export Administration Act gives United States nationality to data of US origin – and that includes intangible data (ideas) in people's heads – and then gives the US absolute control over how that data is to be transmitted and who shall receive it. The US law makes no distinction between data which has originated abroad, and data which originates in the United States, and in practice has successfully imposed controls on data not of US origin. The US, therefore, is manifestly seeking to censor and control ideas and information, the very charge that country seeks most vehemently to level against other states.

Article 27(1) says in part that, 'Everyone has the right freely to participate and to share in scientific advancement and its benefits.' Over the past 2 years the US has been engaged in a major programme aimed at excluding some of its own citizens and all foreign visitors from open scientific conferences. These exclusions have been based on the Export Administration Act, Part 379, which has been unopposedly construed by officials to mean that if a US citizen mentions an item of US data in the presence of a foreigner, he or she is exporting it. Even the Soviet Union has not quite reached this level of bureaucratic absurdity.

So far, the US can claim not to have signed the Universal Declaration, and not to be bound by it. What it can not do is make that claim for those states which deem themselves bound by the Universal Declaration, and which have signed the two covenants.

Since the covenants seek only to clarify and make concrete the broad and general language of the Declaration, I will simply list those articles of the covenants which European governments breach by failing to oppose and end the extra-territorial extension of US law.

The First Convention: International Covenant on Civil and Political Rights.
Adopted by the following European countries: The UK, Austria, Bulgaria, Czechoslovakia, Denmark, Finland, France, East and West Germany, Hungary, Iceland, Italy, Luxembourg, the Netherlands,

Poland, Portugal, Norway, Romania, Spain, Sweden, USSR, Yugoslavia.

Article 14

1. 'All persons shall be equal before the courts and tribunals. In the determination of any criminal charge against him, or of his rights and obligations in a suit of law everyone shall be entitled to a fair and public hearing by a competent, independent and impartial tribunal established by law.'
2. 'Everyone charged with a criminal offence shall have the right to be presumed innocent until proved guilty by law.'

Article 15

1. 'No one shall be held guilty of any criminal offence on account of any act or omission which did not constitute a criminal offence, under national or international law, at the time when it was committed.'

Article 16

'Everyone shall have the right to recognition everywhere as a person before the law.'

Article 19

2. 'Everyone shall have the right to freedom of expression. This right shall include freedom to seek, receive and impart information and ideas of all kinds, regardless of frontiers, either orally, in writing, or in print, in the form of art, or through any other media of his choice.'

Article 24

'All persons are equal before the law . . .'

This provision is quite specific in its application and meaning within one sovereign state. Because about half a million or so people in the UK are deemed, by US legislation, to be subject also to its provisions, and because the majority of US computer and electronics subsidiaries impose those regulations, all the states who have failed to end the reign of US law are in *de jure* and *de facto* breach of this article. Article 24 continues, 'In this respect, the law shall prohibit any discrimination and guarantee to all persons equal and effective protection against discrimination on any grounds such as race, colour, sex, language, religion, political or other opinion, national or social origin, property, birth or other status', ie such as being an employee of an American computer company or buying products or data of American origin.

The European Convention for the Protection of Human Rights and Fundamental Freedoms.

It is very difficult to force governments to take action over the various breaches of their international obligations already identified. However, here in Europe there is a very powerful structure for the protection of human rights and freedoms, complete with its own commission and court, and with a well worn path from the UK to judgment. At the time of writing no action has been commenced in pursuit of a remedy for the following five, possibly six, breaches of the Constitution by the UK and other European countries who have failed to end the violation of their citizens' rights by the United States of America. (By the time this book is in print I hope those actions will be underway.)

The first article violated by the American intrusion and which all the European signatories breach by failing to enforce, is Article 6, section 1, which states the following:

Article 6.1

'In the determination of his civil rights and obligations or of any criminal charge against him, everyone is entitled to a fair and public hearing within a reasonable time by an independent and impartial tribunal established by law.'

None of the signatories to the European Convention can claim that US courts are 'tribunals established by law' as the Convention intends, which is by the law of the signatory states. And when Article 6 is read with Articles 7 and 18, the utter illegality of the breach by the US and the depth of violation by the signatory states in failing to mend that breach is clearly seen.

Article 7 says that (1) no one shall be held guilty of any criminal offence on account of any act or omission which did not constitute a criminal offence under national or international law at the time it was committed. Article 13, which is the most vital element introduced with respect to this problem states categorically that, 'Everyone whose rights and freedoms as set forth in this convention shall have an effective remedy before a national authority notwithstanding that the offence has been committed by persons acting in an official capacity.'

With the discovery of this article, it would seem that the case against the UK government is sewn up. This of course remains to be seen. At the time of writing both the EEC Commission and the UK government had been provided with the kind of irrefutable evidence which should have led to action. Nothing has so far happened. It falls, as so often, upon the ordinary, concerned citizens to fight for the rights that, in part, the government is paid taxes to defend.

But before moving to ways in which the US intrusion should have been opposed and ended by those paid and elected to do it, we should not omit Article 17, since it positively prohibits the US intrusion, and equally clearly prohibits the US corporations and their managers and agents from imposing US law on either their employees or their customers.

Article 17

'Nothing in this Convention may be interpreted as implying for any state, group or person any right to engage in any activity or perform any act aimed at the destruction of any of the rights and freedoms set forth herein or at their limitation to a greater extent than is provided for in the Convention.'

Nothing could be clearer and nothing could more clearly strike down any attempt by the US to impose any of its laws in Europe, much less so onerous a one as the Export Administration Act. But the beauty of Article 17 is that it strikes quite directly at the agents of US imperialism, the US subsidiaries. When Mr Peter Hodge of Texas Instruments sent out his letter in May 1984 insisting that his customers should make themselves subject to US law in relation to technical data, he was inviting his customers to place themselves in jeopardy of a law for which no effective remedy before a national authority in the UK exists. This is an attempt to have Texas Instruments' customers, and more particularly anyone unlucky enough to have signed such an assurance, abort their rights under Article 13 of the European Convention of Human Rights. However, Article 17 with great clarity prevents not only states but any individual from making any such incitement or invitation. The Texas Instruments' letter of May 1984 is wrong under the European Convention of Human Rights and falls under the declaration concerning the IBM letter made by the Attorney General of the United Kingdom, Sir Michael Havers.

The IBM letter is similarly wrong, particularly in relation to the person signing any contract containing attempted binding to US law. Apart, however, from breaches of the Human Rights Convention, the IBM letter also reflects a breach of Protocol 1, Article 1, of the European Convention of Human Rights. The protocol was an additional elaboration of certain rights and Article 1 states that:

'Every natural or legal person is entitled to the peaceful enjoyment of

[143]

his possessions except in the public interest and subject to the conditions provided for by law and by the general principles of international law.' Peaceful enjoyment means use, ownership and disposal on the basis of laws laid down in the country of residence at any one time. Under international law nationality does not attach to goods, and no person or persons may import for operation in their own country the laws of another state. Although it is possible to envisage a private contract in which limited ownership was passed to a purchaser, as with a lease, no private contract which sought to void all local jurisdictions that might apply to goods under local laws could ever be valid in law.

The most immediate local 'law' disrupted by the IBM letter is the right of UK courts to make disposals in receiverships or liquidations. Based on the IBM letter, no judge could order an IBM advanced computer system sold to a willing buyer in a liquidation without first obtaining permission to do so from Washington. The second and far more contingent law which, by implication, the IBM letter seeks to void, is the Treaty of Rome. The Treaty of Rome is the higher sovereign authority when it comes to trade regulations between EEC countries. There is no bilateral agreement between the EEC and the United States to treat IBM's commercial computer systems as tactical nuclear weapons, when it comes to reselling them or moving them from one EEC country to another. However, more of the Treaty of Rome later.

It would be wrong to move on to remedies against the American illegalities without noting a fine piece of hypocrisy. Not to be outdone, either by Europe or Africa or by the rest of the world, the United States drew up an American Declaration of the Rights and Duties of Man and added a Convention which would make that Declaration a binding international law. So far seventeen American states, many of them with appalling human rights records, have signed the Convention but not the United States, which drafted and promoted it. There are several good reasons for this, including:

Article IV
'Every person has the right to freedom of investigation, of opinion, and of the expression and dissemination of ideas, by any medium whatsoever.'

Article XVIII
'Every person may resort to the courts to ensure respect for his legal rights. There should likewise be available to him a simple, brief procedure, whereby the courts will protect him from acts of authority that to his prejudice violate any fundamental constitutional rights.'

[144]

Article XXVI
'Every accused person is presumed to be innocent until proved guilty. Every person accused of an offence has the right to be given an impartial and public hearing and to be tried by courts previously established in accordance with pre-existing laws and not to cruel, infamous or unusual punishment.'

And amen to that.

Now to the vexed question of remedy or, how to fix these imperialists who have half occupied Europe by dint of stealth and treachery.

The first set of ramparts are already provided in this book and they begin at the root of the problem which is the employment contracts used by most American subsidiaries. These contracts usually insist that the would-be employee observe certain American laws, usually anti-trust and corruption laws. More recently, and endemic in the computer and electronics industry, are clauses relating to the Export Administration Act. Far from putting your own head or potential job on the line, you sign them and then, with the utmost concern for the legal health and safety of your new employer, you point out that, as your girlfriend/wife/father/mother/brother has pointed out, any clauses which try to bind you to a foreign law are a breach of Article 13 of the European Convention of Human Rights. You don't mind of course, you're not going to tell anyone. On the other hand, the Convention is a binding undertaking in international law, and were the government to find out, both the company and any manager who had signed for the company would be open to action. Nay, the government would have a binding legal obligation to act, under Article 17 of the Convention. You wouldn't want your company ever to be subject to such an action, of course. If you wish to get heavy, you can always increase the panic by noting that Articles 6 and 7 also apply, and the net effect of Article 7 is to make any such contract, not just the part containing the American references, null and void. The argument is simply that the contract was made under duress of an illegal nature, ie if you hadn't signed the American law clauses, which are illegal under Articles 6, 7, 13 and 17 of the European Convention, you would not have got the job.

Remember that at this point we are simply considering basic human rights violations in American contracts and not the far more powerful commercial law violations which we will come to in due course.

Moving on to the question of the machine and data restrictions imposed in purchase and vendor contracts by all American computer companies, there are one or two fine points to consider. First, copies of

[145]

all contracts and the name of the person signing them are lodged with the US Department of Commerce in a computer system to which both the Pentagon and US Customs have regular access. It is the common practice of each of these departments, when making investigations under the EAA, to take action against companies, their directors and all or any employee named or signing contracts. Now, take the case of an employee of a fairly large company buying a fairly small portable computer, like a DEC PDP/11. The company goes into liquidation or is merged, the PDP/11 is sold off, a job lot, without any reference by the liquidator to the original contract. One day a sharp eyed CIA bagman spots a PDP/11 in a small hotel in Bulgaria. He takes the serial number, sends it back to the States and lo, there you are, Joe Bloggs, three companies later, but the last known person responsible for that machine. Your name will go on to one or maybe all of the grey lists held by each of the three departments. Should you ever go to the States, you run the serious risk of being picked up and you will then find yourself maybe 6,000 miles from being able to prove either that you had nothing to do with the machine or that the company went into liquidation. You will probably find yourself on the vastly expanded US Denials List, which is circulated to all US high technology subsidiaries in Europe. That way you may find that, quite illegally, you are in effect blackballed from eighty-five per cent of Europe's high technology companies.

There is nothing fictional about any of this: it has happened to a significant number of people I know, including two of the most eminent and honourable high technology managing directors in the UK.

Now, no company has the legal right to expose either themselves or any of their employees to such real and growing hazards. And the alternative doesn't have to be a local purchase, or a no buy. The inclusion of all such clauses is, as we have shown, a violation of the European Convention of Human Rights, which the UK government is legally obligated to uphold. On those grounds alone most such contracts are void, or close to it. However, there is the Attorney General's declaration, and it is a very powerful one, even if it does not as yet have the full force of UK law. But no lawyer, for a vendor or purchaser, can afford to overlook the view any British judge is likely to take of a contract which contains clauses that would void or limit the jurisdiction of a UK judge or court in the matter of the contract. For all practical purposes, such contracts are a dead letter even before the question of public policy in the UK, or of the Treaty of Rome, are brought into it. It would be the simplest matter in the world for a purchaser, armed with the information in this book, to have a contract containing such

[146]

clauses struck down. No competent lawyer could, after the publication of this book, advise any company, whether vendor or purchaser of a US computer, that a contract containing clauses which make it subject in whole or in part to US jurisdiction would stand up in a European or British Court. Nor could any competent lawyer advise his company directors that they are on secure legal grounds in seeking to impose US law in employment contracts. They are not.

But there is a third category of person who would seem to be in double jeopardy under the current US mode of operation: the enforcers. They are usually European employees of the subsidiaries and their job is to ensure that all other employees and customers observe US law. Starting from the US side they are held to be directly responsible under the export regulations for enforcement of the regulations, and specifically punishable by US law if there is any breakdown in the procedures. First of all, their European employer is in breach of the European Convention in placing them in this position. Secondly, they themselves are in the most serious breach of Article 17 of the European Convention, not to mention their position under Sir Michael's declaration, though it is notable that only the US goes for the people as well as the company. European law, in the general context in which Sir Michael was writing, tends to halt at the corporate personality.

But there are far more powerful remedies around, some of which may well have been applied by the time this book is published. Though Sir Michael placed the impositions of US law well outside the bounds of legality, he fought shy of taking any action himself. This does not mean that action cannot be taken against the Attorney General himself, over the breach of sovereignty. Such an action, probably an application for a judicial review, is already in preparation. The grounds which have been advanced to the lawyers are several. First, using the IBM letter and the Attorney General's own letter, Paddy and I suggest that the High Court should be invited to consider (*mandamus*) Sir Michael's inactivity over this unconstitutional attempt to limit the power of the judiciary. Secondly, we alternatively invite a High Court judge to examine Sir Michael's failure to uphold the government's legal obligations under the European Convention of Human Rights. Thirdly, and separately again, we could invite a High Court judge to consider Sir Michael's and the Prime Minister's failure to make a restoration of UK law to the computer and electronics industry by immediately invoking the Protection of Trade Act. Fourthly, we could invite a High Court judge to inspect the IBM letter, the Texas Instruments' letter and the GIM letter and consider whether the Queen's writ can any longer be

[147]

deemed to be running in her realm. We could then invite, or rather our lawyers could then invite the judge to consider the status of all ministers of the Crown in Government who have sworn as Privy Councillors to ensure that Her Majesty's writ runs in her realm. Assuming that the judge was swayed by the evidence, Paddy could then invite in Parliament, all named parties, being all the ministers of the Crown, so sworn, from the Prime Minister down, to mend forthwith the rent in the fabric of sovereignty, and the default in their oath of office.

Those are just the simpler actions. In contemplation of his action against General Instruments Microelectronics UK for their breach of contract evidenced in their letter to him of 9 October 1984 Brian Butcher has also been invited to seek an injunction restraining a series of named parties, including the Managing Directors and staff of a large selection of US subsidiaries and the Department of Trade and Industry from circulating the US Denials List in the UK.

Then there are the injury actions, contingent upon a complaint made under Article 85 of the Treaty of Rome. At this time the EEC is contemplating such a complaint and over 300 pages of evidence. Officially, since a number of points need tidying up, it is best simply to say that the complaint has been lodged. Should that complaint proceed then someone, somewhere, could be liable for fines up to, or in excess of, $10billion.

Looking at the two notes which were separately delivered to the US government by the EEC and the UK in 1982, in the wake of the Siberian gas pipeline fiasco. Taking the EEC note first, the legal arguments are limited to two points, the first being the breaches of international law as the EEC sees it, and the breaches of the US law itself, inherent in the way the United States is attempting to project its laws.

First, the Commission says that the extra-territorial projection of US law breaches the established international legal principle of territoriality. As stated in the EEC Note of 22 June 1982:

'The *territoriality principle* (ie the notion that a State should restrict its rule-making in principle to persons and goods within its territory and that an organization like the European Community should restrict the applicability of its rules to the territory to which the Treaty setting it up applies) is a fundamental notion of international law, in particular insofar as it concerns the regulation of the social and economic activity in a State. The principle that each State – and *mutatis mutandis* the Community insofar as powers have been transferred to it – has the right freely to organize and develop its social and economic system has been

[148]

confirmed many times in international fora. The American measures clearly infringe the principle of territoriality since they purport to regulate the activities of companies in the European Community, not under the territorial competence of the United States.'

Secondly, the Commission asserts that the US projections are contrary to the established principle of nationality:

'The *nationality principle* (ie the prescription of rules for nationals, wherever they are) cannot serve as a basis for the extension of United States jurisdiction resulting from the Amendments, ie (i) over companies incorporated in European Community Member States on the basis of some corporate link (parent-subsidiary) or personal link (eg shareholding) to the United States; (ii) over companies incorporated in European Community Member States, either because they have a tie to a United States incorporated company, subsidiary or other "United States controlled" company through a licensing agreement, royalty payments, or payment of other compensation, or because they have bought certain goods originating in the United States.'

Some American lawyers still contest the EEC note, even on these points. Or rather, to support the untenable position of the US government and the Export Administration Act, they claim that both the status of the EEC note and its contents are 'arguable' in law. This is of course true, but any company of whatever origin wishing to avoid the risk of the mass voiding of all its contracts, would do well to read the remainder of the EEC note.

This note, in a less specific but not less compelling argument, points out that the US attempt to enforce its laws extra-territorially, is probably contrary to US law, in the form of paragraph 40 of the Restatement of the Law Second, Foreign Relations Law of the United States. It is worth reading both this section and the next two which deal with the question of compensation to European companies, which the US government had evidently forgotten, and with the contradictions in the EAA in relation to boycotts, and the constraints in the EAA which the US government was supposed to consider before it acted.

Moving on to the UK note, the tone is essentially tougher and any company or company lawyer who still thinks that he could successfully argue a case should look very carefully at the paragraph which says:

'Furthermore, Her Majesty's Government also observes that a provision in a contract between two private parties providing that an overseas party will observe the law of the United States in regard to any re-export of items of US origin is not capable of replacing or overruling the national law of the country concerned.'

[149]

The note might also have added that such arrangements cannot void international treaty obligations, but that point was assumed in the reference to national law. The note continues:

'Any attempt by a state to further the use of such clauses in private contracts concluded by its nationals for the purposes of extending the jurisdiction of the state would be objectionable.' So, while both the EEC and the UK were prepared to go to law against the US over a contract, limited in time, and confined to an essentially non-high technology industry, why has the very heart of Europe's future, the human rights of its workers, and its key exports, been abandoned to the jurisdiction of a foreign state?

One answer is stupidity. Faced with a slowly developing situation, European bureaucracies, including that at the EEC, have reacted at the one-yard-per-year pace of their slowest clerical assistant. The second answer is fear. A senior executive in ICL once told me that the company had no alternative but to comply with US requirements. That is not true. The essential price of giving into a bully, particularly a government-backed bully, is massacre. This is what happened to ICL, which nowadays does little more than market other people's products. Yet the law was always there, and the means to have it enforced, if necessary by third parties. But with the natural industrial leaders behaving like craven cowards, the die, particularly in the UK, was cast.

The US subsidiaries seem never once to have considered the legal consequences of creating a totally illegal environment in which to employ people and to trade. No doubt the ultimate theory is that the Seventh Cavalry, in the form of Richard Perle, will come riding over the hill just as the Europeans are closing in for the kill. However, low flying Perles these days are in serious danger of high flying landmines, not to mention jet propelled and very angry NATO governments, which should keep the Pentagon safely tied up while the lawyers count the fine up to the eleventh or twelfth digit – in dollars of course.

---

[1] See Paul Sieghart, *The Lawful Rights of Mankind*, Oxford University Press, 1985.

CHAPTER 9

Active Foreign Espionage

THE CIA IS THE ACTIVE foreign espionage arm of the US government. It is based in Langley, Virginia, has a staff of 30,000 and recruits openly through advertisements in papers such as the *Wall Street Journal*. It is governed by a charter which among other things prohibits CIA activity in the US against US citizens. The agency has been in constant violation of its charter with many of the violations becoming public in the sixties and seventies through US congressional investigations. More recently the CIA have been involved in a series of criminal acts under international law, including the mining of harbours in Nicaragua and a series of assassination plots in third world countries. Less well known, though long suspected, is the high level of CIA activity in the UK, Northern Ireland and the Irish Republic.

For those who seriously doubt Enoch Powell's revelations that the CIA provided the mechanism the IRA used in the bomb which killed Earl Mountbatten of Burma, they should consider carefully the case of the Air India super constellation, the *Kashmir Princess*. The plane due to carry the Prime Minister of Communist China, Chou En Lai, from Hong Kong to the first third world conference in Bandung in 1955 crashed in the Java Sea. Chou En Lai was not on board, having taken due note of a warning which was also passed to the British authorities, that an attempt would be made to sabotage the plane. When British divers fished the wreckage out of the sea it was to discover that a bomb, supplied to the Taiwanese front by the CIA, had exploded in a wing fuel tank, destroying the aircraft.[1]

In Ireland, the CIA have been engaged in supplying the IRA, principally the Provisional IRA, with weapons and bomb mechanisms, similar to those which killed both Earl Mountbatten and Airey Neave MP. They have also actively disrupted various parts of the internal peace movement in Northern Ireland. Seven months after the fall of

Saigon in 1974, a CIA officer, last seen in uniform in Saigon, turned up in Northern Ireland, posing as the leader of a peace group then engaged in the collection of names and addresses on a peace petition to be given to both the IRA and Protestant terrorist organisations. At the height of a sectarian tit for tat murder campaign, the delivery to both sides of the names *and addresses* of those who objected was an act of criminal irresponsibility. It was stopped, but in the course of stopping it the American promoting the petition accidentally came face to face with a journalist who had known him in Saigon, in uniform. Not unexpectedly the American disappeared.

To most people in the UK such actions on the part of an agency of a friendly foreign government are inexplicable. The explanation however is surprisingly simple and goes some way to set the scene for CIA activity in relation to UK high technology. US policy is, and always has been, aimed at the creation of a united Ireland, with the subordinate aim of having that united Ireland join NATO. The destruction of the Protestant Parliament at Stormont, which the IRA effectively accomplished, was the first real step in that direction in fifty years, and it was logical that the US should seek, albeit covertly, to assist those engaged in this activity. In addition, it was a work of wondrous ease to use the Irish groups in the US, many with family members in the CIA, to pass the ammo and money to 'the lads'. It is also worth noting that it is the fascist-inclined, overtly Catholic Provisional IRA, and not the socialist-inclined old IRA, which gets the supplies. The US policy of pressurising the government in the Republic, even to the extent of encouraging the Provisionals and the INLA to plot a coup, as a move preparatory to the country's ending its neutrality, are well within the actions permitted under this undeclared US strategy. And it must always be remembered that the CIA have a dangerously high level of 'freedom of action' in pursuit of agreed American government policy abroad.

The CIA operation in Ireland appears to be run directly from the United States. In the UK, however, at least part of the operation is conducted from the third floor of the American Embassy in Grosvenor Square, with one or more operational control centres elsewhere in the city and individual CIA officers stationed at Intelligence centres such as GCHQ in Cheltenham. In theory and as a matter of legal principle, the CIA should never undertake any activities on UK soil. The British government possesses no normal constitutional power which would enable it to sanction an operation by the CIA within its borders. In practice, any such situation would probably be defended by the government on the basis of the virtually unlimited powers it does

[152]

possess under the doctrine of the Royal Prerogative. Such a situation has never arisen, because the first party to any injury in these circumstances is the government itself, since it is the government's duty to ensure that the law is upheld and sovereignty maintained. As with the more obvious intrusion which is the main subject matter of this book, successive UK governments seem to have been totally inactive in ensuring that the CIA kept within the guidelines laid down for their activities in the UK.

My first run in with the CIA occurred over the 11 ASA smear. One of the smaller IPC computer magazines, *Computer Talk*, had published a resume of the case, including the phone number of the CIA HQ in the United States. The latter is, of course, in the public phone book, but nonetheless its appearance in the magazine caused quite a few giggles. It was no giggle however when it came to trying to extract any information from the CIA Press Office. It seemed to be peopled entirely with Ivy League accents, each belonging to a name out of a Hollywood script. At that stage all I wanted to know was whether the CIA would be following up the document which had been declassified to Congress in 1982.

'I really couldn't say sir.'

'It was a CIA report?'

'I really couldn't say sir.'

The document had been declared in the Congressional record to be a CIA production but the CIA press office were playing somewhat cautious. It did rather beg the question of why they had a press office.

The second run in was a more serious matter. In the second issue of the paper we were faced with an intriguing story from our contacts in the US. It mainly arose from the indictment of a man called James Harper on charges of selling missile secrets stolen from a company called Systems Control Technology, to Polish intelligence. By the time Harper was indicted in late 1983 the company from which the secrets had been stolen, SCT, had been bought by the British computer company Scicon. But that wasn't the immediate British connection. In his statement to the Grand Jury, Harper claimed that a Californian entrepreneur, William Bell Hugle, had introduced him to his contacts in Polish intelligence. Bell Hugle is, or perhaps was, one of Silicon Valley's more colourful characters. Indeed, he was a founder of one of the original Silicon Valley wonder companies, Siliconix, and also a founder of the now very powerful Semiconductor Industry Association. In 1972 he obtained the Democratic nomination for the Congressional district of Southern California, which he contested that year, but lost. According to some sources Bell Hugle, like Richard Perle, who

[153]

also claims to be a Democrat, was active in anti-Vietnam war protests in the sixties.

When the British government decided to invest $200million in its own independent chip making company, Inmos, it hired another of Silicon Valley's founding fathers to run the American end of the business. This was Dr Richard Petritz, who had founded Mostek, another early entrant into the field of silicon chips. Bell Hugle seems to have been active on the international scene since the late sixties, which is hardly surprising since the electronics industry is uniquely international. In particular, he installed himself in the UK. One of the allegations made in the United States during the Grand Jury hearings, was that the FBI suspected Bell Hugle of selling chip secrets to the Poles as early as 1974. In fact, the FBI are alleged to have claimed that Hugle fled to the UK to avoid their investigation. The FBI confirmed those allegations when I phoned them in October 1983, but the allegations must be treated with the utmost caution.

There are two reasons for this. Employees of SCT, who were privy to the material Harper had been selling to the Poles, described it on TV as 'fringey' and 'esoteric'. Harper got twenty years for his offence, but the sentence bears a direct relationship to the paranoia whipped up by the likes of Perle and little to the quality of material he sold to the Poles. Secondly, despite all the evidence they alleged they had on Hugle, which sounded quite damning when presented, the FBI were unable to secure a Grand Jury indictment against him. Given a public climate which was highly favourable towards the FBI, this is important. Based on my own extensive contacts in Silicon Valley and three or four days of virtually continuous phone calls to those contacts, I came to three conclusions which did not necessarily agree with each other, but which did at least reflect the conflicts in the evidence.

The first, based on the FBI allegations as told to me directly by them and presumably told to the Grand Jury also, was that there had been a major breakdown in communication between US and UK intelligence. If Hugle was under suspicion for selling chip blueprints to the Eastern Bloc then he should never have been allowed to get as close to the British government as he did. It was variously claimed, confirmed and then denied by the UK high technology funding body, the National Enterprise Board, later the British Technology Group, that Hugle had worked as a paid consultant to the group in 1979 and 1980. The process by which the BTG first confirmed, then denied, that he had worked for them is interesting. When the story broke, the BTG was in the process of being privatised and the government was anxiously looking for a

[154]

buyer for Inmos. A significant obstacle to any sale was the position of Dr Richard Petritz, who held shares and special rights to be consulted in the event of any change of ownership in the company.

There were other difficulties too. Inmos was meant to be a British company. Indeed, there was little else it could be, given that it was created almost entirely with British tax payers' money. Nonetheless, the bulk of the company's investment had been made in plant and facilities in Colorado Springs in the United States. This placed all of Inmos and most of its production, plant and designs, under the jurisdiction of the US Export Administration Act. It emerged clearly from the confirm and deny approach adopted by the BTG that, while they accepted the fact that Hugle had been around, 'had hopped into and out of the BTG's horizons several times' as they delicately put it, the place we should look for Hugle's contacts was in Colorado Springs. Petritz was never available personally and all his spokesman would say was that Dr Petritz had not seen Hugle since 1979. That claim was flatly contradicted by a friend of mine who joined both of them in a conversation about Inmos at a semi-conductor show in 1981. And there were also claims that in the course of his BTG connection, Hugle had met Sir Keith Joseph, then Secretary for Trade and Industry. Provided the FBI allegations were true, this indeed was a serious breach of security.

The second conclusion which directly contradicts the FBI allegations and which is partly supported by the FBI's failure to get an indictment, is that Hugle had been singled out simply because he professed an open belief in trade with Eastern Europe, as do so many distinguished American computer bosses. As the figures show the current US Administration is a dedicated believer in that proposition too, but only under its total and absolute control. No entrepreneurs please. Hugle may well have looked a very convenient target for the FBI because, popular though he was, he lacked the kind of institutional protection available to the President of, say, DEC or IBM. There were plenty of people in Silicon Valley who warned me that the attack on Hugle had at least as much to do with sending out warning signals as it did with any real evidence against him. It did not greatly matter that the FBI never got an indictment from the Grand Jury, as his business career in Silicon Valley was utterly ruined by the allegations.

Once more, the US Intelligence community and a gullible US media had established a UK connection, however tenuous, which tended to support Richard Perle's allegations that Britain was the leakiest country in the world when it came to leakages of US technology to the Eastern Bloc. This overlooked the fact that the FBI had ignored an attempt by

[155]

Harper to give himself up in 1981, and had had the matter pressed upon them by a UK intelligence source, who had come across Harper's trail in Warsaw in 1982.

The third conclusion is more of a question, or rather a number of questions. According to William Casey, Director of the CIA, in a speech given in Silicon Valley in April 1984, the agency gets its information on the Soviet technology acquisition programme thus: 'We tap scientists and businessmen who roam the world in their professional capacities, for the information that comes their way and for the insights and understanding they develop.'

Ignoring for the moment the jeopardy in which this places every US businessman and scientist travelling abroad, it does raise the question of whether Casey's bagmen had been using, or perhaps abusing, Hugle in that way. It is perfectly natural for the good citizen to pass on to his or her government information that might be useful. But there is a safe and neutral way to do it, and that is through bodies like the Department of Trade and Industry. The onus of passing the material to the Intelligence services then falls on the government itself.

The appalling danger for any business person or scientist dealing directly with the CIA is that the agency is the active, not passive, external espionage arm of the US government (the passive arm of US external intelligence is the National Security Agency). The way Harper operated placed him under the proper jurisdiction of the FBI in relation to his internal activity in the US, and under the jurisdiction of the CIA in relation to his activity outside the country. If Hugle did introduce Harper to the Poles, and if Casey's operatives were 'tapping' Hugle, as Casey's speech implied, then the CIA should have been on to Harper quite early on. It should not have fallen to a drunken fit of guilt on Harper's own part to bring him before the US courts. So the question that remains is this: had the CIA been told that Harper was in touch with the Poles? If they had, did they make any attempt to check out either his contacts or his activities? The fact that Harper gave himself up, compares interestingly with the manner in which Geoffrey Prime was turned in by a relative in the UK. In both cases the huge machinery of CIA and MI6 had failed to detect what we are led to believe were very serious breaches of Western security. As the CIA involvement in the post mortem on Harper grew, Hugle seems to have become a side issue and eventually he left the United States to return to the UK where he now lives.

Let me now take you forward to mid-April 1984 by way of a detour through Leap Year day, February 29 of that year. It was on that evening

[156]

that the meeting of the Computer Leasing Association took place. At the back of the gathering there were a number of 'unknown faces' and there were more guests present than had actually signed in for the discussion. One of my own industry friends, the managing director of a large computer company, became uneasy about the interest that strangers were taking both in the remarks I had made and in the reaction from the floor. As soon as the discussion broke up he immediately asked a US Embassy official who had identified himself if there were any CIA officers present. The Embassy official muttered that he couldn't answer that question and walked quickly and nervously away. At more or less the same moment a small group of excited people gathered around Colin Moore, and pressed him, angrily, to explain where or how he got hold of all the information he claimed to have on them and their computers. Remembering that this was moments after the ending of a meeting in which the word 'treason' had twice been audible to the speakers' table, what Moore said next is open to some dispute.

All five people standing around him remember the incident, and the questions. Three of the five say they don't recall what the answers were. Two of them say they remember the following: 'We have two people in an office . . .' The next words they claim they didn't catch.

There was a sixth party to the conversation: me. This is what I heard and passed to Paddy Ashdown as soon as I realised that the American Embassy had a complete report on the meeting and was actively seeking to mollify the dissidents: 'We have two people in an office in the Ministry of Defence who gather this information for us.'

Everything hinges on the three words, 'Ministry of Defence' which apparently only I caught.

It matters little now how accurate my memory was. When Paddy wrote to Geoffrey Pattie, then a junior minister at the MoD, asking for an explanation, he got an extremely rapid response which clearly indicated that Pattie himself, a very decent politician, was utterly unaware of the extent to which his own Ministry was cooperating with the United States in the imposition of US law in the UK. He did not need to tell Paddy that he was launching an investigation. He could easily have stonewalled but the *FT* and *Guardian* rightly made that assumption that something was wrong. A hideous amount was wrong and the question of whether it was two CIA men or ten was not the relevant point. The MoD, with an utter lack of perception about where its duties under the law lay, were busy setting up a regime for the UK computer industry based on the US model of universal militarisation

[157]

and denial of civil rights. This was laid out in page 56 of the 1984 defence estimates, which repeat the mission of the UK military in the language of the Pentagon, though with much improved grammar. The ministers responsible did not know this was happening as Pattie's letter makes clear.

In fact, Paddy's release of the letter to the *Financial Times* rather spoilt a plan we had to photograph two CIA men we believed we had discovered in the MoD. Assuming that Moore's remark, whether or not I heard it totally correctly, pointed in the right direction we had set out to find, first of all, the offices containing the fifteen people in the MoD responsible for the attempt to import the US regime into the UK, and then to examine the precise credentials of the American 'tutors' to the group. Help was given, enabling me to pinpoint two uniformed American officers who were operating in that role and who could be CIA. They left the MoD the day after the story appeared and while I was still in the United States. Thus I was never able to complete my investigations.

I always held the view that Moore's remark was intended to address two problems. At the end of his address he was under intense pressure to explain himself and the claims he had been making. Rather than reveal how the US was getting this information from the US subsidiaries, he may have thought it safer to imply that there was authorised support for the US position from the British Ministry of Defence. In general, of course, he was quite right. There was support, assistance and activity on behalf of the US, at the Ministry of Defence. The first problem was that this was support for an intrusion into UK sovereignty which was, and remains illegal under international law. The second problem was that the United States had the information, coerced illegally from the subsidiaries of US corporations, and the MoD did not. Indeed, according to a parliamentary written answer given by Paul Channon, the UK government does not even know which of its own machines are covered by US restrictions, much less how many computer installations throughout the country are little sub statelets of the US.

There was an awful fuss over another of Moore's remarks. He had said that he had enough information on all of those present to 'slap the irons on most of you'. I understood this remark to mean that most of those present were not observing the internal movement regulation in relation to changes of use and movement in the UK. It was the only remark I actually wrote down at the time, since the Chairman had asked us to be 'off the record', even though Moore formally waived this and said he didn't mind if he was reported. I preferred to observe the 'off the

[158]

record' request however, and merely duplicated for an elected representative in the UK what I knew to have been circulated in the Embassy the next day. In fact, so rattled was the Embassy by the reaction from the Leasing group, that apart from trying to have the dissent toned down at the Ambassador's breakfast party, they also phoned me to try to sow confusion as to what had actually been said. In a four-way conference call, with only one of the Embassy voices identified, I was asked to confirm, or perhaps not confirm, several remarks alleged to have been made by Moore. I saw no reason to cause trouble for him because he had spoken frankly, bluntly and with total candour. Despite my unease over the MoD remark, I felt that Colin Moore had performed quite a service to the UK computer industry and acted with considerable courage, given the palpable hostility his remarks were generating. No one left that room in any doubt about US law, intention or will to enforce that intent.

In the conference call I attempted to indicate that certain things had been said, but to avoid confirming that they had been said by Colin Moore. It was quite obvious from the call that someone at the Embassy was having a real go at Moore, who had not said a single thing that was incorrect in relation to US law. The MoD remark was not an issue at that point, indeed it was never an issue since the defence estimates appeared two months later and confirmed the general policy at the MoD. It was my incomplete investigations which had begun to show that two of the fifteen people who were liaising with the US on the issue might not be UK citizens and might indeed be CIA personnel. But it was a real pain to know that a private meeting of the UK computer industry was under surveillance by the CIA. However, there was much worse to come.

On 3 April 1984, in the Commonwealth Club of California, at Palo Alto, in the heart of Silicon Valley, William Casey, the head of the CIA, rose and gave an apparently anodyne speech, warning of the usual things, communism, communism and communism. However, the written text of his speech is quite fascinating. He claims that deals with Japanese computer companies are contrary to US national security, he predicts the appointment of Gorbachev and he boasts of having spied on almost the whole of the European computer industry. Naturally, the latter claim is the one most pertinent to this book, but for the record it is worth quoting his prediction for the Soviet succession:

'We see two men competing to come out on top in the successor generation. One is Romanov, First Secretary of the Leningrad district party, and the other is Gorbachev, whom Andropov was grooming to succeed him.'

[159]

One year later, Gorbachev succeeded Andropov who, like the American vice president George Bush, had come to the top post from within the world of international espionage. (George Bush is a former Deputy Director of the CIA.)

Having made his prediction, Casey then moved into what is best described as the 'crank up'. He sought to induce the right degree of fervour and patriotism to get his audience to swallow a half true presentation of the international scene. First of all, he attempted to justify the US attempt to break out of the 1972 ABM treaty.

'The Soviets have a large and growing arsenal of nuclear weapons which are aimed at the United States, Western Europe and East Asia. On top of that, new missiles and missile carrying planes and submarines are being designed, developed, tested and deployed in amazing profusion. This is compounded by the work the Soviets have carried on over the last decade to improve their capability for missile defence while we have done little or nothing. Recently we have seen alarming signs of radar deployments, which may go beyond the 1972 treaty limiting missile defence, the testing of interceptors and other activities which would give them a running start if they decided to break the treaty and establish a nationwide missile defence. This could heavily tip the strategic balance against us.

'On the European front, the Warsaw Pact forces outnumber us in troop strength, tanks, guns and planes. These weapons are being deployed in an increasingly aggressive way and backed up with long-range missiles which can reach European capitals.'

No doubt all this is more or less true, just as similar statements are more or less true of the United States. With hundreds of Pershing and Cruise missiles stationed in Europe, the US has exactly the same capability against Russian cities. The unsubtle difference is that the US missiles in Europe are hundreds of miles from Russian cities, while most of the Russian missile fleet is three to four thousand miles from US cities. Both Casey's points and the counterpoint facts ignore both sides' strategic submarine fleets. But the half facts continue:

'The Soviets have demonstrated increasing capability to project power over long distances beyond their national borders from bases in Cuba, Vietnam, Angola, Ethiopia and Libya. Over the last ten years we have seen them send weapons thousands of miles away to link up with Cuban troops in Angola, Ethiopia and South Yemen. Soviet power has been established in Vietnam, along China's southern border and astride the sea lanes which bring Japan's oil from the Persian Gulf; in Afghanistan, 500 miles closer to the warm water ports of the Indian Ocean

[160]

and to the Straits of Hormuz through which comes the oil essential to Western Europe; on the Horn of Africa overlooking the passageway of Suez which connects the Mediterranean Sea and the Indian Ocean; in Southern Africa, rich in minerals, which the industrial nations must have; and in the Caribbean and Central America on the very doorstep of the United States.'

Casey conveniently forgets Vietnam, which could never remotely be described as a buffer state on an American land frontier. He overlooks the US forces in Japan, Korea, West Germany, the UK, Spain, Greece, Italy, Turkey and Egypt. As a matter of strategic reality, the US has large land forces in one country with a land border with the Soviet Union – Turkey, and maintains almost a quarter of a million men under arms in West Germany which has a land frontier with a Soviet ally. Armies exist to fight wars and the Soviet Union can be forgiven for supposing that the American military have aggressive aims. Casey makes this assumption on behalf of the Soviet Union's armed forces, but never about his own. In addition, Casey was worried about the Soviet's political missions:

'From these bases we see a process of creeping imperialism to establish subservient governments in other areas of strategic significance. The most effective technique employed in this strategy has been the use of proxies. This is not exactly new in history. The Romans used men from conquered countries to fight their enemies. Later, Swiss and German mercenaries were available to the highest bidder all over Europe. The British army had its Gurkhas and the French their Foreign Legion. But the Soviets use the Cubans, East Germans, Libyans and Vitnamese in a quite different way.

'These proxies act in peace as well as war. Their role is as much political as military. East Germans in Africa, Cubans in Latin America, Vietnamese in Asia have a certain legitimacy and freedom from imperialist taint that Soviet troops would not enjoy. Different proxies have specialised functions. Of the more than 40,000 Cubans in Africa, eighty per cent of the soldiers are on active duty. Vietnam, with the fourth largest army in the world, keeps China and Thailand worried as it solidifies its position in Kampuchea. Most of the thousands of East German experts in Africa or Latin America are active in the security forces which organise block watchers to protect the regimes from the people. Libya, Cuba, South Yemen, East Germany and Bulgaria operate camps for training terrorists and insurgents who are then sent around the world.

'Terrorism has become a weapons system backed and employed by

[161]

sovereign states to destabilise, disrupt and intimidate other governments in their foreign policy. As practised today, terrorism is obliterating the distinction between peace and war. We count over fifty major terrorist organisations and a great many more 'mom and pop shows' which can be hired by Iran, Syria, Libya and other radical governments. US facilities and people here and around the world are a major target and this is a major challenge for our intelligence capabilities.'

Casey again overlooks the fact that his agency was indicted in the US for helping to organise the coup that led to the murder of the elected President of Chile, Salvador Allende, and to the death and disappearance of up to 14,000 people under the Pinochet government. Casey also 'forgets' that his agency trains and supports terrorists all over the world, including the IRA and the Basque separatist movement, so long as it causes trouble for Spain's socialist government.

The CIA were active supporters of two of the most evil and pernicious regimes in South America, that of Batista in Cuba and of Somoza in Nicaragua. Casey's own agents, under his direction, mined Nicaraguan harbours, which is an act of war under international law, and are the main avenue for US aid to a counter-revolutionary army mainly composed of ex-Somoza murderers and torturers. Terrorism is indeed a terrible blot on the face of civilisation, but it hardly behoves the head of a terrorist organisation to say so in public. Unfortunately, the Americans, unlike the Europeans, have never learnt that secrecy helps a nation avoid the moral cesspit of hypocrisy.

Casey then moves to drugs, which are a real and terrible threat to the United States, and are now becoming a similar problem in the Eastern Bloc. However, Casey, obviously a little light on historical analysis, as ever overlooks the fact that the US is the main market for drugs and much, if not most, of the trade is organised by his fellow American citizens. In fact, when US Embassy officials in London found resistance to the intrusions into the computer industry building up, they regularly put out the story that in fact all the high tech smugglers were into illegal arms and drugs as well.

'Narcotics flow into the United States from South America, the Golden Triangle of South-East Asia, from Afghanistan, Pakistan and Iran. They come in containers, they come in aircraft, they even come in stomachs. We see some of the huge amounts of money involved in this activity going into destabilising political and terrorist activity.

'Then we must cope with nuclear proliferation and technology transfer and the Third World debt and international competitiveness problems which could undermine political stability in so many countries, as well as our own security and prosperity.'

I suppose all one can say is, 'Pore ole USA, with all those problems how does it ever manage to survive it all, and maintain all those millionaires, marines, rockets, nuclear weapons, star wars plans and the third world debt?' But, having wound up his audience, Casey then moved directly in on them:

'You in this room are the bull's eye in a massive, well coordinated and precisely targeted Soviet technology acquisition programme. The ability of the Soviet military industrial complex to acquire and assimilate Western technology far exceeds any previous estimates.'

Like everything else Casey said, there is a degree of truth in this statement. Once again, however, it is but half of the truth. The other half is that the USA and particularly Casey's agency, are engaged in precisely the same activities against the Soviet Union. And the West also possesses no mean skills in converting Soviet technology into weapon systems. The skin of the Tornado fighter bomber, NATO's main front line aircraft, is based on a Russian patent. The head up display used to help pilots target their weapons and navigate very fast, in one of NATO's newest fighters, is based on a model acquired from a pilot who defected from the Eastern Bloc with his plane. A guiding principle in the development of the new British army personal weapon system is the simplicity and reliability which has enabled the Kalashnikov assault rifle to become the world's most widely used weapon.

While allowing that most of what Casey has so far said might, upon a very generous interpretation, be put down to partisan special pleading, what he next embarks upon amounts to the lie direct. This statement was made with caution and combined an absolute intention to deceive, with such a prejudicial selection of available facts, that no other conclusion is possible.

'During the late 1970s the Soviets got about 30,000 samples of Western production equipment, weapons and military components and over 400,000 technical documents both classified and unclassified. The majority was of US origin.'

At least ninety per cent of this material was sold to the Soviet Union, for cash, by the United States. The largest armaments supplier in the world is the US, so it is logical that that is where some of the weapon systems acquired by the USSR should come from.

'An increasing share of our technology is obtained through Western Europe and Japan.'

The increase in the share of sales to the Soviet Union achieved by the

[163]

West, as compared with those of the US, was from about fourteen to about eighteen per cent. US technology sales to the Soviet Union, with the exception of the latter half of 1982, which were fully compensated for in 1983, have risen, year by year, by about ten per cent per annum. Casey's next sentence is as close to the facts as he ever gets, but must be viewed in the overall context of deception. Bearing in mind that in the world of superpower politics there is no morality. The way Casey approaches the matter is to make the unjustified moral assumption that if the USSR does it, it is wrong. If we do it, it is right. But Casey himself is the head of the largest espionage organisation outside the Soviet Union, which does not limit its espionage activities to the putative enemy but, as this book shows, is active in the Alliance nations, sabotaging policies of which the US does not approve. And the following statement is simply not true, as to the facts, even if we ignore the intended moral element.

'We estimate that during this period the KGB and its military equivalent, the GRU, and their surrogates among the East European intelligence services, illegally stole about seventy per cent of the technology most significant to Soviet military equipment and weapons programmes.'

There are similarities between the two sides' weapon systems at certain levels, but in general both sides tend to use stolen data to avoid re-inventing the wheel, rather than to initiate wholly new weapon design sequences. But to suggest that about seventy per cent of the most significant Soviet weapon technology comes from the USA is stretching credulity beyond Santa Claus limits.

Casey also has another problem. A significant number of US weapon systems, particularly those which have attempted to incorporate technology, simply do not work. On the one hand, if the USSR has adopted US technology on this scale, it is a good thing. The percentage of Soviet weapons that can be counted to malfunction in any war will be high. On the other hand, if the Allied nations on the central front base their ideas of what they may face in a Soviet attack on Casey's ideas, they are in for a rude shock. Soviet weapon systems are based on a different philosophy from those in the West and that philosophy stresses ease of manufacture, ease of use, utility in a hostile environment and simplicity of function. The US has stressed the need for, but failed to deliver, electronically driven weapons such as the David anti-aircraft gun and the starfighter plane, and made endless other 'experiments' mostly with the lives of Allied pilots and sold on the basis of bribes and coercion. (The Lockhead Starfighter, for instance, known in Germany as the

[164]

widowmaker, was sold to most European countries on the basis of extensive bribery of establishment figures, including Prince Bernhard of the Netherlands.)

The catalogue which follows must be treated with the utmost scepticism:

1 The Soviets had our plans to the C-5A before it flew.
2 The Soviet trucks which rolled into Afghanistan came from a plant outfitted with $1.5billion of modern American and European machinery.
3 The precise gyros and bearings in their latest generation of ICBMs were designed by the US.
4 The radar in their AWACs is ours.
5 Their space shuttle is a virtual copy of ours . . . and the list goes on and on.

Item 1 is uncheckable.

Item 2 is partly true, but then consider that Bendix, that wonderful all-American home appliance company that used to bring you your washing machines and so many other domestic delights, also produced more nuclear warheads than any other organisation in the world. You could argue that every time you bought one of their products you added your ticket to the obscene raffle in which the fate of mankind is the stake. Ford, General Motors (Vauxhall) and IBM are all significant armaments manufacturers. If the US is prepared to tolerate this duality, what is odd about the Russian truck factory supplying the Red Army? The Russians paid for this plant, and the US government negotiated for and won the contract, defeating a series of other countries who also bid for it.

Item 3 is unprovable but logically unlikely. The Soviet Union created its strategic rocket force before the US saw the value of such a move and have the expertise of captured German scientists, as well as the resident expertise of the East Germans, to draw on, much as the US did. The probable explanation for any similarity is that there was a common source: German scientists.

Item 4: This again is thought by reputable scientists to be of the lowest order of likelihood. Notably, neither Casey nor any other Pentagon official has ever shown any inclination to prove this claim.

Item 5 has been dealt with in chapter 2, page 38.

The next section of Casey's speech began with a question: 'Just how do the Soviets get so much of our technology?'

[165]

'First of all, they comb through our open literature, buy through legal trade channels, religiously attend our scientific and technological conferences, and send students over here to study. Between 1970 and 1976 the Soviets purchased some $20billion of Western equipment and machinery, some of which had potential military applications. In addition to exploiting all open, legal channels, they use espionage.

In the first part of his answer, Casey resorts to the half fact as the most convincing form of deception. Every single activity he mentions is based on reciprocal treaties between the USSR and the USA. American students study in the USSR, American scientists regularly visit the USSR and 'religiously' visit scientific and technological conferences. All purchases of technology by the Soviet Union are subject to US veto in Cocom but much, perhaps the major proportion based on the $20 billion figure given by Casey, came from the USA itself. As to espionage: as the Economic Alert List, and the CIA operation which saw the UK ejected from its oil concessions in Dahan show, this is a stool Casey uses evenhandedly against both 'friend' and 'foe' alike.

The claim Casey makes in the next paragraph is interesting: 'There are now several thousand Soviet bloc collection officers at work primarily in the United States, Western Europe and Japan.'

Earlier CIA statements, including some made in Congress, had used a figure of 20,000 Soviet bloc collection officers. This figure had been so widely perceived as absurd that here we have Casey trying to meet scepticism with a degree of reason. The only problem is that Casey is supposed to be in the business of facts, and not in the business of misleading his own Congress and the Alliance nations.

'And as I stated before, your firms here in Silicon Valley are at the very top of their list. The Soviets especially pinpoint and target small, highly innovative companies in the computer and micro-electronics field, not only because they are at the leading edge of the technologies that Moscow is most in need of, but also because such firms' security procedures are usually inadequate to protect against penetration by a determined, hostile intelligence service.'

The volume of internal industrial espionage, combined with the volume of extravagant, not to say overstated, public relations that is endemic to Silicon Valley, puts this particular statement in a curious category. That and the fact that in the electronics age it is the idea and not its implementation that counts. In one sense Casey may be right. The Soviet Union, out of normal competitive interest, could hardly avoid Silicon Valley. On the other hand, a ruthless military analysis of that place would show that neither the US supercomputer industry, nor

[166]

the mainframe industry, nor the main centres of the minicomputer industry are located there.

To get that combination of brain and sand that is the microchip operational in weapons systems you need the design power of the other three computer categories, super, main and mini. You also need the weapon development systems centres themselves and they too are notably lacking in Silicon Valley. There is always the possibility that Casey was attempting to tap the overweening vanity of Silicon Valley in order to try to float a red herring before the Soviet Union. He must think that all his adversaries are as stupid as he. One quick survey of the Valley by a military technology expert and he would happily forget the place, or relegate it to the level of clerical perusal of the open literature.

In closing this chapter, it is essential to consider carefully whether the West can afford to tolerate the likes of William Casey as a significant influence on any of its governments, much less that of the leading government in the Western alliance. Indeed, it is essential for the peoples of the Western democracies to consider carefully the relationship between their own governments and that of a state that is prepared to authorise and license CIA operations against them. The strengths of the West lie in the simple perceptions of liberty, truth and justice, the ones you find clearly understood in the humblest village pub in Britain; that take the gravest exception to the second sentence in the IBM letter; that spring from an uncluttered sense of 'fair's fair', and upon which the nation can rely and has relied, twice in this century, to defeat the forces of evil. William Casey and the CIA represent those same forces of evil that have placed the socialist nations in the grip of the KGB and the Communist Party. They represent the same tendencies to control, secrecy, tyranny and illegal acts that have characterised the secret police throughout history.

Towards the end of his speech, Casey claims that 'intelligence is our first line of defence'. He claims that the CIA carry out this mission 'with the highest standards of integrity, morality and honour and according to the spirit and letter of the law'.

Based on the attempted deception and the total disregard for facts shown in his speech, Casey's notion of integrity gives grounds for a certain degree of considered scepticism.

The next chapter deals with the manner in which Casey's agents have observed the law in the Allied nations.

[1] *Intrepid's Last Case*, William Stephenson, Sphere Books.

[167]

CHAPTER 10

The CIA in the UK

A GOOD TALE OF THE OLD fashioned sort has a beginning, a middle and an end. This book, at the time of writing, lacks a proper ending. Court action to force the UK government to restore sovereignty, though in preparation, has not been commenced. Action by the Commission of the European Community, again in preparation, to force the US Corporations to end their illegal activity, has not been commenced publicly. And yet there had, by the end of 1985, been four significant debates in Parliament on the issue and three television programmes, each uniformly hostile to the American position. There had been endless articles in the trade press and in the *Financial Times*. But the IBM letter, like Macaulay's vision of the Catholic Church after the destruction of St Paul's Cathedral, still stood extant in all its ugly splendour. The US government imposed, unopposed, its new audit rules, requiring every US subsidiary abroad to list, in documents to be available to the US authorities in Washington, the fullest details of all their customers on 23 December 1985. Those details include the names and addresses of all directors, their bank accounts and the company bank accounts. Copies of assurances, similar to those requested in the Texas Instruments letter of May 1984, have to be lodged in Washington.

There is a chilling phrase in the Garvey memorandum which speaks of the UK being immune from forcible federalisation. Whether it was true in April 1954 is open to question. In January 1986 there is no question. The UK and Europe have become, in law, an annexed territory of the United States of America. This has happened because the elected governments of Europe have, in collaboration with their civil servants, betrayed the people who elected them.

To illustrate this point further it is necessary to go back to 17 July 1985, to an historic moment in the House of Commons. That day, for the first time ever, the House of Commons publicly examined the legislation which had governed the UK's most important exports for forty-seven years. The setting, which had taken Paddy Ashdown eighteen months of unremitting effort to arrange, was enough to deaden the most enthusiastic heart.

The notice concerning the meeting said it all. 'The Fifth Standing Committee on Statutory Instruments etc: Export of Goods (Control) Order 1985. Committee Room 12. 10 a.m.' Here, it seemed, relegated to the obscurity of Committee Room 12, the most mind-bogglingly boring debate conceivable would be held.

That, presumably, was what Paul Channon and his advisors thought, as they swung into the long Gothic corridor that gives access to the main committee rooms of the Commons. Watching Paul Channon slow down and his advisors, all seven or eight of them, virtually run into their minister, was straight out of a silent comedy film. There were fifty or sixty people standing in the corridor outside the door of Room 12. The DTI party goggled in amazement.

Paul Channon is an elected Member of Parliament and no fool. The crowd sent out a signal that would be very plain to any politician: something unexpected was happening. It was clear to everyone present, and even clearer from Paul Channon's drafted speech, that he had been given no clear warning that the issue before the committee was of far more general interest than the title of the order implied. If the DTI ministerial advisors had not twigged it, everyone else had. The substance of the Export of Goods (Control) Order was a national issue and no longer just a departmental one, limited to one area of trade, high technology.

The Minister and his minions went into a huddle about twenty feet back from the main body of those waiting to enter Room 12. Channon, looking visibly flustered, appeared to ask a question, which was obviously something like, 'Why is that crowd of people here for this obscure, boring meeting?'

We didn't hear the answer but several of us did hear the next question. 'What letter? Someone get me a copy of that letter.' Paul Channon demanded.

The letter in question was Sir Michael Havers' letter, which had been run as a story in the *Financial Times* that Monday. That was what had drawn the national press. The trade press were there in force anyhow. A fair number of other parties, including company representatives, had also shown up. There were also a significant number of foreign diplomats, including, one assumes, some from the American Embassy.

[169]

Unfortunately, no attendance book is kept, so the identity of most of the crowd remains unknown. On the other hand, eighteen MPs had been named to attend, and fifteen did so, which must be something of a record for a Statutory Instruments Standing Committee.

The Chairman called the Committee to order at 10.30 am and Paddy moved the formal motion 'That the Committee has considered the Export of Goods Control Order 1985.' The assumption is that every member of the Committee had examined the 165 pages of the order itself, the twenty pages of clarification added in the Department of Trade and Industry publication *British Business*, and that the members had also considered the hundred pages of enabling legislation which was drafted in haste in 1939 and which is known as The Defence of the Realm (Emergency Powers) Act 1939. The specific legislation which enables a senior civil servant to sign the Export of Goods Control Order into law without the benefit of ministerial or parliamentary scrutiny is known as the Emergency Powers (Customs and Excise) Act 1939. The fact that the Order was being debated at all was a kindness on the DTI's part which it did not need to exercise, as Paddy noted in his opening remarks.

The debate, and indeed the Committee, lacked an essential discipline, similar to the lack of division discipline which had affected the high technology debate in 1984. No matter what the Committee thought, or said, the order would become law ten days later. Parliament, in effect, had no actual power over this piece of critical trade legislation, which in its 1985 form had finally seen the light of day on 3 June 1985. The interesting thing about 3 June was that it represented the fifth deadline set by ministers in writing, starting with a first deadline in December 1984. Seldom can a piece of legislation have had such a fraught and rocky passage through the government drafting departments, as the United States rejected version after version produced in the UK. And the US version was doing no better. Rushed into law on 31 December 1984, it was withdrawn from the statute book (the Federal Register) three times before June 1985, and was still in suspense as Paul Channon finally imposed what amounted to American legislation on the UK high technology industry. A fine irony indeed.

Paddy's speech lasted twenty-four minutes. It contained forty or fifty hours of research and possibly a day of Paddy's time in drafting. It focused, quite deliberately, on the substance of the Order and not the technicalities. Having stated his clear and unequivocal support for the principle of control of militarily sensitive high technology, Paddy noted that the Order, 'places under licence control, to all destinations,

[170]

virtually all technology relating to computer and electronics goods made in and traded in the United Kingdom, except for some very low level material.'

The key problem that this presented, Paddy said, was that, 'the order defines military technology so broadly that it is . . . practically unenforceable and so does not achieve its aim . . . of protecting our high technology secrets from falling into the hands of potential enemies.'

That point has been laboured elsewhere in this book, but to understand fully just what the relics of the UK high technology were about to face, it is necessary to go on to a later section of Paddy's speech, where he deals with the consequences of the legislation on small firms trying to export even to France.

'There are three levels of licensing control. At the lowest level are goods that can be exported from the United Kingdom without a licence. They include very few items – probably just a few raw chips. The next level is the so-called discretionary level at which the Department of Trade and Industry can, at its own discretion, issue licences to exporters. According to the Minister at a recent press conference, licence applications for 46,000 of these items were received by the Department in the first six months of this year. One of his officials said that he expected about 100,000 applications for licences over the whole year. I understand that the total number of staff available to handle those applications is nineteen. That means that each official will have between five and six minutes to review each licence application.

'That would be bad enough, but the order will make the position worse by making it more complicated. There are now three types of country to which exports need to be rigorously controlled. There is the Eastern Bloc, as before; a second category of twelve nations known as diversionary destinations which must be scrutinised, and a third group subject to control for foreign policy reasons, which includes South Africa and Israel. To compound confusion further, it states that there are no fewer than seven different licences for which application can be made. The Minister has not yet finished formulating one of them – the so-called flexible licence – although he intends to make the order effective from next week. All of that will have to be judged and decided by a Department of Trade and Industry official in just five or six minutes.

'I understand that DTI officials have said that it might be necessary to provide the specifications for computers or software for which a licence was sought. Specifications for a PDP11 – a very old computer – run to about 400 pages. How can nineteen people do that job with such a volume of detail?

[171]

'The simplest application form to be filled in by the exporter comprises about eighty questions spread over four pages with twelve pages of notes. That will be difficult enough for the large firms, but for the small firms it will represent an almost impossible burden in extra bureaucracy. If it were not tragic, it would be ironic that today's newspapers are full of the government's attempts to lift the burden on small industry, when the Minister is planning to bring into effect an order that will massively increase those burdens on the industry that provides the new technology on which we depend so heavily.

'That adds up to a horrendously complicated matrix of licensing and regulation, which will be barely understood by the DTI and be altogether impossible for the industry. The number of staff available to run the system is hopelessly inadequate and delays will be inevitable. Even now, there are licence applications that have been outstanding for more than a year. The order can only make the position worse, and British high-tech companies will pay the price in lost orders and lost exports.'

If this is not the Roman yoke of old, renewed by the United States in a novel form and imposed on the subject peoples by their own sovereign body, nothing is. And it is vital to know just what this immense burden of bureaucracy was aimed at protecting. The hardest elements of this legislation are aimed at protecting hardware from just one company, DEC. Paddy quoted the Lord Chief Justice:

'Individuals who have in the past exported PDP11s (from the UK) have been prosecuted and gaoled under the predecessor of this order. In a recent famous case concerning Mr Michael Ludlam, the Lord Chief Justice, Lord Lane, commented in a judgment, "Let it be said at once, it is almost certain that they (that is, the PDP11s) were of no direct military use." '

Paddy continued: 'The Lord Chief Justice had before him the testimony of Professor Martin Healey, a professor of microprocessing engineering. Professor Healey concluded that the computers were totally unacceptable for military work.'

The absurdities were indeed multiplying, but only because the UK Civil Service were seeking to introduce laws alien in origin and deeply inimical in purpose, into the UK. There is no way a minister charged with running a department staffed by a cast of thousands can be expected to understand technical legislation in detail. For that he employs experts and lawyers and on this one both those parties grievously defaulted. They defaulted thus: the legislation is both inaccurate and incomplete. A non-statutory publication, *British Business*, is needed to provide exactness and precision. How is a judge to try such a

[172]

case? Does he sentence the victim for failing to observe the EGCO? In the case of Brian Butcher, before Judge Ellison in Reading Crown Court, on 18 and 19 November 1985, this very point arose. The Order would have all semiconductor testers licensable. *British Business* categorically stated that only those with a wafer-carrying capacity of 3 × 3 or greater needed a licence. The case did not hinge upon this point, and Judge Ellison's eminently common-sense judgment eliminated the need for an appeal, but one could have been made on just that point. Men cannot, as Solon the ancient lawmaker noted, be expected to obey inexact laws, yet the British high technology community is expected to do just that and more.

On 17 July 1985, just eight days before the legislation came into effect, the DTI had neither published nor made available details of many of the new licence forms which would be needed from that day. Apart from those technical deficiencies, there was another serious flaw in the order.

Paddy reminded the Minister that, 'At a press conference to announce the order, the Minister's officials admitted in his presence that material which can be freely (and undetectably) transmitted over the telephone as software is not policeable.'

Software is the name given to the instructions which tell computers what to do. The instructions can be fed into a machine orally, visually or via a keyboard. They look, in print, like a cross between shorthand and English, which is more or less what they are. They can be sent by radio and transmitted by phone. The EGCO set a number of restrictions on certain kinds of software, without providing a scientifically acceptable definition of what software is, thus leaving the judiciary with a very amusing little legal problem somewhere out there in the future.

It is not unfair, I hope, to say that Paul Channon did not answer the vast majority of points made by Paddy. How could he? He arrived with a prepared speech, which added a surrealistic element to the proceedings. Paddy's speech, carefully designed to last less than the thirty minutes he had been allocated, had been specific. Paddy dealt with what was actually in the order, and with the strict consequences of those contents in terms of their application to the computer and electronics industry. Paul Channon's speech gave few clues as to what would happen under the new regime. The high technology industries may be roughly divided into five different areas: electronics, software, computers, telecommunications and robotics. Software was brought into the net for the first time, so was telecommunications. The regulations on robotics were extended. To claim that fewer products were now

[173]

included in the licensing regimes was flying in the face of the facts. The narrow point on which Paul Channon was hanging by the skin of his platitudes in order to suggest that the new order was less onerous than the old, was an unpublished instrument called an open general licence. Dubious though this device may be in law, it was an administrative and political brainwave. And it came, not from the beleaguered Department of Trade and Industry but from a Conservative backbencher called Spencer Batiste, the MP for Elmet, near Leeds.

A solicitor by profession, Spencer Batiste, like Paddy, was a new MP. With Systime's directors living in his constituency, he had become aware very early in 1983 of the problem of American extra-territoriality. And he had set about doing something about it, behind the scenes as well as in front of them, where he was almost as vociferous as Paddy. Indeed, early on in the saga Paddy had offered to pass the whole issue and all the documents on to Spencer, on the basis that Spencer could achieve a lot more from within the government party than he could from the Opposition front benches. Two sets of political antennae opposed this, for diametrically opposite reasons. I felt that Paddy had done so much, and to such good effect, for both the Liberals and himself, that it was wrong of him to give away an issue with so much mileage still in it. And Spencer, sensing as many of the sharper Conservatives do, that Paddy is a political figure who, in the future, will pose a great challenge to their party, declined the gift.

This did not stop him from being effective, however. If Paddy's persistence yielded the debate on the order, it was Spencer who won the six-week delay between the publishing of the order and its implementation. It was also Spencer who proposed to Paul Channon that he create a special open general licence, which the minister would hold, and under which quite a lot of technology could be shipped to various destinations without the need for any paperwork. Evidently no one told the enforcers about this, however. As late as December angry letters were still appearing in *The Times*, complaining about ignorant Customs officials insisting that anything with a keyboard on it was to be seized and detained, on its way to other EEC countries.

This was another appalling example of the incompetent manner in which the bureaucracy handled this issue. The DTI are responsible for licensing, Customs for enforcement. By 17 July, with much of the documentation neither published nor available, it was quite clear that no real effort had been made to train or educate Customs in the new regulations. As late as June 1985, Customs and Excise had seized a fully declared Apple II computer on its way to Turkey and threatened the consignee with prison and a huge fine on the grounds that Turkey was an Eastern Bloc country. Turkey is one of the oldest and most important members of NATO, and the Apple II computer is the technological equivalent of the penny farthing bicycle. Faced with Customs officials whose judgment on both the technology and the destination is so grievously wrong, is it any wonder that most high technology companies, especially the small ones, don't export at all? Before Spencer Batiste made his key contribution to debate, it is worth briefly mentioning some of the things the three other Conservatives who spoke, said.

Tim Smith, the MP for Beaconsfield, told Paul Channon that he had three worries over the way the UK was applying the existing licensing regime, all expressed to him by the UK subsidiary of a major US electronics and computer manufacturer, Perkin-Elmer.

'Export licences have always been difficult to obtain from the Department of Industry, but recently, due to changes in the rules, the situation has become quite intolerable. Currently, we have a backlog of approximately £1.4 million of goods awaiting licences with delays ranging out to a maximum of seven months.'

Mr Smith was quoting Perkin-Elmer's first worry. Their second was that: '. . . the United Kingdom is almost always more rigorous than other countries in its application of the rule.' And thirdly, the complexity and bureaucracy of the regulations meant that the company had to apply for licences, to export even to other Cocom countries.

Coming back to 17 July 1985, when the disaster of the 1984 agreement had become apparent, Paul Channon found himself surrounded by some very uneasy fellow Conservatives.

Ivor Stanbrook, the Conservative MP for Orpington in Kent, quoting Professor John Ashworth, the Chairman of the Information Technology Economic Department Committee of the National Economic Development Office, said, 'Many information technology firms will find themselves in strategic export controls for the first time from 25 July. Most of those firms do not consider that they are involved in defence or strategic applications.'

Mr Gerry Neal, the Conservative Member for Cornwall North told Paul Channon that, 'Organisations and companies which contribute largely to the country's export effort are asked to give their views on them [new licensing regulations] when it is impossible for them to do so effectively without a draft of the licences which they are expected to accommodate.'

However, it was Spencer Batiste who most strongly expressed the real unease felt on the Conservative backbenches: 'I am,' he said, 'still dubious about including software. I accept that it has strategic value, but no one has explained how software licensing can be effectively policed.'

Later he told Paul Channon that, 'Although the thresholds of control have been raised . . . they are still too low in some instances.' He then added his voice to all the others that had complained about delays. '. . . the majority of severe delays arise when licence applications must be referred to the full Cocom Committee . . . That procedure causes serious difficulties to [companies] in all our constituencies.'

But it was on the extra-territorial issue that Spencer Batiste's warnings were sternest: 'What is the benefit to this country in persevering with Cocom if the US Government demonstrates such little faith in their allies as to ride roughshod over their rules and sovereignty? Why should our companies have to operate a dual licensing system when American companies, which are our principal competitors, operate only one? I understand that the issue has been raised repeatedly with his United States counterpart by my Right Honourable friend [Paul Channon] and the Secretary of State, but the conflict of extra-territoriality remains unresolved. To that extent, we are conducting a dialogue with the deaf.'

Later Batiste added: 'We are responsible partners, and we intend to be treated as such. Unless the United States government are prepared to recognise that, Cocom is running on borrowed time.'

By coincidence, the debate on trade with China took place the following day. Beginning with the Conservative Chairman, Cocom was strafed from every side.

'I am extremely worried,' Ken Warren told a fairly full House, 'at the rumours about substantial American companies engaging in sales drives in China. We fear that soon they will say that the items can be sold, and they will tell Cocom that they can be sold. By then we shall have been outflanked.' (We already have been. See Chapter 6.) There were twenty-one further references to Cocom, eighteen of them negative, three neutral.

To produce the full analysis that would show how the British computer industry was virtually destroyed by the United States would require a different and longer book than this. However, the methods of the United States come into high relief when it comes to Systime PLC. This company was started outside Leeds in 1976 by a wily, aggressive Yorkshireman called John Gow. It grew to a turnover of over £40 million

[176]

and 1,200 employees in 1983. By the end of 1985 the company had been dismembered, and conservative estimates for employment at Systime in 1986 were 200 people.

A number of factors, including over-rapid, under-funded expansion, contributed to the collapse of the company. But despite those factors, the role of the US administration, the Economic Counsellor at the Embassy, the Embassy Customs team, and sundry other US officials at critical moments during attempts to finance the company in the normal way, can fairly be blamed for the direct loss of 1,000 jobs in the Leeds area. It happened like this.

Systime grew initially from its beginnings as a reseller of DEC equipment. John Gow found a way to obtain DEC equipment from vendors in the United States, at a discount of between twenty and thirty per cent on the price the DEC subsidiary in the UK was charging. By 1980, John Gow was looking for new export markets. He discovered the illegal double licence bind. He also discovered that DEC had become extremely vicious and had begun a 'Kill Systime' campaign, starting at a conference at Gleneagles in Scotland in 1979.

Part of the campaign by DEC was a series of actions in the US to cut Systime off from its suppliers there. Systime fought the DEC restrictions in the US, but eventually ran out of money. So John Gow looked for markets in which DEC was not active, having also discovered that any market in which DEC was active was effectively closed to him because of the way in which the US operates the distribution licence system. That system works like this: DEC in the United States operates its exports to other countries based on a series of US Commerce Department distribution licences. These licences relate to specific countries or groups of countries. Within any one country, say the UK, a secondary vendor like Systime, if it wishes to export a DEC machine to France, has to get two licences, one from the United States and one from the Department of Trade and Industry. That can take up to a year, while DEC, with its general distribution licence to France, can export direct into France, from the US, without an individual licence application to any other country. If that sounds unfair, rest assured, it is. It is also illegal. It is a multiple breach of the Treaty of Rome and at the time of writing the whole position of how the distribution licence set up works against EEC Companies is under investigation by the Commission.

John Gow's solution to these constraints was to export DEC equipment from the UK to India, Pakistan, Libya and Iran, using only UK export licences. This is perfectly legal, but as soon as DEC heard about

[177]

the situation, they called in a firm of private detectives. One outcome of this was a direct intervention by DEC's lawyers in Systime's financial negotiations in January 1983. When John Gow decided to use only UK export licences he had calculated that discovery by the US authorities would cost him around $400,000. He made provision for this, and when the crunch came in 1982 he and his finance director, the Hon. Andrew Kaberry, made a voluntary disclosure to the US authorities. But the allegations made by the DEC lawyers were more serious and amounted to a claim that Systime had shipped up to 400 DEC systems to the Eastern Bloc via Switzerland, disguised as juke boxes. UK financiers fought shy of supporting Systime in 1983 and a large US corporation, CDC, which was owed $9million by Systime, took a forty-two per cent stake. From there on, it was disaster all the way.

In the US a grand jury investigation was launched into Systime's exports. On 19 July 1984, acting on information supplied to them by US Customs, UK Customs raided Systime. They found the horse gone. Key export documentation was missing. This was the material that the Prime Minister refused to confirm had not been removed by US officials. That did not stop UK Customs officials from detaining the Managing Director's secretary incommunicado for approximately eleven hours. Sue Arnold was eventually allowed home in an hysterical state, having been refused permission to contact her husband and having been threatened with instant arrest if she stopped talking. Her detention has led to questions in Parliament which had not been answered at the end of 1985.

Systime was effectively cut off from all US supplies. Overall, the US Department of Commerce received three sets of Systime documentation, or documentation relating to Systime. The first set were the voluntary disclosures made by John Gow and the Hon. Andrew Kaberry. The second set, assumed to be the private investigator's report into Systime done for DEC UK, was assumed to be delivered by DEC since that is what DEC lawyers implied they would do to Systime's bankers. The third set are the documents found to be missing when the UK Customs raided Systime in July 1984.

With access to US supplies cut off, and with a major fine in the United States in prospect, CDC, which already owned forty-two per cent of Systime, was forced to increase its stake to over ninety per cent in 1985, when the UK investors took their losses and refused to come up with further finance. The threat of further US action was a total deterrent. As the letters between John Gow and Tim Deal show, Deal was well aware of the US attempt, not merely to cut off all supplies to

Systime, but to fine the company, and to place all its future sales, both internally in the UK and exports from the UK, under American control. When Deal got up in Cambridge and said that all the US would do in such situations was cut off supplies, he was telling a categoric lie. Not only that, but he had full and total knowledge of the export restraints imposed on ICL, which again means his statement was deliberately untrue.

And Deal was not the only one telling lies to the Allied peoples in 1985. In his *Today in Politics* encounter with Richard Perle on 7 December 1984, Paddy had told him that, 'I believe that you are just about to publish some guidelines on how you will actually license people with that information, moving out of the United States.'

To this assertion Perle responded, as he responded the following day to a gathering of very senior UK government and industry executives: 'That's complete rubbish and I'm delighted to have an opportunity once and for all to set it to rest, because it's been repeated on a number of occasions. We have no intention of restricting – have never suggested we restrict – the personal freedom of individuals.'

According to the ICL memorandum on US trade law, drawn up for ICL by a team of US attorneys: 'If ICL employs an American engineer to write a report or a piece of software, that report or software is controlled under US law – ICL has in fact had to obtain US export licences to cover knowledge carried in the heads of American engineers.'

On 8 December 1984, during the conference at which Perle spoke, the Chairman of ICL confirmed that in practice American engineers had to get an export licence to leave the United States to work for ICL in the UK. Perle's assertion that the US has made no move to restrict personal freedoms is doubly spurious. In 1984 the Pentagon issued Directive 2040.2. According to Professor Heinrich Vogel, this memorandum, which is understood to have originated in Perle's department, 'tries to militarise large areas of R&D and severely limits exchange of information in scientific co-operation with non-US corporations or individuals.'

Aside from the eight open scientific conferences to which access was denied to European scientists by the Pentagon, and which the UK listed to the EEC Commission, there was the extraordinary case of the Society of Photo-optical Instrumentation Engineers.

In the second week of April 1985, an open conference being run by SPIE was taken over by the Pentagon. During registration for the conference, all foreigners, including a number of UK engineers, were turned away and told they would not be admitted unless they were

[179]

vetted by their embassies, and signed US Export Control agreements prepared by the Pentagon. No foreign embassy had been warned of the US action and none had any means of carrying out the vetting. US nationals were themselves refused admission to the suddenly closed sessions, unless they too signed the Pentagon sponsored Export Control forms and registered on a special Pentagon computer.

When I contacted the Pentagon two weeks later I was told that the restrictions were part of a nationwide programme being run by the international policy department of the Department of Defence. Richard Perle was then the assistant Secretary of Defence for international security policy.

The following week, 23 April 1985, Jack Robertson, the government correspondent for the US trade paper *Electronics News*, which first reported the SPIE incident, wrote that 'the ominous DoD plan to control unclassified open technical and scientific discussions at industry and professional meetings poses one of the greatest threats to scientific and personal freedom . . . more than that, it is just plain stupid.' He referred to the DoD personnel involved in the issue as the 'DoD technical thought police'.

In the wake of this incident, the first of several emergency visits to Europe by senior American academics took place. Dale Corson, the president elect of Cornell University made a flying visit to the Royal Academy in Sweden and to the Royal Society in London. What transpired is not known, except that a much larger team from the US National Academy of Sciences flew into London on 14 January 1985. They spent a whole day at the Royal Society and a day with the government at the Department of Trade and Industry. On the 15th they were presented with an utterly uncompromising message at a meeting at the House of Commons with Opposition MPs, including Paddy Ashdown (Liberal), Brian Gould (Labour), Ian Wrigglesworth (SDP), and Spencer Batiste (Conservative). They were told that unless the US took immediate steps to correct the basic illegalities under international law, counter-action would be taken.

'If we leave you gentlemen under the impression that there is any basis for reasonable negotiations while the US government maintains its breach of this country's sovereignty, and its unchallenged suppression of the constitutional rights of UK citizens, then we do us both a grave disservice.

'The fact that the UK government has taken no legal action to restore the jurisdiction of this House in the UK, is the constraint on us. Measures leading to extensive legal action are in hand.'

[180]

The delegation were later informed that the US action had placed the UK in breach of five major international treaties, three of them specifying the fundamental right to academic and scientific freedom.

Before moving to the larger scheme of things it is worth considering several other statements made by Perle in his *Today in Politics* programme. Perle claimed that, 'We have no desire to extend America's law abroad.'

This, in the light of the Export Administration Act, the IBM letter and finally the new controls imposed on 23 December 1985, is another downright lie. Pressed by Peter Jay, who suggested that if the US did not get its way in multilateral negotiations, it would pass the law and so far as it was physically able, apply that law in Europe. Perle denied it, but the United States then did just that, under direct pressure from Perle himself or his department in the Pentagon, when they passed a new Export Administration Act, even more extra-territorial in its effect than any previous act. A little later, and despite the Root letter, and the direct evidence of the DTI Cocom negotiators given to twenty UK journalists, Perle denied that the US was acting unilaterally in relation to the Cocom agreement.

Paddy then questioned Perle on the US Export Denials List. According to Perle it was a list of firms which had violated the Cocom regulations, and generally consisted of fly-by-night operations that buy equipment from the United States for the sole purpose of passing it on to the Soviet Union at inflated prices. The US Export Denials List has got nothing whatsoever to do with Cocom and is created specifically by the US Export Administration Act, an Act that is publicly repudiated by most of the Cocom member states, including the UK. Piher, the largest electronics company in Spain, is no fly-by-night operator and was put on the Denials List for allegedly supplying US origin technology to Cuba.

Later again Paddy raised the question of the US government agents running around the UK. Perle said that the US 'does not conduct investigations in this country without the full cooperation and consent of the British government'.

The British government issued a prompt denial and Paddy was able to point out to Perle that the Prime Minister had described such claims as 'unsubstantiated'.

When they were discussing the question of US shipments of PDP11 computers into the Eastern Bloc, Perle said that it was the VAX 11/780s that really mattered. 'Those computers are now being used to programme missile trajectories, that are aimed at London and Washington.'

[181]

This is a gross exaggeration. Soviet missiles were targeted on to London and Washington fifteen or twenty years before the first VAX was built. A VAX could be used for that purpose but it is unlikely that the Soviet Union would use computers of uncertain continuity of supply for any functions connected with intercontinental ballistic missiles.

It is no secret that there are a number of NATO governments who would be very grateful to the United States government if it made Richard Perle a prohibited export from the United States. The US Embassy in London used to speak of 'damage limitation exercises', after Perle had been let loose in the UK, particularly in the media. Now that he travels as President Reagan's minder at summit talks (in Geneva 1985, Perle replaced Caspar Weinberger) he has learned a lot more diplomacy. This does not alter the fact that Perle, more than any other member of the present US administration, has driven NATO to the brink of destruction over the extra-territorial and high technology issue.

It is curious to watch Perle on TV when he is faced with an informed opponent like Paddy Ashdown. The normally confident champion of America and its allies looks distinctly shifty. Nor did he look any happier when the Chairman of the Congressional Foreign Trade Subcommittee, Congressman Don Bonker, challenged the legality of the Pentagon's funding for Operation Exodus and of its interference in the Commerce Department licensing process. Bonker suggested that companies affected by either operation should sue the Pentagon. Of the six speakers who addressed the meeting five attacked Perle, some, like Professor Vogel, with a great deal more vehemence than others. Perle was the sixth speaker. His worst moment came in response to his claim that the Soviet Union was virtually totally dependent on stolen US technology for its computer needs. Tony Ebel, the Chairman of Quest Automation, a small UK company with extensive Soviet business, got up and addressed Perle. There was a real smell of cordite in the air and a sense that we were hearing the man from the trenches.

'When I was in the Soviet Union three years ago, there was very little computer technology visible.' He paused. 'When I was in the Soviet Union three months ago I saw computer factories that I would like to have here in the UK. Computers similar to the PDP/11 are in volume production. We have seen prototypes of the Soviet equivalent to the VAX.'

When Ebel sat down, Perle's head had sunk deep between his shoulders and he was staring at him as though he were something from Planet X.

Perhaps the most bizarre of all the events surrounding the activities promoted by Perle was the arrest in Britain by the UK Customs high technology team, of one of MI6's sources in the Eastern Bloc. Indeed, when the government was asked in Parliament if any of those arrested in the Customs operations were employees of government departments, the reply that such information was not collated centrally and could only be obtained at disproportionate cost, was deemed confirmation of the allegation by one *Times* correspondent, as well as by *Computing*, the paper that ran the story.

In fact, an attempt by the US intelligence agencies to eliminate all, or most, UK high tech sources in the Soviet bloc, was thoroughly logical after Perle's reception on 7 and 8 December 1984. His discovery of the rising level of informed opposition to his policies – or US policies, depending on which way you wish to look at it – obviously shocked him deeply. In fact, some time in April 1985 I was told that one of the UK liaison officers to US Intelligence, presumably the CIA, had asked for my records and those of Paddy Ashdown and Spencer Batiste. We had all three spoken at a seminar on 14 February at which we had been very critical of US policy. My records, which I was once told were very obvious 'because they come in two wheelbarrows' have been requested at least twice via the liaison arrangements.

The interesting question here is just what laws govern the transfer by the government of my country of my personal and military records to the (unfriendly) intelligence services of a foreign power. A nice one for the lawyers, that.

But looking out into 1986 I am more optimistic about the ending of the United States intrusion into the United Kingdom than I have ever been. A number of things make me feel this way.

During 1985 the UK government made a series of very unhappy discoveries. The Trident submarine programme, in the course of which the UK will spend over $10billion with US missile contractors, will generate about $60million of work for UK companies, not at all what the best endeavours work-sharing clause in the agreement implies. The Prime Minister, in a bid to maintain the tempo of her political relationship with President Reagan, virtually ordered Michael Heseltine to get an agreement for UK participation in Star Wars (SDI) at any price. That was how Heseltine came around to seeing what Paddy and I had been seeing and saying for two years, namely that the US is not in a legally workable mode in relation to high technology.

The memorandum of understanding that Weinberger and Heseltine signed in November 1985 is one of the most meaningless bits of paper ever to be signed by Allied nations. Michael Heseltine simply got nowhere. Weinberger and his staff never budged from the principle of total US control, including direct Pentagon supervision of contracts and censorship of publication for all Star Wars work. Further, just as in the Cocom negotiations, if such they can be called, Weinberger insisted on the movement control of those with Star Wars data in their heads, and, unlike the Cocom negotiations where this issue was dropped, there was no give on the American side at all. It was take it or leave it and the leave taking that Michael Heseltine so spectacularly took during a Cabinet meeting concerning Westland later in the year is reliably understood to have commenced psychologically during the 'negotiations' with Weinberger. What happened to Heseltine was that he discovered what UK civil servants had known for years, but due to poor political guidance or interference from the higher levels of the civil service, had not been allowed to convey to Ministers or to the public. This was, namely, that the US does not negotiate; it bullies, blackmails and blusters, especially with the Allies.

In the background there was Heseltine's spectacular failure to secure the US battlefield communications system order for the UK bidder Plessy, and the political egg he collected on his own and the Prime Minister's face when he persuaded her to write to President Reagan to try and secure the order.

It is reliably reported from Paris that the US Embassy there, in conjunction with the French Government and the French bidders, had secured the order for France, partly based on alleged French willingness to place all 3,000 members of the French Secret Service at the disposal of the American campaign to deny high technology to the East Bloc – from anywhere except the US. According to one source close to the Embassy, Timothy Deal (he of several appearances in the UK and this book) is supposed to have complained bitterly that all the UK would provide for the campaign was nine people.

It is not clear how much of this was known to Heseltine when he made his spectacular exit from the Cabinet, but if the echoes of Paddy's words in his farewell speech on the day after his departure are anything to go by, then he too has come to see the dangers of working too closely with an ally that has now become so overbearing and illegal in its international operations.

The curious thing is that Paddy had been warning Heseltine for over a year that Westland was in serious difficulties, and he had been ignored. He has been warning the Prime Minister on the computer issue for a little longer, though no less emphatically.

[184]

Will the final denouement be as spectacular? Time will tell, and that time may be soon.

As this book indicates, the legal tide in the UK and in Brussels and Strasbourg is moving in our direction. In itself, that is neither one thing nor another, unless it persuades Europe to consider carefully the following disastrous balance sheet which shows the number of manufacturers of computers and other related high-technology products.

	Mainframe Manufacturing	Minicomputer Manufacturing	Supercomputer Manufacturing
JAPAN	5	3+	3
USA	6–7	10+	2
USSR	2	5	2
EUROPE	—	1	—

	Independent Microprocessor Chip Design	Manned Space Vehicles	Submarine Projects	Large-scale Civilian Aircraft Manufacturing
JAPAN	2–4	Nil	3	3
USA	8–12	1 (disabled)	4	5
USSR	6–10	2	4	3
EUROPE	(1)	Nil	2	1

APPENDIX I

Shotgun Diplomacy

SHOTGUN DIPLOMACY

Telegrams Nos. 1534 and 1535 to Washington, of which I attach copies, represent the latest move in the campaign for reducing East-West trade controls. To clinch the argument the President of the Board of Trade reverts to his favourite theme that, if the Americans do not accept our point of view, and that quickly, we shall advertise our disagreement to the other dozen or so members of the Paris Group, and endeavour to unite the Europeans against the United States. I think it is fair to describe this as the "favourite theme" of the President of the Board of Trade, since he has been playing variations upon it ever since March 22 (see this minute to the Prime Minister of that date at Flag A), and he continued to do so throughout the conversations in London with Mr. Stassen and M. Schumann at the beginning of this month.

2.   This policy of holding the Americans up to ransom is not, as might be thought, some aberration of the President's, resulting from lack of coordination between the Board of Trade and the Foreign Office. On the contrary, the commercial appetites of the Board of Trade have been harnessed to the Prime Minister's notions about domesticating the Russians by turning the U.S.S.R. into a welfare state, and about the possibility of "friendly infiltration" through trade: with the result that it is now evidently the considered policy of H.M. Government to go after a massive reduction of strategic export controls regardless of the consequences elsewhere.

3.   It is not the purpose of this minute to suggest that we should attempt here and now to reverse this state of affairs. The present policy has been opposed by the Foreign Office all along the line, but we have been steadily defeated. We should however not delude ourselves that it is a right policy, and should be on the alert for any turn of events which might enable us to reverse it.

4.   The case for not behaving as, under the impulse of the President and the Prime Minister, we have recently been behaving, is this. Britain claims, in her dealings with the United States, what we have frequently called a "special relationship". This is, in a small measure, a matter of sentiment (common ancestry, common law, etc.,), but rests mainly with a certain amount of justification, to be America's only reliable ally, the only one that will fight, the only one that really tightens its belt and so on. The Americans also rely on us quite a bit, though they do not admit it, for political know-how and common sense. It is on the basis of our "special relationship" founded upon these real, or supposed, qualities that we have had the Loan, the lion's share of Marshall Aid, comparative immunity from forcible federalisation, and so on.

5.   Few things could be more destructive of the "special relationship" than a demonstration, on a matter of real importance to the United States Government, that Britain is not merely in herself no better than the squalling and selfish Europeans, who are continually trying to blackmail and brow-beat the United States into doing things for them, but is also prepared to desert the side of the United States, and rouse the Europeans to revolt against her.

6.   It has always been the custom for the business of the Paris Group to be pre-digested at an Anglo-American meeting a few days in advance.   Thereafter, the two of us have squared the French (who hold the Chair in the Group), and thereafter i has generally not been too difficult to get the right decision from the plenary.   It is against this background of especially close Anglo-American consultation that Mr. Thorneycroft's tactic of threatening to raise the crew to mutiny must be judged.   Nor indeed is this matter one on which the United States Government have much latitude. Mr. Stassen has by a skilful publicity campaign improved the atmosphere very markedly in the last twelve months.   But American opinion is simply not ready for a de-control of East-West trade on the lines which commend themselves to Ministers here, and pressure on the Administration, while undermining our relationship and weakening our general bargaining position, is unlikely even so to achieve its objective.

T.W. Garvey
April 12, 1954

    Mr Garvey is quite right to draw attention to this danger. It has not arisen yet.   But it may, if the President of the Board of Trade does not consider that Mr. Stassen's reply is satisfactory.

    In that case I take it that there can be no question of our tabling our short list on machine tools and rolling mill items without the question being considered by Ministers.   In a previous minute you agreed that such proposed action should go to the Secretary of State personally before it was taken.   On that occasion it related to the whole list.   But in my own view it should equally apply to the present list of machine tools and rolling mill items, which is a very important section of the whole.

Lord Reading
March 14, 1953.

APPENDIX II

Correspondence between Paddy Ashdown MP and
The Prime Minister

HOUSE OF COMMONS
LONDON SWIA OAA

Rt. Hon. M. Thatcher, MP
Prime Minister
10 Downing Street
LONDON
SW1

Our ref :- JJDA/KAM//21/07/83.
Date :- 6 November 1984

I want to begin my letter by bringing to your attention a speech by Mr
William Casey, the Director of the CIA, given at the Commonwealth Club,
Palo Alto, California, on 3rd April 1984.

In my role as opposition spokesman, it has fallen to me to investigate
part of the contents of this speech, on page 7 and page 10. I have
established to my own satisfaction, and have had the CIA admit, that there
are a number of UK companies amongst the 300 Mr Casey says he has
identified as trading illegally with the Eastern Bloc. My subsequent
investigations have led me to conclude that the CIA got the information
on the UK companies in the course of an operation in this country, an
operation which, it seems, is still continuing. I therefore attach to
this letter a number of instances of interference with UK companies by US
officials of unspecified agency background.

I am sure that you will appreciate that my resources are not sufficient to
conduct a full investigation into these matters. However, I am clear that
there is sufficient evidence, albeit some of a circumstantial nature, to
pose very serious questions which ought to be investigated, about the
possibility of CIA activity on this matter in Britain.

Needless to say, I support appropriate controls to prevent high
technology which has military or security value from falling into the
hands of the Eastern bloc. However, I am sure you would agree that this
is a matter which, within the UK, is for the UK Security Services alone to
consider. Any interference from another nation, even a friendly one, in
the operations of UK companies and actions which are subject to UK law is
something which must raise very grave concern indeed.

I hope that you will agree that there are now serious and important
questions to be answered and will institute an enquiry into this whole
affair.

Yours sincerely

Paddy Ashdown MP
Encs.

1O DOWNING STREET

THE PRIME MINISTER

27 November, 1984

Dear Mr. Ashdown,

Thank you for your letter of 6 November about a possible CIA operation against British companies in the computer technology field.

The points raised in your letter, and your letter of 27 March to Norman Tebbit, have been carefully examined by the appropriate departments. As Paul Channon told you in his letter of 9 May, allegations about the involvement of the CIA are unsubstantiated. There is no evidence of improper activity by the CIA or that the law has been broken. As you are aware, there is close co-operation between the British and American authorities on the enforcement of multilaterally agreed export controls which is in the national interest.

It follows that there is no need for an inquiry. However, I would naturally expect the police to investigate any substantiated charges that the law had been broken in this country.

Yours sincerely

Margaret Thatcher

Paddy Ashdown, Esq., M.P.

HOUSE OF COMMONS
LONDON SWIA OAA

The Prime Minister,
10, Downing Street,
London, SW1

2nd December 1984

COCOM and US Extra Territorial activity in Britain.

I am very grateful indeed for your letter of the 27th of November and your
assurance that the matters which I brought to your attention have been
carefully examined by the appropriate department.

Your letter indicates that you have concluded that there has been no
inappropriate activity on the part of US government officials in Britain .
Nevertheless, I am convinced that US government officials did visit among
other firms DEC in Reading. The details of this were in my original letter
to you. I presume from your letter that you knew of these visits and have
decided they were " appropriate ". In this case I would be grateful, if
you could tell me where the officials came from or what was the official
basis of their visit and whether they had the approval of the UK
government.

Your letter says that "the involvement of the CIA are unsubstantiated"
I note that you are unable to substantiate such activity. Surely this
is a matter upon which the UK government has sought assurances from the US
government ? I should be grateful if you could indicate to me that this
has happened and that such assurances have been given in an unequivocal
fashion.

I also note from your letter that you say that "there is close
co-operation between the British and American authorities...". I have for
sometime been pressing both Paul Channon and Barney Hayhoe to provide me
with details of this co-operation. Barney Hayhoe has indicated that   e
co-operation is merely of a "routine". He has specifically told me that
there is no UK US customs operation aimed at enforcements of multilateral
agreed export controls. I should be very grateful if you could ask for
full details of the nature of this co-operation to be given including at
what level it is conducted, how many people are involved in it and what is
the nature of the operation. I should tell you that I have recently
received information that the UK customs could not move against a UK firm,
Systime, who, it was claimed, had broked the COCOM regulation, because
US customs had removed key documentation from one of its customers (DEC).
This does not sound to me very much like "close co-operation".

I am sorry to have to burden you with this, but I feel that this important
matter still requires further investigation.

Yours sincerely

Paddy Ashdown MP.

10 DOWNING STREET

THE PRIME MINISTER

24 December, 1984

Dear Mr. Ashdown,

Thank you for your letter of 2 December about COCOM and US extra-territorial activity in Britain. I shall answer your points in the order in which you made them.

As to DEC in Reading, officials from the US Department of Commerce visited the firm earlier this year. They did so after the US authorities had been in touch with the DTI and, as is usual in such cases, the latter had consulted DEC. Officials of other governments of course have no legal powers in the UK to require information of British companies; but we do not in general object to enquiries being pursued on a voluntary basis. We do however expect to be informed in advance and assured that all concerned understand the nature and voluntary character of the enquiries. As to matters discussed with DEC, it would be for the company itself to comment.

The reference in my letter to the earlier statement that allegations about the involvement of the CIA were unsubstantiated meant, quite simply, that no evidence had been produced, so far as I am aware, to the effect that there was CIA involvement. That is still the position. You would not expect me to go into details about any exchanges with the US intelligence authorities which may have taken place, but I can assure you that the British authorities are satisfied that the CIA are not involved in improper activities in this country.

The affairs of Systime Computers are at present under consideration by HM Customs and Excise but they assure me that there has been no lack of co-operation on the part of the US authorities and that they are not aware of any documents which would be of assistance to them being removed from other companies by US Customs.

I consider that, in the light of the foregoing, the matters which you have raised do not require further investigation.

Yours sincerely

Margaret Thatcher

P. Ashdown, Esq., MP

10 DOWNING STREET

THE PRIME MINISTER

19 May 1986

Dear Mr. Ashdown,

Thank you for your letter of 22 April.

The Government's objections of principle to the extra-territorial implications of the new distribution licence regulations are firmly on record. But the new regulations will not have the sweeping effects which you ascribe to them. Nor are they to be imposed on unwilling companies as you imply.

The US authorities have introduced the distribution licence as a system of bulk licensing that allows approved US exporters to export specified goods to approved foreign consignees, (who may in turn re-export to certain destinations) without the individual transaction approval that the US authorities normally require for security reasons. The system is designed by the US authorities to free the companies concerned from the delays and expense of applying for individual licences. The US authorities have made clear that participation is voluntary, and there is no reason to suppose that UK companies will seek consignee status unless they regard it as in their commercial interests to do so.

The US Department of Commerce have sought the Government's agreement to Department of Commerce officials visiting the companies to check their compliance with the new regulations. The Government are currently consulting industry about the US request. No decision has yet been taken on whether to agree to it.

Yours sincerely

Margaret Thatcher

Paddy Ashdown, Esq., M.P.

APPENDIX III

Foreword to the Economic Alert List

CONFIDENTIAL

FOREWORD

The Economic Alert List (EAL) highlights the current
economic information needs of all members of the Washington
economic community.* It is intended to be a current guidance
document for use by field reporters of all agencies participating in the Combined Economic Reporting Program (CERP). Individual collectors may determine in view of their local situation the manner and extent to which they respond to EAL items
in their formal program of reporting. *When field reports are
prepared in response to EAL items, however, the EAL should be
shown as a reference. Department of State posts are reminded
that telegrams and airgrams prepared in response to EAL
guidance should show the reference tag EALR.*

The Western Europe EAL is published triannually. Items
are classified separately and bear the classification (C)
CONFIDENTIAL or (U) UNCLASSIFIED. Field reporters may find
related political, military, and scientific questions in the
companion publication, the Current Intelligence Reporting
List (CIRL).

The EAL is coordinated and produced by the Secretariat
of the Subcommittee on Requirements and Coordination of the Economic Intelligence Committee of the United States Intelligence
Board (USIB). *Economic topics of major concern are identified
in the EAL section on Key Intelligence Questions (KIQ's).
When the interagency panels charged with reviewing submissions
for the EAL feel it is appropriate, special attention may be
directed to particular aspects of KIQ questions. These statements of emphasis relating to the KIQ's may appear at the beginning of country and/or regional sections.* Overseas distribution is made through the auspices of the Department of State
as executive manager of the Combined Economic Reporting Program.
Comments and suggestions are encouraged and should be directed
to:

Secretariat, EIC Subcommittee
Room 2G40
CIA Headquarters Building   or   c/o EB/OCA/CM
Washington, D.C. 20505   Department of State
Code 143, extension 5577

---

*State, Treasury, Commerce, Labor, Agriculture, Interior, Army,
Navy, AF, CIA, DIA, NSA, Export-Import Bank, Federal Reserve
Board, ACDA, OPIC, OMB, AID, STR, CIEP, CEA, International Trade
Commission, Transportation

INDEX

Anning, Nick, 66
Aldrich, Winthrop W, 22
Allende, Salvador, 131
Amdahl, Gene, 39
American Bar Association, 90–96
American Declaration of the Rights
    and Duties of Man, 144–5
Arnold, Sue, 178
ASEA, 127
Ashdown, Paddy; and CIA, 126–30;
    and EEC, 86–7; and IBM
    letter, 62–5; at PITCOM, 118;
    as MP, 87; his enthusiasm, 73;
    in Parliament, 101–7, 133,
    147–8, 169–74; writes to
    Havers, 76–9, 92–3, 95–8;
    writes to PM, 122, 192–6;
    writes to Tebbit, 73–4
Ashworth, John, 175
Attorney General (office), 88, 96;
    see also Havers, Sir Michael
Austria, 1, 3, 8, 51–2, 80, 127, 128,
    135, 140

Baker, Kenneth, 63, 74, 115–16
Baldwin, David, 64
Batiste, Spencer, 174, 176, 180
Beijing (China), 74, 100–101, 111
Beresford, Philip, 9, 63–4, 69, 126
Bonker, Don, 56, 182
Bradshaw, Della, 64
Brady, Larry, 13
British Business, 172–3
British Computer Society, 73
British Technology Group, 154–5
Brittan, Leon, 184
Bucy, J. Fred, 50–51
Bulgaria, 113, 140
Burroughs, 49
Butcher, Brian, 138, 148, 173
Butcher, John, 69–71

Button, The, (Ford), 48

Carr, David, 74, 110–11
Casey, William J, 17, 120–32, 156,
    159–67, 192
CDC Corporation (US), 83
Channon, Paul, 45, 63–4, 158,
    169–70, 173–6, 193–4
Chile, 131, 162
China, 1, 37, 42, 74–5, 94, 100–101,
    109–12, 114, 117, 121, 176
Churchill, Sir Winston, 20–32,
    35–6, 40, 45
CIA (Central Intelligence Agency),
    12, 14, 15, 17, 66–7, 85, 120–32,
    146, 151–8, 168–84, 192–3
Cleaver, Tony, 12
Clement Jones, Tim, 79, 95
Coburn, Andrew, 48
Cocom (Co-ordinating Committee),
    19, 20–27, 30, 33–6, 42–59, 74,
    79, 86, 94, 99–100, 108–14,
    121, 128, 176, 181, 194–5
Combined Customs Agreement
    (US), 85
Commons, House of, procedure of,
    61–2, 86, 101–3
Computer Leasing Association, 156
Computer News, 5, 9, 17, 57, 60, 62,
    68–9, 71, 73, 76, 99, 126
Computer Talk, 153
Computer Weekly, 5, 11, 14, 66
Computer User's Year Book, 16
Computers; Apple, 175; main
    frame, 20, 39–40, 49, 70, 72,
    126, 185; PD 11, 112, 146,
    171–2, 181–2; super, 39–40, 49,
    128, 185; Racal-Redac, 112–13;
    VAX 11, 181–2; ZX, 80, 109,
    112
Computing, 5, 11, 183

[199]

Powell, Enoch, 41, 151
Prime, Geoffrey, 17, 66–8, 156
Protection of Trade Act, 79, 90, 93, 147

Quest Automation, 182

Reagan, Ronald, 18, 52, 58, 96,
  99–100, 110, 130, 182, 183
Rhyolite surveillance system, 66–7
Robertson, Jack, 180
Romania, 99–100, 141
Rome, Treaty of, 61, 71, 84, 93,
  133, 144, 146, 148
Root, William, 45, 52–8

SAL, 94
Scicon, 153
Seighart, Paul, 136–7
Semiconductor Industry Assoc, 153
Siliconise, 153
Sinclair, Sir Clive, 75
Smith, John Pridmore, 138
Smith, Nigel, 104
Smith, Tim, 175
Society of Photo-optical
  Instrumentation Engineers,
  179–80
South Africa, 83–4
Spain, 127, 128, 131, 141
'Special relationship', 188
Sperry, 49
Stranbrook, Ivor, 175
Star Wars, 183–4
Stott, Roger, 69–73, 115, 116, 118
Sunday Times, 6, 9, 16, 56, 63–9,
  74, 95, 126–7
Sunitron, 8
Sweden, 7–8, 51, 74, 80, 112,
  127–8, 141
Switzerland, 51, 80, 127
Systems Control Technology, 153
Systime PLC, 85, 88, 138, 174, 176–8

Tasbian, 112–13
Tebbit, Norman, 4, 9–18, 63–4, 71,
  73, 74, 76, 88, 105, 184, 193
Technobandits (Malvern), 68

Texas Instruments, 50, 123, 143,
  147, 168
Thatcher, Margaret, 17–19, 45, 62,
  79, 96–7, 110, 113, 122, 124,
  127, 147, 183, 192–6
Thorneycroft, Peter (Lord), 20, 23,
  30–37, 40, 45
Threat, The, (Coburn), 48
Times, The, 6, 41, 174, 183
Today (BBC), 9, 12, 18, 88
Today in Politics, 123, 179, 181
Turkey, 174–5

United Kingdom; Civil Service, 41,
  56, 58, 61, 75; Constitution,
  77–9, 97, 152; Customs and
  Excise, 12, 85, 87, 123, 128,
  174, 178, 183, 195;
  Sovereignty, 6, 11, 18–19,
  60–61, 71, 76–9, 88–9, 93–7,
  105–7, 115, 118, 147, 153, 158
United Nations Charter, 134–7
USA; Customs, 12–14, 85, 94, 121,
  123, 146, 178; Dept of Defense
  see Pentagon; exports, 109–12,
  124; extra-territoriality, 3, 17,
  74, 105–6, 115, 139, 148–9,
  174–8, 195–6; officials visit
  UK firms, 91, 94, 96, 120–23;
  space programme, 38–9
USSR; Siberian pipeline, 79, 82,
  133, 148; and Western
  technology, 14, 15, 22–4,
  26–34, 66–8, 71, 86, 118, 163–7
Vogel, Heinrich, 124, 179

Warren, Ken, 176
Warsaw Pact, 27, 99, 160
Weinberger, Caspar, 47, 184
Weinstock, Arnold (Lord), 84
Westinghouse, 88
Westland Helicopters, 87, 184
Wrigglesworth, Ian, 69, 180

Yeovil, 62, 87
Yugoslavia, 51, 112, 141